BY *Special* REQUEST

OUR FAVORITE RECIPES

PRODUCED BY PIGGLY WIGGLY CAROLINA EMPLOYEES

The information contained in this publication is accurate to the best of our knowledge. All recommended directions and ingredients are made without any guarantees on the part of authors. The authors and publishers disclaim all liability in connection with the use of this information.

Cover design "Fresh Cut" detail
by Mike Kennedy

All proceeds from the sale of this book will go to community causes and charities in Piggly Wiggly areas of operation, designated by Piggly Wiggly employees.

Printed in the USA by

WIMMER
The Wimmer Companies, Inc.
Memphis • Dallas

Table
OF
CONTENTS

DEDICATION

By Special Request!

To

Mr. Joseph T. Newton, Jr.,

founder of Piggly Wiggly Carolina Co., Inc.,

with Love, Respect, and Admiration to a very *Special* man.

From your family of proud employees.

"By Special Request" began as an idea inspired by the well known generosity of our Piggly Wiggly Company. From that point on, little did we know what lay ahead.

We wish to thank the following with our deepest appreciation, Mr. Joseph T. Newton, III, President, and Mr. Burton R. Schools, Executive Vice-President for Piggly Wiggly's support. The recipe contributors, the tasting committee, all our fine Pride Representatives and everyone's patience and sacrifices in dealing with piles of recipes and copies going in every direction.

We are profoundly indebted to the **"By Special Request Committee"**:

Rita Postell, Chairman

Theresa Blacklocke	True Henderson
Jennifer Dingler	Lavon Hood
Lorraine Dubose	Lane Spell
Carroll Godwin	Jeanette Stancil
Dottie Hardin	Eileen Stellefson

Without our "Special Employees", this project would not have been possible. We are truly grateful for everyone's assistance. Thank you!

THE BEGINNING

It started as a struggling young enterprise in an old cotton warehouse located on the banks of the Cooper River in Charleston, S.C. The year was 1947. It was the beginning of a dream long envisioned by its founder, Joseph T. Newton, Jr., and it bore the unusual, but memorable name, of Piggly Wiggly.

Having lived through the great depression, and the deprivations of World War II, Joseph T. Newton, Jr., knew the meaning of hard work and personal sacrifice.

As the war ended, he was a young married man with a growing family. Merchandising, and the grocery business in particular, was his trade. He worked hard, long hours as a butcher and grocer to make a living and support his young family.

It occurred to Mr. Newton that there should be a central source to supply grocery stores with all their needs, rather than each store having to deal with 20 or more different suppliers for their merchandise. He was convinced that with a central buying office, he could bargain for lower prices on volume purchases from all suppliers and supply stores at lower cost.

Having scrimped and saved every penny possible during those early years, Mr. Newton set out to purchase a Piggly Wiggly grocery franchise from the Piggly Wiggly Corporation. One by one, Mr. Newton convinced owners of small grocery stores to join the franchise, and very soon the familiar round sign with the smiling Pig's head became a familiar landmark throughout South Carolina and later in Savannah, Ga.

As each journey begins with one step at a time, the early years of Piggly Wiggly Wholesale were skimpy and frugal, to say the least. The little warehouse operation in Charleston had a mere handful of employees. Mr. Newton called on stores for orders personally, at the same time contacting others to join the Piggly Wiggly group. There was one delivery truck and workdays that stretched far into the night.

Under Mr. Newton's guidance and leadership, Piggly Wiggly Carolina experienced phenomenal growth and the name Piggly Wiggly soon became a household word, known for its national brands, fair prices and friendly service. Customers in ever-growing numbers depended on the self service supermarket for their total food needs.

Mr. Newton was gifted at enlisting the services of some of the most dedicated employees in shaping the growing company into, not only the friendliest place in town to shop, but also the most generous in returning much of the company's earnings back into each community through charitable causes and agencies that supported the needy and the overall betterment of each community in which Piggly Wiggly operated.

Today, Piggly Wiggly Carolina is among the state's 5 top privately owned firms in volume sales every year, with a work force exceeding 5,000 employees, and still growing.

The legendary generosity of Piggly Wiggly Carolina prompted its legions of loyal, proud employees, both in retail and wholesale, to create this cookbook, *"By Special Request"*, with the stipulation that all proceeds from sales will go directly back into the community to support noble and charitable causes. Those causes and agencies selected by the employees.

We sincerely hope that this unselfish effort by the employees of Piggly Wiggly Carolina and its subsidiaries will double your pleasure in owning and using our cookbook.

Special MENUS

"NOON" By Mike Kennedy

"NEW YEARS DAY BUFFET"

*Served mid-afternoon due to the prior "Eve" celebration.
Casual and laid back, but a must for the Southern tradition
that promises luck and money for the New Year.*

Pickled Shrimp

Smoked Boston Butt

Spicy Bar-b-cue sauce

Hoppin John
(for luck)

Collard Greens
(for money)

Pepper relish

Pineapple and Cheese Casserole

Sweet Potato Crunch

Cornbread

Carrot Cake

*Hot Specialty Coffee, Iced Tea,
or your favorite beverage*

*Pig out! Make your New Years resolutions. Then occupy
your favorite seat (grab the remote) for an afternoon of
football with everyone.*

"DINNER PARTY FOR EIGHT PEOPLE"

Coquille St. Jacques

Roast Beef

Potato and Onion Casserole

Hearts of Palm Salad

String Beans

Rolls

Key Lime Pie or Chess Pie

Cocktails, candlelight, soft music, interesting guests and good food are the makings for an enjoyable dinner party.

"SUMMER FEST"

Any occasion or excuse will do to relax and enjoy friends and family on a lazy summer afternoon. Always outdoors where no restrictions or formality apply. Everyone pitches in and no one worries about the mess afterwards.

Dave's Frozen Margaritas

Cold Salsa with large Corn Chips

Broccoli Salad

Tomato Pie

Donald's Island Stew

Lowcountry Beer Bread

Chewy Cake

Blackberry Cobbler with ice cream

Variety of iced down beverages

Everything prepared in advance, except for the stew. Let the kids run wild, enjoy the party, and just keep cool.

"ST. PATRICK'S DAY"

(Everybody's Irish on March 17th)

Green Salad

Pistachio Salad

Jimbo's Irish Glazed Corn Beef

Cabbage

Potato Wedges

Irish Soda Bread

"Green" (Red) Velvet Cake (Use green food coloring)

Irish Coffee

Decorate with Shamrocks. Do the Irish Jig and pinch anyone who doesn't wear green.

"BABY SHOWER"

Party sandwiches

(Shrimp Sandwich Paste & Pimento Cheese Spread)

Vegetable Tray with Pineapple Cheese Dip

Fruit Tray with Apple Dip

Crab Cheese Ball & Crackers

White Chocolate covered Pretzels

Piggly Wiggly decorated Baby Cake

Mints - Nuts

Party Punch

Decorate in pretty pastel colors. Everyone joins in the fun with a "Relay baby changing contest". The Mother-to-be will bring that new baby into the world with lots of nice gifts, best wishes, and fond memories.

"PIG PICKIN"

*Traditional Cooked Whole Pig or smoked Boston Butt
with Barbecue Sauce*

Kelly's Barbecue Hash

Rice

Italian Slaw

Southern Baked Beans

Sally Lunn Bread

Pig Pickin Cake

Iced Tea and Lemonade

Great for all occasions, family reunions, engagement announcements, block parties, etc. Be sure to leave some meat on the grill just for "Pickin".

"PIGNIC"

Hamburgers and Hot Dogs on the grill

Fried Chicken Wings

Copper Pennies

Marinated Vegetables

Potato Salad

Pickles

Chips

Brownies

Whether it be at the seashore, at the lake or at the river, all ages like to get together for picnics. The atmosphere is very casual, the food is good and everyone helps with the preparation, young and old.

ESPECIALLY LIGHT MENUS

A Cool Summer Supper
Chilled Strawberry Soup
Grilled Fish
Parslied Potato Salad
Cucumber Salad with Mint
Fresh Fruit Cup

A Warm "Heart"-Y Meal
Swiss Steak
Onion Roasted Potatoes
Zucchini Spears Olé
Low Fat Vanilla Cake

A Light Chinese Buffet
Bok Choy Soup
Stir Fried Beef and Pea Pods
Chicken Fried Rice
Fortune Cookies

ESPECIALLY LIGHT MENUS

A Housewarming Drop-In

Spinach Dip

Cream Cheese and Pineapple Spread

Pasta Salad

Low Cal Reese's Cup Pie

Low Fat Brownies

Gourmet On A Budget

Gourmet Catfish

Parslied Potatoes

Sesame Broccoli

Raspberry Sherbet

Ballgame Best Bets

Crockpot Chili

Rice

Mixed Green Salad

Baked Apples

Special STARTERS

BANANA PUNCH

1½ quarts water
3 cups granulated sugar
1 (12 ounce) can frozen
    orange juice, thawed
1 (46 ounce) can pineapple-
    grapefruit drink

4 mashed bananas
1 quart club soda for two
    quarts of banana punch
vodka (optional)

Mix water and sugar together. Add orange juice, pineapple-grapefruit drink and bananas. Pour into appropriate freezer container. Add 1 quart of club soda for 2 quarts of banana punch mix. Add vodka if desired. Freeze. Take out of freezer about 2 hours before using and chip to have a crushed effect.

Great for all occasions

Yield: 1¼ gallons

MAMA'S CHRISTMAS TEA

1 teaspoon whole cloves
1 (2 inch) cinnamon stick
3 quarts water
2½ tablespoons black tea or 3
    tea bags

3 oranges juiced or 1 cup
    orange juice
¼ cup lemon juice
½ to 1 cup granulated sugar
    (to personal taste)

Tie spices in clean cheese cloth pouch. Bring water to full boil, remove from heat. Let spice pouch and tea steep for 5 minutes. Remove pouch and tea and add juices. Serve hot.

Perfect for after shopping.

Yield: 3 quarts

FESTIVE PUNCH

2 cups cranberry juice
2 cups pineapple juice
1 cup sugar

1 tablespoon almond extract
6 (12 ounce) cans ginger ale
    (chilled)

Mix first 4 ingredients and chill. Just before serving, add ginger ale.

You can also make an ice ring out of the first 4 ingredients. It looks festive in the punch bowl and also keeps the punch cold.

Yield: 16 servings

HOT PUNCH

1 quart cranberry juice
1½ quarts apple juice
⅓ cup brown sugar

½ teaspoon salt
3 cinnamon sticks
12 whole cloves

Pour fruit juices into 12 cup coffeemaker. Place remaining ingredients in coffee basket. Cover and plug in; complete the cycle as for coffee. Remove basket as soon as perking stops; discard spices. Serve in heated mugs.

Yield: 8 to 10 servings

DAVE'S FROZEN MARGARITAS

1 (6 ounce) can frozen
   limeade
½ can Tequila and a splash
   (use limeade can to
   measure)

½ can Triple Sec and a splash
1 whole fresh lime, peeled and
   sliced
Ice, as needed

Place first four ingredients in blender. Add ice and blend until smooth. Serve in salt rimmed Margarita glasses. Garnish with lime slices.

There's a story behind each batch.

Yield: 4 servings

WHISKEY SOUR PUNCH

1 quart lemonade
1 quart orange juice
1 quart whiskey (bourbon)

2 quarts soda water
cherries

Combine all of the above. Pour over ice and add a cherry to each glass.

Yield: 50 servings

TEMPERANCE PUNCH

½ pound powdered sugar
½ (6 ounce) can frozen
   lemonade

2 quarts red grape juice
2 cups cut-up fruit
1 quart sparkling water

Combine sugar, lemon juice, grape juice and pour over ice in large bowl. Chill and toss in cut-up fruit. Add sparkling water before serving.

1 (16 ounce) can fruit cocktail can be used instead of fresh fruit.

Yield: 12 servings

PARTY PUNCH

1 (46 ounce) can pineapple
   juice
juice of 4 lemons
1 small can frozen orange
   juice

1 package lemon-lime drink
   mix (Kool-Aid or Wylers)
⅓ of a 5 pound bag of sugar
water
1 quart ginger ale

Mix all ingredients except ginger ale in a gallon jar. Add water to completely fill jar. Pour into punch bowl and add ginger ale when ready to serve.

Garnish with fruit.

You can make a ice ring with water and fruit, or you may want to use crushed ice. For a party you need to make 3 gallon jars full.

Yield: 100 servings

IRISH COFFEE

1 jigger Irish whiskey
1 teaspoon sugar

1 cup brewed coffee
Whipped cream or Cool Whip

Heat whiskey in coffee cup in microwave. Add sugar and stir. Pour hot coffee into mixture and top with whipped cream. (Do not stir.)

You'll bless the Irish for this coffee.

Yield: 1 serving

RUSSIAN TEA MIX

1 cup instant unsweetened tea
1 (18 ounce) powdered orange
   juice mix
2 cups granulated sugar

1 (6.2 ounce) lemonade mix,
   unsweetened
1 teaspoon ground cloves
1 teaspoon cinnamon

In a large container mix all ingredients thoroughly. Store in tightly sealed container. To serve, add 2 teaspoons of mixture to 8 ounces boiling water, stir.

Put in pretty container. Great as a gift.

Yield: 6 cups

HOT CHOCOLATE MIX

10⅔ cups powdered milk
1 pound powdered sugar

1 pound powdered chocolate
1 (3 ounce) jar coffee creamer

Thoroughly mix all ingredients. Use 2 to 3 tablespoons per 8 ounces of water.

Keep on hand.

DOLLY'S KAHLÚA

14 cups boiling water
10 cups granulated sugar
8 ounces instant coffee

6 tablespoons of vanilla
   extract
2 pints grain alcohol or vodka

Dissolve above ingredients into boiling water. Let cool completely then add alcohol or vodka. Pour into plastic milk jugs and let stand for about a week or longer.

Poured in fancy bottles make perfect Christmas gifts.

Yield: 2 gallons

ARTICHOKE DELIGHT

1 cup mayonnaise
1 cup Parmesan cheese
½ teaspoon garlic powder

1 (14 ounce) can artichoke
hearts, drained and
chopped

Butter a shallow baking dish. Combine all ingredients and mix well. Bake at 350 degrees for 15 to 20 minutes. Serve, warm as a dip or spread.

Yield: 6 to 8 servings

SHRIMP DIP

1½ cups precooked salad
shrimp, chopped
1½ cups medium Cheddar
cheese, grated
1½ cups mayonnaise

1 tablespoon horseradish
1 tablespoon French salad
dressing
1 tablespoon Worcestershire
sauce

Combine shrimp, cheese, mayonnaise, horseradish, salad dressing, and Worcestershire sauce. If the mixture seems to liquidy, add more shrimp and cheese. Refrigerate overnight and serve with Ritz crackers.

Good at any occasion.

Yield: 12 servings

OAK ISLAND CRAB DIP

1 (8 ounce) package cream
cheese, softened
1 cup shredded, sharp
Cheddar cheese
1 heaping tablespoon
mayonnaise
2 teaspoons lemon juice

1 teaspoon Worcestershire
sauce
1 cup crab meat, canned or
fresh
1 teaspoon horseradish
garlic powder to taste

Mix all ingredients together, chill and serve with chips or crackers.

You may substitute shrimp for the crab.

Yield: 6 to 8 servings

BECKA'S HOT CRAB DIP

1 pound crab meat, picked
    over
1 (8 ounce) package cream
    cheese
1 medium onion, grated

½ stick butter
1 dash soy sauce
1 dash Worcestershire sauce
½ teaspoon garlic powder, or
    salt

Place cream cheese, onion, butter, soy sauce, Worcestershire sauce and garlic in baking dish. Place in microwave to melt, approximately, 1½ minutes. Add crab and mix well. Bake at 325 degrees for 30 to 35 minutes or until brown on top. Serve with crackers.

Yield: 8 to 10 servings

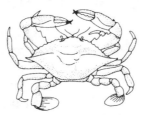

CRAB DIP MANKIN

½ cup Cheddar cheese, grated
2 cups mayonnaise
1 cup crab meat (white, not
    claw)

1 teaspoon salt
½ cup French dressing
horseradish to taste

Mix all ingredients together and chill for several hours. Serve with crackers.

Yield: 1 quart or 4 cups

HICKORY-SMOKED CHEESE

2 cups cottage cheese
1 cup sour cream
2 tablespoons minced scallion

½ teaspoon minced garlic
1 teaspoon hickory-smoked
    salt

Blend cottage cheese and sour cream. Add remaining ingredients and mix thoroughly. Cover and chill for several hours. Serve with party crackers.

Serve on crackers or as a dip.

Simply Good.

Yield: 8 to 10 servings

DIP IT

1 package dry Italian salad
   dressing mix
½ cup mayonnaise

½ cup sour cream
1 tablespoon lemon juice

Combine all ingredients and mix well. Chill for about 2 hours. Serve assorted vegetables or fruit.

Yield: 1 cup

SPINACH DIP

1 package frozen chopped
   spinach, cooked and
   drained
½ cup water
½ teaspoon salt
1 cup sour cream

1 cup mayonnaise
¼ teaspoon thyme
1 tablespoon onion, chopped
1 package Knorr's Vegetable
   Soup mix

Cook frozen spinach in water with salt; drain thoroughly in colander. Add sour cream, mayonnaise, thyme, onion and soup mix. Mix thoroughly. Chill and serve with crackers.

May add ½ small can water chestnuts, sliced very thin.

Good and Green.

Yield: 4 to 6 servings

SALSA AND CREAM CHEESE DIP

1 (8 ounce) package cream
   cheese, softened

1 (8 ounce) jar chunky salsa
tortilla or corn chips

Place softened cream cheese in a flat dish. Top with ½ jar of salsa. Serve with sturdy chips. Add more salsa as needed.

Quick Fix.

Yield: 6 to 8 servings

PINEAPPLE CHEESE DIP

1 (2 ounce) package cream
cheese, softened
1 (4 ounce) can crushed
pineapple, drained
1 tablespoon chopped bell
pepper

1 tablespoon onion, chopped
fine
1 teaspoon "Season All"
dash of cayenne pepper
¼ cup pecans, chopped

Mix all ingredients together and place in bowl. Refrigerate for several hours or until ready to use.

Yield: 4 to 6 servings

TANGY TACO DIP

1 (15 ounce) can refried beans
1 (1½ ounce) package taco
seasoning mix
1 medium tomato, chopped
1 medium onion, chopped
1 (8 ounce) container sour
cream

1 (8 ounce) jar of chopped
green chilies
1 (6 ounce) jar of chopped
black olives
1 (8 ounce) package of
Monterey Jack cheese,
shredded

Combine beans and taco mix together, and spread it evenly in bottom of baking dish. Layer tomatoes, onions, sour cream, green chilies, black olives, then cheese. Be sure to layer in this order. Bake at 350 degrees for 25 to 30 minutes.

Serve with tortilla chips

Enjoy.

Yield: 8 servings

CLAM DIP

1 (6.5 ounce) can minced
clams
2 (8 ounce) packages cream
cheese

2 tablespoons Worcestershire
sauce
½ teaspoon red pepper
(cayenne)

Drain clams, save juice. Combine remaining ingredients and add small amount of clam juice to make a smooth dip. Add clams and chill. Serve with chips or crackers

Yield: 2 cups

1-2-3 PARTY CHEESE DIP

1 cup green onions, chopped
2 cups mayonnaise

3 cups sharp shredded
Cheddar cheese

In medium size bowl, combine all ingredients and mix well. Cook 7 minutes in microwave or at 350 degrees for 25 minutes in regular oven. Serve with corn chips or tortilla chips.

Simple but delicious.

Yield: 10 to 12 servings

APPLE DIP

1 (8 ounce) package cream
cheese
1 cup brown sugar

1 tablespoon vanilla extract
⅓ cup sour cream
apple slices

Mix cream cheese and brown sugar together. Add vanilla and sour cream and whip with mixer until light and fluffy. Chill. Use as a dip for apple slices or other fruit.

Nice touch for the summer.

Yield: 2 cups

BOURBON SPREAD

1 cup (2 sticks) of butter or
margarine, softened
1 cup shredded Cheddar
cheese
¼ cup bourbon

1 teaspoon dried oregano or
dill flakes
½ teaspoon parsley flakes
¼ teaspoon garlic salt

Cream butter (or margarine) and cheese until mixture is fairly smooth. Add remaining ingredients, continue beating until light and fluffy. Store in refrigerator in air tight container.

Spread on crackers.

Yield: 2 cups

SHRIMP SANDWICH PASTE

1 pound medium shrimp,
   peeled and cooked
1 (8 ounce) package cream
   cheese
⅓ cup sour cream
⅓ cup mayonnaise

1 tablespoon lemon juice
1 tablespoon Worcestershire
   sauce
1 teaspoon seasoned salt
½ teaspoon white pepper
1 cup celery, chopped fine

Chop shrimp into small pieces. Mix remaining ingredients and stir until smooth. Add shrimp and chill. Make into small party sandwiches or serve with crackers.

Yield: 2 dozen sandwiches

PIMENTO CHEESE SPREAD

1 (7 ounce) jar pimentos
1 (12 ounce) package mild or
   sharp Cheddar cheese,
   grated

1 cup mayonnaise

Mash pimentos into small pieces. Add cheese and mayonnaise, mix well. Spread on bread or crackers.

Yield: 2 cups

SMOKED SALMON PARTY BALL

1 (8 ounce) package cream
   cheese softened
1 (16 ounce) can salmon,
   drained and flaked
1 tablespoon finely chopped
   onion

1 tablespoon lemon juice
1 teaspoon prepared
   horseradish
¼ teaspoon liquid smoke
⅓ cup chopped nuts
¼ teaspoon parsley flakes

Mix all ingredients except nuts and parsley. Shape mixture into a ball. Cover and refrigerate at least 8 hours, but no longer than 4 days. Mix nuts and parsley flakes and coat ball.

Super.

Yield: 12 servings

CRAB CHEESE BALL

8 ounces crab meat (1 cup)
1 (8 ounce) package cream
   cheese

4 tablespoons ranch dressing
1 green onion, finely sliced
½ cup sliced almonds

Mix first 4 ingredients. Form into a ball. Roll in sliced almonds. Cover with plastic wrap and refrigerate for at least 3 hours. Serve with crackers.

May also substitute chopped shrimp or ham for crab.

Can't go wrong.

Yield: 10 servings

OYSTER ROLL

2 (8 ounce) packages cream
   cheese
2 teaspoons Worcestershire
   sauce
⅛ teaspoon garlic powder

2 cans smoked oysters,
   drained and finely
   chopped
½ small onion, grated
3 tablespoons mayonnaise
⅛ teaspoon salt
¼ cup fresh parsley, chopped

Cream together cream cheese, Worcestershire, garlic powder, onion, mayonnaise, and salt. Spread mixture on waxed paper until it is about 12 x 8 inches and less than ½ inch thick. Chill in refrigerator about an hour. Spread oysters on top of cheese mixture, and roll up into a log. Roll log in chopped parsley and chill in refrigerator for 24 hours before serving. Serve with crackers.

Yield: 10 to 25 servings

CHEESE SNACKS

½ pound butter or margarine
1½ cups plain flour
½ teaspoon red pepper
½ teaspoon salt

½ pound New York sharp
   cheese, grated
3 cups Rice Krispies

Cream butter with an electric mixer until lightly fluffy, then mix by hand, gradually add flour, pepper, salt and cheese. Mix in Rice Krispies. Make small balls. Bake at 400 degrees for 8 to 10 minutes.

Yield: 90 balls

SAUSAGE BALLS

3 cups Bisquick
1 pound sausage, mild or hot

2½ cups shredded Cheddar
cheese
dash Tabasco

Thoroughly mix all ingredients. Form into small balls. Place on cookie sheet and bake at 350 degrees for 20 minutes or until brown.

Kids can help too.

Yield: 4 to 6 servings

SAUSAGE STUFFED MUSHROOMS

1 pound hot sausage
1 (8 ounce) package cream
cheese, softened

1 pound fresh mushrooms,
cleaned and stems
removed

Brown sausage and drain well. Mix cream cheese and sausage. Stuff each mushroom with one teaspoon sausage mixture. Bake at 350 degrees for 15 minutes or until mushrooms are cooked through.

Yield: 6 to 8 servings

SHRIMP BREAD

1 loaf French or rye bread, cut
into 4 pieces
½ cup mayonnaise
½ cup chopped parsley
2 (8 ounce) packages cream
cheese, softened

1 (7 ounce) package Italian
salad dressing mix
1 (4 ounce) jar pimentos,
chopped
1 pound boiled shrimp, finely
chopped

Hollow out bread and spread with mayonnaise. Sprinkle interior with parsley. Combine remaining ingredients. Pack mixture into loaf and wrap in plastic wrap. Chill then slice approximately ⅜ inch thick.

Yield: 8 to 10 servings

PIZZA CUPS

¾ pound ground beef
1 (6 ounce) can tomato paste
1 tablespoon instant minced
   onions
1 teaspoon Italian seasoning

½ teaspoon salt
1 (10 ounce) can refrigerated
   biscuits
½ to ¾ cup shredded
   Mozzarella cheese

Brown and drain ground beef. Stir in tomato paste, minced onions and seasonings (please note: mixture will be thick). Cook over low heat for 5 minutes, stirring frequently. Place biscuits in a greased muffin tin, pressing to cover bottom and sides. Spoon ground beef mixture into each biscuit-lined cup. Sprinkle shredded Mozzarella cheese on top. Bake at 400 degrees for 12 minutes or until golden brown.

Yield: 12 pizza cups

VEGETABLE BARS

2 packages crescent rolls
1 (8 ounce) package cream
   cheese
1 envelope of Hidden Valley
   Ranch dressing
½ cup mayonnaise

1 cup green pepper, chopped
   fine
1 cup carrots, chopped fine
1 cup grated cheese
1 cup tomatoes, chopped fine
1 cup olives, chopped fine

Cover bottom of jelly roll pan with rolls. Press together to form crust. Bake at 350 degrees for 8 to 10 minutes, let cool. Mix cream cheese, mayonnaise, and ranch dressing. Spread over rolls. Sprinkle vegetables and cheese over dressing. Press down and chill for 1 to 2 hours. Cut into small squares. Serve cold.

This is great for parties or any kind of gathering, pretty too.

Yield: 36 squares

PICKLED SHRIMP

2 pounds shrimp, peeled and
  cooked
1 cup catsup
1 cup vinegar
½ cup vegetable oil
1 tablespoon sugar
1 tablespoon Worcestershire
  sauce

1 dash Tabasco
1 teaspoon celery salt
2 tablespoons mustard
2 bay leaves
1 clove garlic, minced
1 bell pepper, chopped
1 onion, chopped
salt and pepper to taste

Place shrimp in container with lid. Add remaining ingredients and toss to cover shrimp. Marinate in refrigerator overnight. Before serving stir.

Can keep for seven days.

Delicious. Have lots of toothpicks handy.

Yield: 6 servings

SWEDISH MEATBALLS

2 pounds ground beef
1 pound pork sausage
1½ cups dry bread crumbs
⅓ cup minced onions
¼ cup milk
2 eggs
1 teaspoon salt

½ teaspoon Worcestershire
  sauce
⅛ teaspoon black pepper
¼ cup vegetable shortening
1 (12 ounce) bottle barbecue
  sauce
1 (10 ounce) jar grape jelly

Mix ground beef, pork sausage, bread crumbs, onion, milk, eggs, salt, pepper and Worcestershire sauce. Gently mix and shape into 1 inch balls. Melt shortening in large skillet, brown meatballs evenly and drain fat from skillet. Heat barbecue sauce and grape jelly in deep saucepan, stirring constantly until jelly has melted. Add meatballs and stir until coated. Simmer for 30 minutes over low heat. Serve hot.

Great for any occasion.

Yield: 5 dozen

BARBECUED FRANKS

1 (6 ounce) jar prepared mustard

1 (10 ounce) jar grape jelly
1 pound of franks

In medium saucepan heat mustard and jelly. Cut franks into bite-size pieces and add to mixture. Place in chafing dish and serve hot with toothpicks. May add more franks to sauce as needed or may reserve sauce for another party.

Yield: 6 servings

HAM AND CHEESE QUICHETTES

1 stick margarine
1 cup water
2 teaspoons sugar
1 cup all-purpose flour
4 large eggs

2 cups shredded Cheddar cheese
2 cups thinly sliced and diced cooked ham

Bring margarine, water and sugar to a boil in a medium saucepan. Remove from heat and add flour. Mix well. Cool 5 minutes. Add eggs, one at a time, beating well after each one. Add cheese and ham and mix well. Drop by rounded tablespoon onto greased baking sheet. Bake at 375 degrees for 20 to 25 minutes or until brown.

Could also use muffin pan.

Don't worry when beating in the eggs, it will look like it will never mix up, but it will. Be persistent.

Yield: 2 dozen

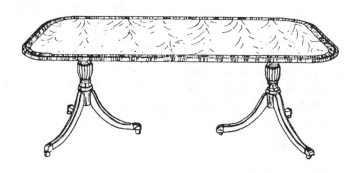

HAM AND CHEESE PARTY ROLLS

½ pound whipped margarine
3 tablespoons mustard
3 tablespoons poppy seed
1 medium grated onion
1 teaspoon Worcestershire
  sauce

1 pound boiled ham (sliced
  thin)
½ pound Swiss cheese
5 packs small party rolls

Combine, margarine, mustard, poppy seeds, onion, Worcestershire sauce and mix well. Spread on split rolls. Add slices of ham and cheese. Put top on roll and place in pan the rolls came in and cover with foil. Bake at 400 degrees for 15 to 20 minutes or until cheese melts.

Can be made the night before and used the next day.

Yield: 40 servings

FIVE VEGETABLE SANDWICHES

1 (1 ounce) envelope Knox
  gelatin
½ cup cold water
¼ cup boiling water
1 cup mayonnaise
2 medium tomatoes, chopped
2 green peppers, chopped

1 cup celery, chopped
1 onion, chopped
1 cucumber, chopped
salt and pepper to taste
1 loaf of white bread
1 loaf of brown bread

Soften gelatin in cold water. Add boiling water and stir to dissolve. Cool. Add mayonnaise and mix well. Add chopped vegetables, salt and pepper to taste. Refrigerate for several hours and spread on bread, trim, cut and serve.

Yield: 30 to 40 servings

TERIYAKI CHICKEN WINGS

1 (4 to 4½) pound package of
  chicken wings
1 (10 ounce) bottle teriyaki
  sauce

½ teaspoon garlic salt
¼ teaspoon black pepper

In large bowl combine teriyaki sauce, garlic salt and pepper. Add wing pieces, cover and marinade several hours or overnight. Place wings and marinade in baking dish. Add more garlic, salt and pepper if desired. Bake at 350 degrees for 50 to 60 minutes. Pour marinade in small bowl for dipping.

Yield: 40 pieces

BUFFALO WINGS

4 pounds chicken wings
½ cup melted butter
¼ cup hot pepper sauce

3 tablespoons vinegar
1 (4 ounce) package dry ranch
  dressing

Place chicken wings in baking dish. Mix butter, hot pepper sauce and vinegar, pour over chicken. Sprinkle with ranch dressing. Bake at 350 degrees for one 1 hour.

Yield: 6 to 8 servings

SHRIMP BALLS

1 pound cooked shrimp
1 tablespoon chili sauce
  (from a jar)
1 hard-boiled egg, chopped
salt and pepper to taste

3 tablespoons cream cheese
2 teaspoons horseradish
¼ cup celery, chopped
1 tablespoon onion, grated
parsley, finely chopped

Must prepare 1 day ahead. Finely chop cooked shrimp. Blend together remaining ingredients and add to shrimp. Form into small balls. Roll these balls in fresh chopped parsley and chill. Serve with crackers.

Spicy and Delicious.

Yield: 30 balls

EASY SAUSAGE CIRCLES

**2 (8 ounce) cans crescent
    dinner rolls**

**2 tablespoons hot or mild
    mustard
1 pound hot pork sausage**

Separate rolls into 4 rectangles and spread with mustard. Spread with thin layer of sausage. Roll and chill until ready to serve. Thinly slice each roll (10 circles to a roll) and place on ungreased pan. Bake at 400 degrees for 18 to 20 minutes. Serve hot.

2 packages of ham slices can be substituted for pork sausage.

These circles roll.

Yield: 20 pieces

CURRY GLAZED SESAME WINGS

**¼ cup sesame seeds
2 tablespoons butter or
    margarine, melted
½ cup honey
¼ cup prepared mustard**

**1 teaspoon salt
1 teaspoon curry powder
1 dozen chicken wings
    (approximately 2 pounds)**

In a wide frying pan, over medium heat, toast sesame seeds, shaking pan often, until golden (approximately 2 minutes), set aside; in a small bowl, stir together melted butter, honey, mustard, salt and curry powder until smooth, set aside. Arrange chicken wings on a broiler pan and broil about 4 inches from (or cook on a grill about 6 inches above a solid bed of medium glowing coals) turning once, for 15 minutes. Baste wings with honey mixture and continue cooking, turning and basting occasionally until done. Dip wings in sesame seeds and arrange on a serving platter.

Yield: 1 dozen

CEREAL TID BITS

⅓ cup margarine
1½ teaspoons garlic salt
1½ teaspoons onion salt
1¼ teaspoons celery salt
2 teaspoons Worcestershire
   sauce

½ of (12 ounce) box Cheerios
½ of (12 ounce) box Wheat
   Chex
½ of (12 ounce) box Rice Chex
1 small package pretzels
2 cups pecan pieces

Melt margarine, add next four ingredients to margarine. Stir well and pour over cereal and pecans. Bake at 200 degrees for 2 hours stirring every 20 minutes.

Makes a great gift in a pretty tin.

CHOCOLATE FONDUE

1 can prepared chocolate
   frosting (white or dark)

1 tablespoon instant coffee
fresh fruit

Heat frosting and coffee on low in microwave and stir occasionally until completely melted. Transfer into fondue pot. Serve with fresh fruit.

Yield: 1½ cups

Soups
& SALADS

FRESH VEGETABLE SOUP

1 pound ground round or 1½
    pounds stew beef, cut into
    bite size pieces
1 tablespoon olive oil
3 quarts water
1 large onion, chopped
1 tablespoon salt
½ teaspoon dried thyme,
    crumbled
½ cup dried split peas
5 medium carrots, sliced
2 cups sliced celery
3 medium tomatoes, peeled,
    seeded and coarsely
    chopped

1½ cups fresh corn
1 large potato, peeled and
    chopped
1 large green pepper,
    chopped
1 cup fresh green peas
1 cup shelled fresh
    butterbeans
1 cup fresh green beans,
    broken in small pieces
1 cup chopped fresh spinach
2 tablespoons chopped fresh
    parsley
salt to taste
freshly ground pepper to taste

Brown beef in olive oil in large stockpot. Add onion, sauté. Add water and bring to a boil. Add split peas, cover and simmer 2 hours. Add remaining ingredients, cover and simmer 1 hour or until vegetables are tender. Flavor is best if prepared ahead, refrigerated (removing fat from surface when chilled) and reheated the following day.

To prepare in the winter when fresh vegetables are not available, use canned tomatoes and frozen vegetables.

Yield: 6 quarts

MUSHROOM AND BARLEY SOUP

1 pound fresh mushrooms,
   sliced
2 tablespoons butter
1 onion, finely chopped
¼ cup bacon drippings
4 cups beef broth

1 cup barley
1 tablespoon lemon juice
1 cup whipping cream
3 egg yolks
salt and pepper to taste

Sauté mushrooms in butter. Set aside. In a medium-size saucepan, sauté onions in bacon drippings. Stir in beef broth and barley. Cook covered about 45 minutes or until barley is tender. Add mushrooms and lemon juice. Cook covered for 15 minutes on low heat. Combine cream and egg yolks and stir slowly into soup. Season with salt and pepper. Continue heating, but do not boil. Serve hot.

Yield: 10 servings

FRENCH ONION SOUP

1½ pounds sweet onions
¼ cup butter
1 tablespoon flour
4 cups beef broth
½ cup dry white wine

1 teaspoon Worcestershire
   sauce
salt and pepper to taste
8 slices French bread,
   cut ½ inch thick
2 cups grated Swiss cheese

Peel and dice onions. Melt butter, add onions and sauté 20 minutes. Stir in flour, gradually stir in beef broth and wine. Cover and simmer 10 minutes. Season with Worcestershire sauce, salt and pepper. Layer half the bread in a 3 quart casserole or oven proof soup dish. Add ½ the cheese. Pour in soup and top with remaining bread and sprinkle with cheese. Bake at 400 degrees for 12 to 15 minutes or until bread is golden.

Yield: 4 to 6 servings

NAVY BEAN SOUP WITH HAM AND KRIDLERS

Bean Soup

1 pound Navy beans	1 ham bone or ham hock
10 to 12 cups water	1 teaspoon salt
1 onion, chopped	½ teaspoon pepper

Kridlers

4 large eggs, beaten	1 teaspoon salt
2 cups flour	¼ teaspoon pepper

Soak Navy beans in water overnight. Drain. Place beans, water, onion, ham, salt and pepper in a large stockpot and cook for 2 hours or until soft. To prepare Kridlers combine eggs, flour, salt and pepper. Drop by teaspoon in soup. Kridlers will come off easily if you put the spoon down in the soup. Cook 5 to 10 minutes.

Yield: 6 to 8 servings

SPLIT PEA SOUP

1½ cups green split peas	1 stalk celery, chopped
3 quarts water	3 medium size potatoes, peeled and cubed
2 pig's feet, optional	leafy top of 1 bunch of celery
1½ teaspoons salt	½ pound fat ham or 1 large smoked sausage
3 leeks, thinly sliced	slices of pumpernickel bread
2 medium sized yellow onions, sliced	

Soak the peas in water overnight in a covered pan. Drain the peas and place them in a large pan with 3 quarts of water, pig's feet and salt. Bring to a boil, lower the heat and simmer slowly for 3 hours. Add leeks, celery, potatoes and celery tops and simmer another 30 minutes, stirring occasionally. Add ham or sausage and simmer 10 more minutes. Discard the pig's feet. Remove ham or sausage. Slice ham or sausage and serve on pumpernickel bread, accompanied by bowls of hot soup.

Yield: 6 to 8 servings

CORN CHOWDER

2 cups potatoes, cubed
1 large onion, chopped
1 cup water
2 pounds smoked sausage,
   chopped
2 (16 ounce) cans whole
   kernel corn

1 (16 ounce) can cream corn
2 cups milk
½ stick margarine
2 teaspoons cornstarch,
   optional

Place potatoes, onion and water in pot and boil for 10 to 12 minutes or until potatoes are cooked. Drain. Add remaining ingredients and let simmer for 30 minutes. Add 2 teaspoons of cornstarch if it needs thickening.

You may want to top it off with shredded Cheddar cheese.

Yield: 6 to 8 servings

CAMPERS TOMATO SOUP BASE

3 (28 ounce) cans tomatoes,
   chopped
5 stalks celery, finely chopped
1 large onion, chopped
2 cups chicken bouillon
1 teaspoon garlic salt
7 bay leaves
1 tablespoon dried parsley

dash cayenne pepper
1½ teaspoons basil
1 teaspoon allspice
½ teaspoon black pepper
2½ teaspoons granulated
   sugar
1 stick butter or margarine
1 teaspoon baking soda

Combine all ingredients except baking soda. Bring mixture to a boil, remove from heat and add baking soda. To serve add equal amounts of tomato soup base to 2 percent milk. Heat until hot, but do not boil.

Yield: 12 servings

SPRING LAMB STEW

1 tablespoon vegetable oil
2 pounds lamb shoulder, cut
   into 2 inch pieces
2½ cups beef stock
salt and pepper to taste
2 cloves garlic, crushed
½ teaspoon dried rosemary
1 bay leaf

6 small whole, white onions,
   peeled
6 small turnips, peeled
6 baby carrots, peeled
½ cup green peas (fresh or
   frozen) or ½ cup of fresh
   snow peas

Heat the oil in a large heavy gauge Dutch oven. Trim excess fat away from lamb and sauté in the oil until nicely browned. Add the beef stock to the pot and season with salt, pepper, garlic, rosemary and the bay leaf. Cover and simmer gently for 1 hour. Add the onions, turnips and carrots. Serve by the bowl with wedges of Rosemary Bread.

Yield: 6 servings

JACK'S BRUNSWICK STEW

1 large hen
1 large Boston Butt
1 pound pork liver
1 large onion, chopped
6 potatoes, chopped
2 (16 ounce) cans lima beans,
   drained

2 (16 ounce) cans tomatoes
2 (16 ounce) cans whole
   kernel corn
salt and pepper to taste
okra, if desired

Boil meats until they are tender. Remove bone and fat. Grind meat and add to broth and combine remaining ingredients. Cook slowly until done.

Serve with rice, barbecue and a green vegetable.

Yield: 8 servings

CHUCKWAGON STEW

2½ pounds beef cubes
2 tablespoons all-purpose
   flour
1 tablespoon paprika
1 teaspoon chili powder
2 teaspoons salt
oil
2 sliced onions
1 clove garlic, minced

1 (28 ounce) can tomatoes
2 cups chopped potatoes
3 tablespoons chili powder
1 tablespoon cinnamon
1 teaspoon ground cloves
½ to 1 teaspoon crushed red
   peppers
2 cups chopped carrots

Coat beef in a mixture of flour, paprika, 1 teaspoon chili powder and salt, brown in oil in a large Dutch oven. Add onion and garlic and cook until soft. Add tomatoes, 3 tablespoons chili powder, cinnamon, cloves and pepper. Cover and simmer 2 hours. Add potatoes and carrots and cook until vegetables are done, about 45 minutes.

Yield: 6 to 8 servings

DONALD'S ISLAND STEW

Crab boil or Creole seafood
   seasoning, 2 teaspoons
   per quart of water
¼ pound smoked beef
   sausage per person
2 to 3 small red potatoes,
   unpeeled, per person

1 ear of corn per person
   or 3 inch cobbettes
¾ pound large shrimp per
   person
crab claws, optional

Bring large quantity of water to a boil. Add seafood seasoning and stir. Add sausage and red potatoes. Cook for 15 minutes. Add corn and cook for 10 minutes or 15 if corn is frozen. Add shrimp and cook only 5 minutes. Drain and serve yourself.

A variation of "Frogmore Stew".

Perfect for outdoor and casual company. Fun, easy and delicious one pot party.

CATFISH STEW

2 pounds catfish
1 cup water
2 slices salt pork, cut in
   1 inch squares
1 onion, chopped
1 bell pepper, chopped
chopped celery to taste

2 medium potatoes, diced
4 cups tomatoes
1 teaspoon Worcestershire
   sauce
1 teaspoon Creole
1 teaspoon Cajun seasoning
dash of Tabasco sauce

Simmer catfish in water until it comes off bone. Remove bone and put meat back in liquid. In a skillet fry pork slowly adding onions, bell peppers and celery to sauté. Combine potatoes, tomatoes, Worcestershire sauce, Creole, Cajun seasoning and Tabasco sauce in fish and liquid. Simmer for 30 to 45 minutes or until potatoes are tender. Serve with white rice or cornbread.

Yield: 8 servings

FISH CHOWDER STEW

¼ pound salt pork or bacon
2 to 3 pounds fish, fillet and
   cut in small pieces
5 medium large potatoes,
   diced
4 large onions, chopped
1 (16 ounce) can tomato
   sauce

¼ cup Worcestershire sauce
1 quart cut tomatoes
black pepper to taste
hot sauce to taste
1 (46 ounce) can tomato juice
½ cup celery, chopped

Cut pork or bacon into small pieces and brown. Add all remaining ingredients. Cook on medium to high heat. Stirring occasionally to prevent sticking. Reduce heat and simmer until potatoes are tender. Serve as stew or over rice.

For variation you may add shrimp or oysters.

Yields: 4 to 5 quarts

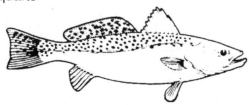

SARAH'S CRAB STEW

1 medium onion, minced
½ cup celery, finely chopped
2 tablespoons butter or
    margarine
3 tablespoons cornstarch
4½ cups milk

1 pound claw crab meat
1 teaspoon seafood season
1 teaspoon salt
½ teaspoon pepper
½ teaspoon parsley

Sauté onions and celery in butter until tender; set aside. Mix cornstarch with ½ cup milk; set aside. In a heavy saucepan combine 4 cups milk and crab meat. Add seafood season, salt, pepper and parsley. Gradually stir in onion mixture and cornstarch. Heat over low heat until hot (do not let stew come to a boil).

Yield: 4 servings

SALMON STEW

6 potatoes, cubed
1 large onion, chopped

1 large can of salmon
1 cup of ketchup

In a large pot boil potatoes until almost done. Add onion and cook on medium until tender. Add crumbled salmon mixing well. Stir in ketchup and simmer for 15 minutes.

More ketchup may be added if desired.

This is a quick and easy meal for the whole family.

Yield: 10 servings

TURKEY VEGETABLE SOUP

1 pound ground turkey
1 (16 ounce) can cut green
    beans
1 (16 ounce) can whole kernel
    corn
1 (16 ounce) can cut carrots

1 (15 ounce) can early peas
2 (15 ounce) cans whole
    potatoes, drained
2 teaspoons cornstarch
1 tablespoon Kitchen Bouquet
    browning sauce

Brown turkey in large saucepan. Drain. Add remaining ingredients. Bring to boil and simmer for about 15 minutes. Serve with crackers or cornbread.

Yield: 8 servings

GAZPACHO

6 cups tomato juice
1 Vidalia onion, finely
 chopped
6 tomatoes, chopped
1 green pepper, chopped
1 cucumber, chopped
2 green onions, chopped
¼ cup chopped fresh parsley

¼ cup lemon juice
2 tablespoons cider vinegar
1 teaspoon dried tarragon
1 teaspoon dried basil
1 teaspoon cayenne pepper
3 tablespoons olive oil
salt and pepper to taste

Combine all ingredients. Chill thoroughly before serving.

For a creamier texture, purée in blender.

Yield: 8 to 10 servings

TRUE'S SOUP

1 (10½ ounce) can tomato
 soup
1 (10½ ounce) can split pea
 soup

1 can milk
1 can water
1 pound crab meat
Parmesan cheese

Combine soups, milk and water in saucepan. Heat but do not boil. Add crab meat and stir. Just before serving sprinkle with Parmesan cheese.

Easy and tasty.

Yield: 4 servings

EASY CHILI CON CARNE

½ cup onion, chopped
½ cup green pepper, chopped
2 tablespoons vegetable oil
1 pound ground beef
2 (15 ounce) cans tomato
 sauce

1 (6 ounce) can tomato paste
2 (16 ounce) cans Bush's chili
 hot beans
1 (1½ ounce) package Sauer's
 chili seasoning mix

Heat oil in 4 quart pot. Sauté onions, peppers and brown ground beef. Drain well. Add all remaining ingredients and bring to a boil. Reduce heat and simmer for 1 hour. Serve in bowls with crackers or serve over yellow rice and top with shredded cheese.

Yield: 6 to 8 servings

SISSY'S SURE FIRE CHILI

1 pound ground beef
1 onion, diced
¼ teaspoon meat tenderizer
½ teaspoon onion powder
1 can sliced potatoes, drained
½ teaspoon salt
¼ teaspoon pepper

3 (16 ounce) cans red kidney
  beans
1 (10.75 ounce) can tomato
  soup
¼ teaspoon chili powder, if
  desired

Brown ground beef with diced onion, when beef is completely browned add 1 can tomato soup. Stir in meat tenderizer, onion powder, salt, pepper and chili powder. Add sliced potatoes and kidney beans. Cook on medium heat for approximately 45 minutes or until potatoes are done.

Yield: 8 to 10 servings

QUICK OKRA SOUP

1 medium onion, chopped
1 chunk of fat back
1 (16 ounce) can tomatoes,
  okra and corn

1 (16 ounce) can tomatoes
  and okra
1 (16 ounce) can tomatoes
2 tablespoons hot sauce

Sauté onions and fat back in a 2 quart pot. Combine remaining ingredients except hot sauce and simmer for 30 to 45 minutes. Add hot sauce 5 minutes before ready.

Serve with cornbread.

Yield: 4 servings

AVOCADO SOUP

2 avocados
1 cup chicken broth
1 cup half and half
1 teaspoon salt

¼ teaspoon onion salt
dash white pepper
1 teaspoon lemon or lime
  juice

Peel avocados and remove seeds. Blend avocados and chicken broth in blender until smooth. Combine with remaining ingredients except lemon or lime juice. Chill thoroughly; stir in lemon or lime juice. Garnish with grated lemon rind, lemon slices, watercress, a spoonful of sour cream or a combination of garnishes.

Yield: 6 servings

BROCCOLI SALAD

1 bunch broccoli
10 slices bacon, cooked and
    crumbled
½ cup raisins
1 purple onion, chopped

1 cup slivered almonds
1 cup mayonnaise
2 tablespoons vinegar
½ cup sugar

Trim broccoli breaking into small pieces. Add bacon, raisins, onion and almonds. Mix together mayonnaise, vinegar and sugar then add to broccoli mixture and toss. Chill ½ hour before serving.

Serve with soup and crusty bread for a light and easy lunch.

Yield: 10 servings

GARBANZO AND WALNUT SALAD

Salad
1 (approximately 1 pound) can
    garbanzos, drained
⅔ cup finely chopped walnuts

Lemon Dressing (see below)
inner romaine lettuce leaves

Lemon Dressing
6 tablespoons lemon juice
¼ cup olive oil or salad oil

2 cloves garlic, minced or
    pressed
1 teaspoon salt

In a large bowl mash garbanzos until they resemble crumbs; stir in chopped nuts. Prepare lemon dressing by combining lemon juice, olive oil or salad oil, minced garlic and salt. Mix until blended. Spoon garbanzo spread into center of shallow bowl or plate and surround with lettuce leaves. Serve at room temperature.

Yield: 6 servings

BEAN AND CARROT SALAD

1 pound cut green beans
1 pound kidney beans
1 pound can carrots
½ cup chopped green peppers
2 tablespoons chopped
   onions

½ cup oil
¾ cup vinegar
¾ cup sugar
½ tablespoon pepper
1 teaspoon salt

Drain juice from first 3 ingredients and toss vegetables together. Add green peppers, onions and toss with oil, vinegar, sugar, pepper and salt. Let stand overnight before serving.

Very easy. Can be made ahead.

Yield: 4 to 6 servings

PEA SALAD

2 (16 ounce) cans early peas
1 cup shredded Cheddar
   cheese
1 (2 ounce) jar diced pimentos

3 tablespoons mayonnaise
½ onion, diced
dash of celery seed

Drain peas well. Place in mixing bowl and add remaining ingredients. Can be made 1 day ahead and served cold.

Terrific dish for family gatherings.

Yield: 8 to 10 servings

3 BEAN SALAD

1 (16 ounce) can kidney beans
1 (16 ounce) can wax beans
1 (16 ounce) can green beans
½ cup onion, chopped or
   sliced
½ cup green bell pepper,
   chopped or sliced

½ cup sugar
1 cup apple cider vinegar
1 teaspoon salt
½ teaspoon black pepper
½ cup salad oil

Combine in mixing bowl all vegetables. In smaller bowl mix together sugar, vinegar, salt, pepper, and oil. Pour liquid mixture over vegetables and store in container with a tight fitting lid. Refrigerate.

Yield: 6 to 8 servings

TOM'S TACO SALAD

1 (16 ounce) can stewed
   tomatoes
1 teaspoon granulated sugar
¾ teaspoon dried oregano
½ teaspoon Worcestershire
   sauce
¼ teaspoon salt
⅛ teaspoon pepper
¼ teaspoon hot pepper sauce

¼ cup green pepper, chopped
¼ cup onion, chopped
1 pound ground beef
½ teaspoon garlic salt
1 (9½ ounce) package corn
   chips
4 to 5 slices processed
   American cheese
2 cups shredded lettuce

To make taco sauce, stir together first 7 ingredients. Using edge of spoon, break up large tomato pieces. Stir in green pepper and onion, then set aside. In medium skillet, cook ground beef until browned, stirring to break up. Drain excess fat. Stir in garlic salt. Coarsely crush corn chips; place in bottom of ungreased 8x8x2 inch baking dish. Spoon hot meat over corn chips; top with cheese slices. Bake at 350 degrees for 10 to 12 minutes. Sprinkle casserole with lettuce and top with taco sauce.

Yield: 4 to 6 servings

MOZZARELLA AND TOMATO SALAD

1 pound tomatoes, cut
   crosswise into ⅛ inch
   cubes or slices
½ pound Mozzarella cheese,
   sliced thin

¼ cup packed fresh basil
   leaves, minced
1 tablespoon wine vinegar
1 tablespoon oil
1 small clove garlic, minced
salt and pepper to taste

On a platter, arrange tomato slices alternately with Mozzarella cheese, overlapping them. In a small bowl, stir together basil, vinegar, oil and garlic. Spoon dressing over the salad and let stand at room temperature covered loosely for 30 minutes.

Yield: 4 to 6 servings

HUZARENSLA HUSSAR'S SALAD

1½ cups chopped cold
   cooked meat (veal or pork)
2 green apples, peeled, cored
   and chopped
1 small beet, cooked and
   chopped
2 hard-boiled eggs
1 small onion or scallion,
   finely chopped
8 new potatoes, cooked,
   cooled and chopped

3 tablespoons oil
3 tablespoons vinegar
½ teaspoon salt
freshly ground black pepper
   to taste
lettuce leaves
mayonnaise
1 tomato, peeled and thinly
   sliced

In a bowl, combine the meat, apples, beef, 1 egg, onion and potatoes. Mix together with oil, vinegar, salt and pepper and pour over salad. Toss to coat the meat and vegetables thoroughly. Place lettuce leaves on flat serving dish. Arrange the salad in a boat shape on the lettuce. Cover the "boat" with a very thin layer of mayonnaise. Decorate with thin sliced eggs and tomatoes.

MUSHROOM SALAD WITH MADEIRA WINE

½ pound fresh mushrooms,
   rinsed and sliced
juice of 1 lemon
½ tablespoon Madeira wine

⅓ cup mayonnaise
1½ teaspoons tomato paste
1 teaspoon fresh tarragon,
   chopped

Combine all of the ingredients with the exception of the mushrooms and lemon juice. Sprinkle the mushrooms with lemon juice. Add to other ingredients. Stir, cover and chill.

Yield: 4 servings

HEARTS OF PALM SALAD

1 (14 ounce) can hearts of palm
3 cups watercress
2 cups torn romaine
2 cups torn iceberg lettuce
pinch of tarragon
pinch of thyme

pinch of basil leaves
2 tablespoons vinegar
⅓ cup olive oil
1 clove garlic, crushed
½ teaspoon salt
½ teaspoon ground pepper
1 tablespoon Dijon mustard

In a lidded glass container soak tarragon, thyme and bail leaves in vinegar. Add olive oil, mustard, pepper and garlic. Shake well. Drain hearts of palm. Cut in serving pieces. Combine with greens. Place in large bowl and gently toss with dressing.

Watercress is sometimes difficult to find. Substitute with green leaf lettuce.

Delicious.

Yield: 6 to 8 servings

LOWCOUNTRY SHRIMP SALAD

½ cup sour cream
¼ teaspoon salt
⅛ teaspoon mace
1 tablespoon fresh lemon juice
1 tablespoon Miracle Whip salad dressing

2 hard-boiled eggs, finely chopped
1 pound medium shrimp, cooked, shelled and deveined

Mix all ingredients together except the shrimp and chill for several hours. Add the shrimp, cut into large chunks or leave whole. Refrigerate again for at least an hour. May be made as much as a day ahead of serving.

Yield: 4 servings

SUMMER SEAFOOD PASTA

1 (8 ounce) package sea shell
   pasta
1½ teaspoons lemon juice
½ cup celery, finely chopped
2 tablespoons onion, minced
6 ounces salad shrimp,
   cooked, peeled

1 (8 ounce) package imitation
   salad style crab meat,
   diced
½ cup mayonnaise
2 teaspoons seafood
   seasoning
⅓ cup thawed frozen peas
1 tablespoon parsley
salt and pepper to taste

Cook sea shells according to package instructions. Drain and rinse in cool water. Immediately toss with lemon juice. Mix in remaining ingredients. Chill for several hours to blend flavors. Serve on bed of fresh lettuce.

Yield: 8 to 10 servings

SEAFOOD SALAD

1 pound shrimp, cooked,
   peeled and deveined
1 pound crab meat
6 eggs, hard-boiled
1 large onion, chopped fine

1 bell pepper, chopped
2 stalks celery, chopped
1 cup mayonnaise
paprika

Cut shrimp and crab meat into little pieces. Mash boiled eggs with a fork. Add eggs, onion, pepper, celery to shrimp and crab. Stir in mayonnaise and blend well. Sprinkle lightly with paprika. Chill and serve.

Yield: 8 to 10 servings

MACARONI GARDEN SALAD

¾ pound shrimp, peeled, deveined and cooked
¾ pound crab meat
1 cucumber, chopped
1 tomato, chopped
½ cup black olives, sliced
1 (8 ounce) package uncooked frozen peas
½ cup onion, chopped
1 (8 ounce) package elbow macaroni (cooked, drained)
¾ cup mayonnaise
½ teaspoon sugar
1 teaspoon salt
½ teaspoon black pepper

Mix first 8 ingredients together in large bowl. Mix together mayonnaise, sugar, salt and pepper and add to seafood mixture. Toss to coat. Cover and chill.

Yield: 12 servings

CHINESE SALAD

Salad
3 to 4 chicken breasts
½ cup freshly grated ginger
1 head of chopped iceberg lettuce
4 to 6 chopped scallions
1 cup slivered toasted almonds
¼ cup toasted sesame seeds
½ (7 ounce) pack rice sticks

Cook chicken with ginger in small amount of water and simmer until done. Drain chicken and shred. Toss together lettuce, scallions, almonds and sesame seed. Keep refrigerated. Deep fry rice sticks.

Dressing
4 tablespoons granulated sugar
2 teaspoons salt
½ teaspoon black pepper
4 teaspoons rice vinegar
½ cup canola oil

Dissolve sugar, salt, pepper and rice vinegar over low heat. Cool mixture and add canola oil. To serve, gently toss chicken, bread sticks and chilled salad mixture with dressing.

Yield: 20 servings

ITALIAN SLAW

1 medium head of cabbage
1 large onion, sliced into rings
⅞ cup granulated sugar
1 cup vinegar
¾ cup salad oil

2 teaspoons granulated sugar
1 teaspoon prepared mustard
1 teaspoon celery seed
1 teaspoon salt

Shred cabbage and place in large bowl. Layer with onion rings and cover with ⅞ cup sugar. Bring remaining ingredients to a boil and pour over cabbage. Let set for 6 hours for best results.

Yield: 10 servings

APPLE COLE SLAW

½ head cabbage, grated
1 medium red apple, unpeeled
   and cut into chunks
1 small carrot, grated

3 tablespoons mayonnaise
2½ tablespoons granulated
   sugar
¼ cup raisins

Combine ingredients in order listed. Mix well and chill before serving.

Yield: 4 to 6 servings

MARINATED PEA SALAD

1 (16 ounce) can garden peas,
   drained
1 (16 ounce) can cut green
   beans, drained
1 (2 ounce) jar chopped
   pimentos
1 medium bell pepper,
   chopped
1 large sweet red onion,
   chopped

1 large sweet white onion,
   chopped
4 stalks celery, chopped
1 cup granulated sugar
1 cup cider vinegar
1 tablespoon water
1 tablespoon salt
½ cup vegetable oil

Mix all ingredients together 24 hours before serving.

Tangy, but delicious.

Yield: 4 to 6 servings

REFRESHING ORANGE SALAD

1 (6 ounce) package orange
   gelatin
1 (8 ounce) carton sour cream
1 (16 ounce) container Cool
   Whip

1 (8 ounce) can crushed
   pineapple, drained
1 (8 ounce) can mandarin
   oranges, drained

Mix gelatin with sour cream and Cool Whip. Fold fruit into cream and gelatin mixture. Refrigerate.

Yield: 8 to 10 servings

PISTACHIO SALAD

2 cups miniature
   marshmallows
1 (3 ounce) package pistachio
   instant pudding
1 (20 ounce) can crushed
   pineapple with juice

1 (8 ounce) jar maraschino
   cherries, drained and cut
   up
1 (9 ounce) container whipped
   topping
1 cup chopped pecans

Combine all ingredients, mixing well. Chill before serving.

Yield: 8 to 10 servings

SEVEN LAYER SALAD

½ head shredded lettuce
1 cup celery, chopped
1 cup bell pepper, chopped
1 cup purple onion, chopped
1 (17 ounce) can peas,
   drained

1½ cups mayonnaise
1½ teaspoons granulated
   sugar
½ cup Parmesan cheese
Bac-o's

Layer ingredients as listed in a 2 quart bowl. Spread mayonnaise over top of peas. Sprinkle with sugar, cheese and then Bac-o's over top of mayonnaise. Cover and chill 8 hours before servings.

Yield: 6 to 8 servings

STRAWBERRY CREAM LAYERED SALAD

1 (3 ounce) package
  strawberry gelatin
½ cup boiling water
2 medium size bananas
1 (10 ounce) package frozen
  sweetened strawberries,
  thawed

1 (8 ounce) can crushed
  pineapple
1 cup coarsely chopped
  walnuts
1 cup sour cream
lettuce leaves

Dissolve gelatin in a small bowl of boiling water. In a large bowl, mash bananas and combine with strawberries and their juice, pineapple, and nuts. Add gelatin. Pour half the mixture into an 8 inch square baking dish; cover and refrigerate until firm (about 1½ hours). Cover remaining banana mixture and let stand at room temperature. Spread refrigerated portion evenly with sour cream, then spoon remaining banana mixture over sour cream layer. Cover and refrigerate until firm (at least 4 hours). To serve, arrange lettuce leaves on 6 individual salad plates. Cut layered salad into 6 portions and arrange on lettuce.

Tastes wonderful on a hot summer day.

Yield: 6 servings

ROSE MARIE'S SALAD

1 (6 ounce) package lemon
  gelatin
1 cup boiling water
1 cup cold water
1 (14 ounce) can sweetened
  condensed milk

1 (8 ounce) can crushed
  pineapple
½ cup chopped walnuts
leafy lettuce, if desired

In a mixing bowl, stir in gelatin with boiling water until dissolved. Mix in cold water, condensed milk, pineapple and walnuts. Pour mixture into a 13x9x2 inch dish and chill until firm. Cut into squares and serve on lettuce.

Excellent with turkey.

Yield: 15 servings

EASY FRUIT SALAD

2 (11 ounce) cans mandarin
oranges
1 (20 ounce) can crushed
pineapple, in juice
1 (16 ounce) jar red salad
cherries

1 (16 ounce) carton sour
cream
2 cups miniature
marshmallows

Drain all fruit except pineapple. In big bowl mix all fruit, sour cream, marshmallows. Chill in covered dish overnight. Stir before servings.

May be prepared ahead of time, the longer the salad chills, the better.

Yield: 8 servings

24 HOUR SALAD

1 (3 ounce) box instant vanilla
pudding
1 cup whipping cream
1 (14 ounce) can fruit cocktail
1 (11 ounce) can mandarin
oranges

1 (4 ounce) jar maraschino
cherries
1 (6 ounce) package
marshmallows
2 medium bananas, sliced

Prepare pudding according to package directions. Whip cream. Drain fruit cocktail, mandarin oranges and cherries. Add fruit and whipped cream to pudding mix. Stir to blend. Refrigerate for 24 hours before serving.

Almost a dessert.

Yield: 14 to 16 servings

FIVE CUP SALAD

1 cup mini marshmallows
1 cup coconut
1 cup pineapple chunks
1 cup mandarin oranges

1 (6 ounce) jar maraschino
cherries
1 cup sour cream

Drain oranges and pineapple well. Mix all ingredients together and chill before serving.

For large crowds double recipe.

Yield: 6 servings

MIXED FRUIT SALAD

2 (17 ounce) cans chunky
    mixed fruit
1 cup chunked pineapple
½ pound green seedless
    grapes
2 unpeeled apples, diced
1 cup mandarin oranges

½ cup chopped pecans
2 sliced bananas
2 tablespoons dry instant
    orange flavored dry mix
2 (3 ounce) packages instant
    vanilla pudding

Drain all canned fruits and reserve liquid. Combine mixed fruit, pine-apple, grapes, apples, oranges with pecans in a large bowl. In a medium mixing bowl combine pudding with 2 cups of reserved liquid, blend with an electric mixer until thickened. Pour pudding mixture over fruit and refrigerate overnight. Just before serving slice bananas and sprinkle orange flavored dry mix over the bananas. (This will keep the bananas from turning dark.) Stir bananas into fruit mixture and serve.

Yield: 6 to 8 servings

COCONUT FRUIT SALAD

2 apples
2 (8 ounce) cans mandarin
    oranges
1 (4 ounce) can drained
    pineapple
1 (16 ounce) can fruit cocktail
1 small can coconut

1 cup pecans, chopped
1 (3 ounce) can chilled
    evaporated milk
1 cup mayonnaise
2 (6 ounce) jars cherries
1 bag miniature
    marshmallows

Mix together all ingredients except cherries and marshmallows. Place cherries and marshmallows on top and chill.

Serves well as a refreshing after dinner salad.

Yield: 10 servings

FROZEN BANANA SALAD

2 (3 ounce) packages cream
   cheese
4 tablespoons mayonnaise
1 (8 ounce) can crushed
   pineapple
1 tablespoon lemon juice

1 teaspoon salt
½ cup maraschino cherries,
   chopped
½ cup pecans, chopped
3 ripe bananas
1 cup cream (whipped)

Whip cream cheese until fluffy. Add mayonnaise, pineapple, lemon juice, salt, cherries and nuts. Fold in thinly sliced bananas. Mix in whipped cream. Freeze in mold or a shallow pan, and cut in pieces.

Yield: 6 servings

FESTIVE CRANBERRY SALAD

2 (3 ounce) packages lemon
   gelatin
1 cup granulated sugar
1 cup boiling water
4 cups fresh cranberries,
   ground

½ cup chopped pecans
lettuce leaves
mayonnaise or salad dressing
orange slices

Dissolve gelatin and sugar in boiling water. Add next 4 ingredients; stir well. Pour into a lightly oiled 6-cup ring mold; chill until set. Unmold on lettuce leaves. Fill center of ring with mayonnaise, and garnish salad with orange slices.

Yield: 6 to 8 servings

Breads

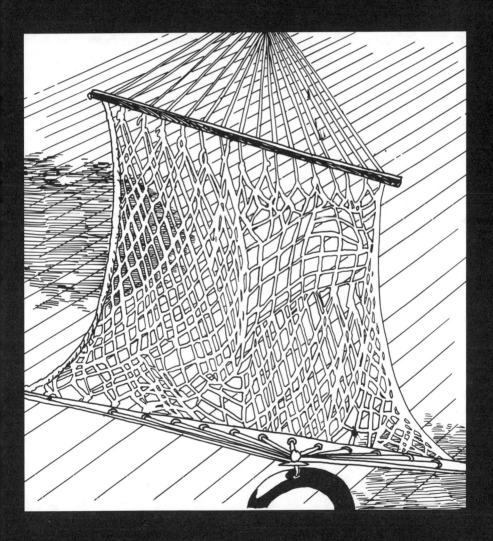

IRISH SODA BREAD

3½ cups all-purpose flour
3½ teaspoons baking powder
½ teaspoon baking soda
1 teaspoon salt

2½ tablespoons granulated
 sugar
½ cup vegetable oil
1 egg
2 cups buttermilk

Preheat oven to 350 degrees. Sift dry ingredients together into a large bowl. Work in shortening and blend into flour until mixture is fine. To one cup of buttermilk add the egg and beat well. Add other cup of buttermilk to this mixture. Slowly add buttermilk mixture to dry ingredients until the mixture resembles biscuit dough; this may not require all of the buttermilk mixture. Knead dough on a floured board and shape to fit into a greased, loaf pan. Bake at 350 degrees for 1 hour.

Yield: 6 to 8 servings

FAMOUS BEER BREAD

1 (12 ounce) can beer
2½ cups self rising flour

1 cup granulated sugar
non-stick cooking spray

Open beer and let stand for 6 hours so it becomes flat. Mix sugar with beer until sugar dissolved. Preheat oven to 250 degrees. Slowly add flour with beer until you have a smooth creamy mixture like melted peanut butter. Pour mixture into loaf pan coated with non-stick cooking spray. Fill each pan ¾ of the way. Let pans sit for 30 minutes for proofing. Place filled loaf pans in oven and allow to cook for 1½ hours. Check for doneness with toothpick.

Excellent with honey butter spread, or as toast for breakfast with cinnamon sugar.

Yield: 6 to 8 servings

BUBBLE BREAD

1 small package pecan chips
1 package Rich's frozen rolls
¾ cup brown sugar

1 small package vanilla
  pudding (not instant, do
  not mix — use powder)
1 stick of margarine
cinnamon, optional

In a bundt pan, place above ingredients in the order they appear and cover with wax paper unrefrigerated. Let rise overnight and bake next morning at 350 degrees for 30 minutes.

Great for any occasion.

Yield: 6 to 8 servings

CINNAMON-NUT COFFEE CAKE

Coffee Cake
2 sticks butter
1½ cups granulated sugar
4 eggs, separated
3 cups flour

¼ teaspoon salt
1 teaspoon baking soda
1 cup buttermilk
2 teaspoons baking powder

Cream butter and sugar. Add egg yolks one at a time. Sift flour with salt and soda 6 times. Add flour to batter, alternating with buttermilk, adding baking powder to flour before the last addition. Beat egg whites stiffly and fold into batter.

Cinnamon Mixture
½ cup granulated sugar
1 cup chopped pecans
1 teaspoon cocoa

¼ cup minced raisins
1 tablespoon cinnamon
butter, as desired

Mix all the above ingredients to form the cinnamon mixture. Then, pour a little of the batter into a greased and floured tube or bundt cake pan. Sprinkle some cinnamon mixture over batter. Alternate batter and cinnamon mixture, ending with cinnamon mixture. Dot generously with butter. Bake at 375 degrees for 1 hour.

This may be made ahead of time and frozen. However, it is better made the day before serving.

When well sealed, this cake keeps over a period of several days.

Yield: 12 servings

MEXICAN CORN BREAD

1 cup yellow cornmeal
1 cup milk
¾ teaspoon salt
½ cup bacon drippings
2 eggs, slightly beaten
½ teaspoon soda

1 (16 ounce) can cream style
   corn
½ pound rat cheese, grated
1 large onion, finely chopped
4 canned jalapeño peppers,
   chopped

Combine cornmeal, milk, salt, bacon drippings, eggs, soda, corn and mix well. Grease a #9 black iron skillet and heat. Sprinkle a very thin layer of cornmeal and let brown lightly. Pour ½ of batter in skillet; sprinkle cheese evenly, then onion, then peppers. Pour on remaining batter. Bake at 350 degrees for 45 to 50 minutes.

If you like spicy food, you'll love this.

Yield: 6 to 8 servings

CAROL'S CORNBREAD

½ cup oil
1 (16 ounce) can creamed
   corn

1 cup sour cream
2 eggs
1½ cups self-rising cornmeal

Combine all ingredients and mix with an electric hand mixer. Pour in a 13x9x2 inch pan and bake at 400 degrees for 30 minutes.

Yield: 12 servings

"OLD" OLD FASHIONED CORN FRITTERS

4 egg yolks, well beaten
1 cup milk
2 cups flour
1 teaspoon salt

1 teaspoon baking powder
1 teaspoon butter, melted
1 (16 ounce) can whole kernel
   corn

Beat egg yolks well with milk. Sift and add flour, salt, and baking powder. Stir in melted butter and well drained corn. Drop by spoonfuls into hot oil (375 degrees). Fry until brown. Drain on paper towels. Serve hot.

Great with maple syrup and butter.

Yield: 4 to 6 servings.

BEER AND TOMATO HUSH PUPPIES

1½ cups self-rising yellow
  cornmeal
4 tablespoons self-rising flour
1 egg, beaten
1½ teaspoons Worcestershire
  sauce
dash of salt

dash of hot sauce
2 medium onions, chopped
1 bell pepper, chopped
1 tomato, cut in quarters
½ cup beer
vegetable shortening

Combine cornmeal, flour, egg, Worcestershire sauce, salt, and hot sauce in mixing bowl. Place onion, bell pepper and tomato in blender and blend for 30 seconds. Combine beer in blended mixture, then add to cornmeal mixture. Heat shortening in deep fat fryer or large frying pan. Drop ½ teaspoon at a time and fry until they come to the top of pan. Remove and enjoy.

Yield: 6 servings

MONKEY BREAD

⅔ cup sugar
1 teaspoon salt
1 cup mashed potatoes
1 package yeast
½ cup lukewarm water

⅔ cup margarine
⅔ cup butter
1 cup milk
6 cups sifted flour
2 eggs

Mix sugar, salt and potatoes in bowl. Dissolve yeast in water. Melt butter and margarine in milk over low heat and add to sugar mixture. Cool to lukewarm. Add yeast and half of flour. Beat eggs; add to remaining flour. Combine the 2 mixtures and mix well. Let rise about 1 hour. Stir down and place in refrigerator. When ready to bake, melt more butter and dip small elongated rolls of dough in it. Place rolls of dough in well-buttered ring mold, making only 2 layers. Bake at 350 degrees for 30 to 40 minutes.

When serving, tear bread off with fingers instead of cutting with a knife.

Yield: 8 to 10 servings

SPOON BREAD

1 cup water
2 cups milk
1 teaspoon salt

1 cup cornmeal (water-ground best)
3 eggs, well beaten
¼ cup melted oleo or butter

Scald water and milk together. Add salt and meal. Cook and stir until thick. Fold beaten eggs and butter and pour into greased 2 quart casserole dish. Bake at 350 degrees for 1 hour. Serve immediately.

Yield: 6 servings

EASY AND QUICK SWEET LOAVES

1 cup nuts, chopped
1 package frozen rolls
¾ cup brown sugar
1 small package vanilla
    pudding (not instant)

1½ teaspoons cinnamon
5 tablespoons butter or
    margarine

Coat two loaf pans with non-stick spray. Layer nuts in pans. Place rolls close to together in pan in a line. Mix sugar, pudding and cinnamon together and sprinkle over rolls. Dot with butter. Cover and let stand overnight to rise. Bake at 350 degrees for 30 to 40 minutes.

Yield: 8 to 10 servings

CHEESE BISCUITS

½ pound grated sharp cheese,
    room temperature
½ pound margarine, room
    temperature

2½ cups sifted self-rising flour
½ teaspoon salt
dash cayenne pepper
pecan halves, optional

Cream together cheese, margarine and salt together. Mix flour and pepper until well blended. Divide into 2 parts. Shape into rolls about 12 inch long. Roll in waxed paper and store in refrigerator overnight or until ready to use. Slice thinly and place on ungreased cookie sheet about ½ inch apart. Top with pecan halves. Bake at 400 degrees for 10 minutes.

Yield: 10 to 12 servings

GARLIC CHEESE BISCUITS

2 cups Bisquick
⅔ cup milk
**½ cup shredded Cheddar
cheese**

¼ cup melted margarine
¼ teaspoon garlic powder

Preheat oven to 450 degrees. Mix Bisquick, milk and cheese until moist. Drop dough by spoonfuls on greased cookie sheet. Bake 10 minutes or until golden brown. Mix margarine and garlic and brush over biscuits.

Variation: onion or broccoli

Quick, easy and delicious.

Yield: 6 to 8 servings

BREAKFAST MUFFINS

2 cups oats
2 cups sour cream
**⅔ cup butter or margarine,
melted**
4 eggs

**2 cups light brown sugar,
packed**
2 cups flour
2 teaspoons baking powder
1 teaspoon soda
½ teaspoon salt

Combine oats and sour cream. Stir in melted butter, eggs, brown sugar until well mixed. Sift together flour, baking powder, soda and salt. Stir into oat mixture just until blended. Put into muffin paper cups or greased muffin tins. Bake at 375 degrees for 20 to 25 minutes.

For a lighter version, substitute 2 cups non dairy imitation sour cream for regular, ⅔ cup diet margarine for butter, and frozen egg substitute equivalent to 4 eggs.

Great for a snack.

Yield: 3 dozen

LEMON MUFFINS

Lemon Muffins

1 cup butter or shortening	2 cups flour
1 cup granulated sugar	2 teaspoons baking powder
4 eggs, separated	1 teaspoon salt
½ cup lemon juice	2 teaspoons grated lemon peel

Cream butter and sugar until smooth. Add well-beaten egg yolks and beat until light. Add the lemon juice alternately with the flour which has been sifted with baking powder and salt, mixing thoroughly after each addition (do not over-mix). Fold in stiffly beaten egg whites and grated lemon peel. Fill buttered muffins pans ¾ full and bake at 375 degrees for about 20 minutes.

Citrus Glaze

¼ cup lemon juice	2 tablespoons butter
¼ cup orange juice	2¼ cups unsifted confectioners' sugar
¼ cup pineapple juice	

Heat lemon juice, orange juice, pineapple juice, and butter. Add confectioners' sugar. Stir till blended. Pour over muffins while it is still warm.

These freeze well and are nice split and toasted for breakfast.

Yield: makes 24

BANANA MUFFINS

1 egg	¾ teaspoon salt
⅓ cup salad oil	2 teaspoons baking powder
½ cup granulated sugar	¼ teaspoon soda
½ cup mashed banana	tart jelly (red currant, quince, guava, cranberry)
1¾ cups sifted flour	

Beat egg slightly; stir in oil and sugar. Add banana and mix well. Sift flour with remaining dry ingredients; add to first mixture and stir until liquid and dry ingredients are combined. Grease muffin tins and fill ⅔ full with batter. Place 1 teaspoon jelly in center of each filled cup. Bake at 375 degrees for 15 minutes.

Yield: Makes about 12

REFRIGERATOR BRAN MUFFINS

1 cup boiling water
3 cups All Bran or Bran Buds
2 eggs
½ cup oil
¾ to 1 cup granulated sugar
1 pint buttermilk

2½ cups flour
2½ teaspoons soda
½ teaspoon salt
1 teaspoon cinnamon
raisins

Put boiling water and All Bran in large boil and let stand while mixing other ingredients. Beat together the eggs, oil, sugar, and buttermilk. Sift together the flour, soda, salt and cinnamon and combine with the egg mixture, All Bran and water. Either store in the refrigerator until cooking time or bake in regular size or miniature muffin tins at 350 degrees for 20 minutes. Add raisins when mixing the batter or when ready to bake muffins. After baking, let muffins stand in the pans a few minutes before removing.

Can be kept six weeks before baking.

Yield: 2 to 3 dozen

SOURDOUGH MUFFINS

3 cups biscuit mix
3 tablespoons granulated
  sugar

¾ can (9 ounces) beer, room
  temperature

Mix together all ingredients until moistened. Grease muffin tins with salad oil. Fill ¾ full and let rise about an hour. Bake at 375 degrees until golden and no white shows through, about 20 to 22 minutes.

Freezes well. Reheat at 325 degrees for 10 to 15 minutes.

A favorite.

Yield: 1 dozen

NUT N' APPLE MUFFINS

Muffins

1¾ cups plain flour
½ cup granulated sugar
½ teaspoon baking soda
½ teaspoon salt
½ teaspoon nutmeg

1½ cups apple, unpaired and
   finely chopped
1 (8 ounce) carton sour cream
½ cup vegetable oil
1 egg
1 teaspoon vanilla extract

Topping

⅓ cup chopped nuts
⅓ cup brown sugar

½ teaspoon cinnamon

Combine flour, sugar, soda, salt, nutmeg and apples in bowl. Combine sour cream, oil, egg and vanilla. Add sour cream mixture to dry ingredients until moist. Fill greased or paper lined muffin tins ¾ full. Combine topping ingredients and sprinkle over muffins. Bake at 350 degrees for 20 to 25 minutes or until lightly browned. Remove from pan and cool.

Honey butter adds extra flavor.

Yield: 1½ dozen

CRANBERRY ORANGE BREAD

2 cups sifted all-purpose flour
¾ cup granulated sugar
1½ teaspoons baking powder
1 teaspoon salt
½ teaspoon soda
1 beaten egg

1 teaspoon grated orange peel
¾ cup orange juice
2 tablespoons salad oil
1 cup coarsely chopped fresh
   cranberries
½ cup chopped walnuts

Sift together flour, sugar, baking powder, salt, and soda. Combine egg, grated orange peel, orange juice, and salad oil. Add to dry ingredients, stirring just till moistened. Fold in cranberries and walnuts. Bake in a greased 9x5x3 inch loaf pan at 350 degrees for 60 minutes or till done. Remove from pan; cool. Wrap; store overnight.

Colorful for Christmas or anytime.

Yield: 6 to 8 servings

BANANA BREAD

½ cup butter
1 cup sugar
2 eggs
1¾ cups all-purpose flour
dash of salt
2 tablespoons buttermilk

3 large bananas, mashed
  (very, very ripe)
1 teaspoon soda
1 teaspoon vanilla
1 cup pecans

Cream butter and sugar. Add eggs one at a time, beat well.

Add flour and milk alternately. Mix in bananas, soda, vanilla and nuts. Bake in greased loaf pan 350 degrees for 1 hour.

Great to wrap up with pretty bow for Christmas.

Yield: 1 loaf

SALLY LUNN BREAD

½ cup melted margarine
½ cup sugar
3 slightly beaten eggs

1 cup milk
2 cups self-rising flour

Combine margarine and sugar and set aside. Mix eggs and milk together. Combine ½ of milk mixture to creamed mixture. Add 1 cup of flour stirring with wire whisk. Add remaining milk mixture and 1 cup of flour. Pour into greased 13x9x2 inch baking dish. Bake at 425 degrees for 25 minutes or until golden brown.

This is sweeter than most breads and goes well with beef or pork roast.

Yield: 15 to 18 servings

SESAME CHEESE LOAF

2 tablespoons sesame seeds
½ cup softened butter
1 envelope cheese sauce mix

1 tablespoon dried parsley
  flakes
1 loaf Italian bread, about 13
  inches long

Preheat oven to 400 degrees. Pour sesame seeds into a small dish and bake about 5 minutes or until golden brown. Blend butter, sauce mix and parsley together. Cut bread in half lengthwise. Spread cheese mixture over cut surfaces; sprinkle with sesame seeds. Cut bread in diagonal slices about 1½ inches apart, being careful not to cut all the way through. Bake 5 to 10 minutes, or until lightly browned.

Yield: 6 to 8 servings

PUMPKIN FRUIT BREAD

1 (15 ounce) can pumpkin
  (approximately 2 cups)
2 cups sugar
⅔ cup softened butter or
  margarine
½ cup water
3 eggs
2½ cups all purpose or
  unbleached flour

2 teaspoons soda
1 teaspoon salt
1 teaspoon cinnamon
½ teaspoon cloves
⅔ cup chopped dates or
  raisins
1 cup chopped nuts

Preheat oven to 325 degrees. In large bowl combine pumpkin, sugar, butter, water and eggs. Beat 1 minute at medium speed with an electric mixer. Add flour, soda, salt, cinnamon and cloves. Beat 1 minute at medium speed. Stir in dates or raisins and nuts. Pour into a greased (not oiled) 8 x 4 inch or 9 x 5 inch loaf pan. Bake for 50 to 60 minutes or until toothpick inserted in center comes out clean. Cool in pan 5 minutes. Remove from pan and cool completely.

Yield: makes 2 loaves

BLUEBERRY BUCKLE

½ cup shortening
¾ cup granulated sugar
1 egg
2 cups sifted all-purpose flour
2½ teaspoons baking powder
¼ teaspoon salt

½ cup milk
2 cups fresh blueberries
½ cup granulated sugar
½ cup sifted all-purpose flour
½ teaspoon ground cinnamon
¼ cup butter or margarine

Thoroughly cream shortening and ¾ cup sugar; add egg and beat till light and fluffy. Sift together 2 cups flour, baking powder, and salt; add to creamed mixture alternately with milk. Spread in greased 11 x 7 x 1½ inch pan. Top with berries. Mix ½ cup sugar, ½ flour, and cinnamon; cut in butter till crumbly; sprinkle over berries. Bake at 350 degrees for 45 minutes. Cut in squares. Serve warm.

Seasonal favorite.

Yield: 8 to 10 servings

BISHOP'S BREAD

2½ cups plain flour
½ cup vegetable shortening
1 teaspoon cinnamon
1 teaspoon nutmeg
½ teaspoon salt

2 cups brown sugar
1 teaspoon baking powder
¾ cup buttermilk
1 egg
½ cup chopped nuts

Mix flour, sugar, salt, shortening and spices thoroughly. Save ¾ cup of this mixture for the top crumbs. To the remainder add baking powder, eggs, buttermilk and soda. Beat briskly until smooth. Pour into 2 well greased layer pans, scatter reserved crumbs and nuts over top. Bake at 400 degrees for 20 minutes.

Yield: 8 to 10 servings

QUICK BREAD

1½ cups milk
½ cup oil
2 tablespoons honey or
    granulated sugar

2 cups all-purpose flour
2 teaspoons salt
2 tablespoons yeast

Combine milk, oil and honey and heat in microwave for 2 minutes. Add flour, salt and yeast. Mix well and place in a greased pan. Bake at 375 degrees until light brown.

It's fast and easy.

Yield: 4 to 6 servings

SWEET POTATO PONE

4 large sweet potatoes (to
    yield 6 cups grated)
1 cup dark brown sugar
1 cup molasses
1 cup milk
1 cup butter (no substitutes)

4 eggs, beaten
½ teaspoon nutmeg
½ teaspoon cloves
½ teaspoon cinnamon
grated rind of 1 lemon
grated rind of 1 orange

Coarsely grate potatoes by hand or in a food processor. Add all other ingredients. Mix well and pour into a well-greased heavy baking pan or iron skillet; bake at 350 degrees for 1½ hours or until knife inserted in middle comes out clean. Serve hot or cold.

Yield: 6 to 8 servings

ZUCCHINI BREAD

3 cups all-purpose flour
1½ cups granulated sugar
1 cup chopped walnuts
4½ teaspoons double acting
   baking powder
1 teaspoon salt

4 eggs
⅔ cup salad oil
2 cups grated zucchini
2 teaspoons grated lemon
   peel

Preheat oven to 350 degrees. In a large bowl with fork, mix flour, sugar, walnuts, baking powder and salt. In medium bowl with fork, beat eggs slightly, mix in salad oil, zucchini and lemon peel. Combine liquid mixture into flour mixture until flour is moistened. Spread mixture evenly in 2 (8½ x 4½ x 2½ inch) loaf pans. Bake 1 hour. Cool in pans on wire rack 10 minutes. Remove from pans.

Can serve hot or cold.

Yield: 2 loaves

BROCCOLI BREAD

1 (10 ounce) package frozen
   broccoli
1 large onion, chopped
1 (6 ounce) container cottage
   cheese

4 eggs
½ cup melted margarine
1 teaspoon salt
1 (8½ ounce) box corn muffin
   mix

Mix first 6 ingredients together in blender for 2 minutes. Then add the corn muffin mix. Pour in a greased 9x13 inch casserole dish. Bake at 400 degrees for 20 to 25 minutes. Do not over bake. Cut into squares and serve while hot.

May substitute spinach for broccoli.

A family favorite.

Yield: 10 to 12 servings

WAFFLES

2 cups flour
½ teaspoon salt
4 teaspoons baking powder

2 eggs, separated
1½ cups milk
1 stick butter, melted

Mix dry ingredients. Beat together egg yolks and milk, and mix with dry ingredients. Pour in melted butter; then fold in stiffly beaten egg whites.

Yield: makes 7 waffles

Entrees...
MEAT

REUBEN CASSEROLE

6 rye crackers, crushed
2 tablespoons butter
¼ teaspoon caraway seed
1 (16 ounce) can sauerkraut,
   drained
4 medium tomatoes, sliced

2 (4 ounce) packages corned
   beef, shredded
4 tablespoons Thousand
   Island dressing
2 cups shredded Swiss
   cheese

Combine together cracker crumbs, butter and caraway seeds and set aside. Spread sauerkraut on the bottom of a 12x18 inch square baking dish. Place tomatoes on top of sauerkraut. Dot dressing on tomatoes. Layer with shredded corned beef. Sprinkle with cheese. Cover with cracker mixture. Bake at 350 degrees for 15 to 18 minutes.

Can be frozen.

Yield: 4 servings

JIMBO'S IRISH GLAZED CORNED BEEF

3 to 4 pounds corned beef
1 onion
1 clove of garlic, sliced
1 teaspoon mixed pickling
   spice

¼ cup brown sugar
1 tablespoon prepared
   mustard
½ cup orange juice

Preheat oven to 325 degrees. Wash the beef, then cover with cold water. Add the onion, garlic and pickling spice. Bring to a boil, cover, simmer over low heat 2 hours. Let cool in the liquid 20 minutes, then drain. Place meat in a shallow roasting pan and score the fat. Cover with a mixture of brown sugar and mustard. Pour the orange juice into the pan. Bake for 45 minutes, basting frequently.

Can be served hot or cold.

Yield: 8 to 10 servings

ANDY'S SPARE RIBS

1 cup water
½ cup ketchup
½ cup vinegar
½ cup sugar
1 teaspoon salt
1 teaspoon allspice

1 teaspoon chili spice
1 teaspoon pepper
1 teaspoon onion powder
3 to 4 pounds of country
   spare ribs

Boil the water, ketchup and vinegar for 3 to 4 minutes. Add remaining ingredients. Boil 20 minutes, reduce heat and simmer 1 hour.

Wonderful.

Yield: 6 servings

SPICY PORK AND PINEAPPLE

2 (8¼ ounce) cans pineapple
   chunks
1 pound boneless pork, cut in
   strips or cubes
2 tablespoons margarine

1 medium onion, chopped
1 cup of barbecue sauce
1 green pepper, cut in strips
hot cooked rice

Drain pineapple, reserving ½ cup juice. In skillet or wok, brown pork in margarine. Add onions, cook until tender. Add pineapple, reserved juice, barbecue sauce and green pepper. Simmer 20 minutes or until pork is done. Serve over hot rice.

You may slice the pineapple chunks in half and use 1½ cups of barbecue sauce for more liquid.

Yield: 4 servings

PORK CHOP CASSEROLE

3 to 4 pork chops
2 tablespoons oil
1 cup uncooked rice
1 (16 ounce) can tomatoes
1 medium onion, sliced

1 (10½ ounce) can beef
   consommé
1 teaspoon thyme
salt and pepper to taste

Brown pork chops in shortening. In a greased 1½ quart casserole dish place uncooked rice. Lay browned pork chops on rice. Add other ingredients. Cook covered for 1 hour at 350 degrees.

Yield: 3 to 4 servings

SAMARIAN PORK

2 pounds Boston Butt (pork)
6 sections of garlic, sliced
   thin
1 medium onion, chopped
⅓ cup soy sauce
⅓ cup white vinegar

2 bay leaves
1 teaspoon peppercorn,
   crushed
dash of paprika
⅓ cup flour
⅔ cup water or milk

In a deep saucepan combine all ingredients except flour and water or milk. Mix well. Cover and cook on medium heat for 45 minutes or until meat is very tender. Bring to a boil and add flour and water or milk to thicken. Stir well and cover. Reduce heat and simmer for 5 minutes. Serve over steamed rice or baked potato.

Yield: 4 to 6 servings

"HOG WILD" BARBECUED BOSTON BUTT

1 (3½ to 4 pound) Boston Butt
   roast
1 medium onion, chopped
4 cloves garlic, crushed
1 tablespoon salt
1 teaspoon pepper
1 cup catsup
½ cup firmly packed brown
   sugar
2 teaspoons salt

1 teaspoon pepper
2 tablespoons chili powder
¼ cup plus 2 tablespoons
   vinegar
2 tablespoons lemon juice
¼ cup Worcestershire sauce
2 teaspoons prepared
   mustard
1 small onion, chopped

Place Boston Butt in Dutch oven and enough water to cover. Add onion, garlic, salt and pepper. Cover and bring to a boil. Lower heat and let simmer for 2½ to 3 hours. Remove from liquid and slice or shred meat and place in a 13 x 9 x 3 inch pan. Combine remaining ingredients in saucepan and simmer for 30 minutes. Pour sauce over meat and bake covered at 370 degrees for 45 minutes. Serve on buns or over rice.

After removing meat from water try to remove as much fat as possible.

Yield: 8 to 10 servings

SMOKED BOSTON BUTT

Boston Butt   **seasoning, optional**

Place pork in smoker for suggested time based on weight. Should be 170 degrees by meat thermometer when well done. Pull apart and add Maurice's Barbecue Sauce to taste.

Cooking time: 3 to 4 pounds - 3 to 4 hours, 5 to 7 pounds - 4 to 6 hours.

Delightful smoked flavor throughout with no trouble.

Yield: 4 to 10 servings

MUSHROOM FILLED MEAT LOAF

2 cups sliced fresh mushrooms
1 cup chopped onion
½ cup sour cream
2 eggs
½ cup milk

½ pound ground beef (chuck)
¼ cup bread crumbs
2 teaspoons salt
1 tablespoon Worcestershire sauce

Preheat oven to 350 degrees. Sauté 1 cup mushrooms and onion in butter. Remove from heat and stir in sour cream. Set aside. Combine remaining ingredients except mushrooms. Place ½ of meat mixture into a 9 x 5 x 3 inch loaf pan. Make a shallow trough down the center of the meat. Spoon sour cream-mushroom mixture into this indentation. Shape the rest of the meat over the filling. Make sure all filling is covered. Seal meat loaf well around edges. Bake for 1 hour. Let stand 15 minutes before slicing. Garnish top with remaining mushrooms, thinly sliced and sautéed.

Sour Cream Sauce
1 cup sour cream
1 teaspoon Dijon mustard
1 teaspoon prepared horseradish

½ teaspoon salt
pinch of nutmeg
pinch of white pepper

Combine together in a small saucepan over low heat. Serve hot with meat loaf.

Try serving with grilled tomatoes, garlic flavored pop-overs, green salad and gingerbread for dessert.

Yield: 4 to 6 servings

STUFFED PEPPERS

8 large bell peppers or 12
   medium (green or red)
2 pounds ground chuck
¾ cup chopped onion
1 tablespoon garlic powder
1 tablespoon salt
1 teaspoon pepper
1 (24 ounce) can tomato
   sauce
1⅓ cups cooked rice
1 (8 ounce) package sharp
   Cheddar cheese, shredded

Boil peppers in salted water for 7 minutes. Cool down with cold water. In pan brown ground beef, onion, garlic powder, salt and pepper. Drain and return to pan. Add tomato sauce, rice, 7 ounces of cheese (save 1 ounce for topping). Simmer 10 minutes. Fill peppers and top with remaining cheese. Place peppers in loaf pans with ⅛ inch water in bottom. Bake at 350 degrees for 20 to 30 minutes or until cheese is melted.

Yield: 6 to 8 servings

CRUSTY BEEF CASSEROLE

1 pound ground beef
¼ cup chopped onion
1 clove garlic, crushed
2 (8 ounce) cans tomato
   sauce
2 tablespoons chili powder
1 cup shredded Cheddar
   cheese
1 (16 ounce) can pinto beans,
   undrained
1 (6 ounce) package
   cornbread mix

Cook ground beef, onion and garlic in skillet until meat is browned. Drain off drippings. Stir in tomato sauce and chili powder. Pour mixture into a lightly greased 12 x 8 x 2 inch baking dish. Top with cheese and spoon beans over cheese. Prepare cornbread mix according to package directions and pour over beans. Bake at 400 degrees or 25 minutes or until cornbread is brown.

Better to use non-sweet cornbread mix.

Yield: 6 servings

SHEPHERD'S PIE

1¼ pounds ground beef
1 teaspoon hamburger
    seasoning
salt and pepper to taste
1 (14 ounce) can whole kernel
    corn, drained

2½ cups mashed potatoes,
    prepared
1 egg
⅛ teaspoon paprika
½ cup grated cheese

Brown ground beef and spread in bottom of baking dish. Stir in hamburger seasoning, salt and pepper. Arrange corn over the beef mixture. Combine mashed potatoes, egg and paprika. Spread potato mixture over the corn. Garnish with grated cheese. Bake at 350 degrees for 25 minutes or until cheese is melted.

Yield: 4 to 6 servings

GROUND BEEF POPPIN FRESH BARBECUPS

¾ pound ground beef
½ cup barbecue sauce
1 tablespoon instant minced
    onions
2 tablespoons brown sugar

1 (8 ounce) can refrigerated
    tender flake baking
    powder biscuits
¾ cup shredded Cheddar
    cheese

In a large skillet, brown ground beef. Drain. Add barbecue sauce, onion and brown sugar. Set aside. Separate biscuit dough into 12 biscuits. Place 1 biscuit in each of 12 ungreased muffin cups, pressing dough up sides to edge of cup. Spoon meat mixture into cups. Sprinkle each one with cheese. Bake at 400 degrees for 10 to 12 minutes or until golden brown.

Yield: 4 servings

HOT PEPPER STEAK

2 pounds round steak
1 hot pepper
2 medium onions

2 medium bell peppers
¼ cup soy sauce
salt and pepper to taste

Brown steak in electric fry pan. Add hot pepper, onions, bell peppers, salt and pepper. Cook on medium heat until onions and peppers are done. Add soy sauce and simmer on low heat. Serve over hot rice.

Yield: 4 servings

EASY BEEF

3 to 4 pounds beef roast
¾ teaspoon salt
½ teaspoon Nature seasoning
¼ teaspoon seasoned pepper
pinch of granulated garlic
2 tablespoons A-1 sauce

1 (1¼ ounce) package dry
  onion soup mix
¼ cup water
1 (10.75 ounce) can
  condensed cream of
  mushroom soup

Place beef in crock pot that has been lightly sprayed with non-stick vegetable spray. Coat beef with salt, Nature seasoning, pepper and garlic. Apply A-1 sauce with spoon, spreading over meat, with back of spoon. Place dry soup mixture evenly over meat, then spread mushroom soup over dry mixture. Add water at side of meat without disturbing top dressing. Cover and cook on high for 30 minutes. Turn to low setting for 8 to 10 hours in crock pot.

Yield: 8 servings

QUICK BEEF STROGANOFF

1 pound round steak (cut into
  ¾ inch cubes)
flour
2 tablespoons oil
½ cup onion, chopped
1 garlic clove, minced
1 (6 ounce) can mushrooms,
  reserve liquid
1 cup sour cream
1 (10.50 ounce) can tomato
  soup

6 to 8 drops of Tabasco sauce
1 tablespoon Worcestershire
  sauce
½ teaspoon salt
dash of pepper
1 (7 ounce) package pasta,
  cooked, or 2 cups rice,
  cooked
Parmesan cheese

Coat meat in flour and brown in oil. Sauté onions, garlic and mushrooms with meat. Combine sour cream, tomato soup, mushroom liquid, Tabasco sauce, Worcestershire sauce, salt and pepper together and pour over meat. Simmer 1 hour or until meat is tender. Serve over hot pasta or rice. Sprinkle with Parmesan cheese.

Yield: 4 to 6 servings

ROAST BEEF

3 to 4 pounds of tenderloin or filet mignon
garlic slivers, to taste

2 tablespoons Mazola
1½ cups bread crumbs

Preheat oven to 350 degrees. Make holes in roast and insert slivers of garlic. Rub Mazola all over roast and roll in plain bread crumbs. Place roast in baking pan and bake for 1 hour and 20 minutes.

Be sure roast has about ½ inch of fat on top, put garlic all over top and sides.

Delicious.

Yield: 6 to 10 servings

STEAK AND POTATO CASSEROLE

2 or 2½ pounds cube steak
6 or 8 medium white potatoes
1 (10.75 ounce) can mushroom soup

1 (10.75 ounce) can French onion soup

Cut steak in bite size pieces and brown in greased fry pan. Layer baking dish with thinly sliced potatoes and cube steak. Pour soups over casserole. Cover and bake at 350 degrees for 1 hour or until potatoes are tender.

Great served with salad and rolls.

Yield: 6 to 8 servings

SWISS STEAK

2 pounds cubed steak
1 tablespoon oil
3 (14.5 ounce) cans tomatoes, chopped

1 medium onion, chopped
garlic salt to taste
pepper to taste
2 cups cooked rice

In a large skillet brown steak in oil. Remove steak from skillet and add tomatoes. Stir well. Add onion, garlic salt, pepper and cubed steak. Stir well, cover and simmer for 1 to 1½ hours. Serve over hot rice.

Yield: 6 to 8 servings

VENISON MEATBALLS

1 pound ground venison
2 tablespoons evaporated
   milk
1 teaspoon salt
3 tablespoons vegetable oil

2 teaspoons lemon juice
1 (16 ounce) can jellied
   cranberry sauce
½ package taco seasoning
   mix

Combine ground meat, milk, and salt. Mix well and form in balls about ¾ inch. Brown slowly over medium heat. Remove meat balls and drain. Combine cranberry sauce, taco mix and lemon juice. Cook over low heat until mixture is smooth. Stir constantly while cooking. Add meatballs and simmer 15 to 20 minutes. Serve warm.

Yield: 8 to 10 servings

VENISON IN A BAG

3 to 5 pound roast, shoulder
   or loin
2 large onions
½ pound bacon
1 (10½ ounce) can onion soup

1 (16 ounce) can mushroom
   slices
1 large oven cooking bag
1 cup vinegar (optional)
1 cup oil (optional)

If marinating meat, place vinegar and oil in plastic bag with meat and let sit overnight, turning meat over 2 to 3 times during process. When ready to cook, sprinkle 1 tablespoon flour in oven cooking bag and shake. Slice onions and layer in bottom of bag. Pat meat dry with paper towels and place on top of onions. Cover meat freely with uncooked bacon strips, onion soup and mushrooms, including juice. Close bag with tie and poke 6 holes in top. Place bag in roasting pan and bake at 275 to 300 degrees about 45 minutes for each pound of meat. When done, remove meat from bag. Leftover ingredients in bag makes delicious gravy stock. If marinade was used, add 1 tablespoon of sugar to cut taste of vinegar.

Yield: 6 to 10 servings

SLAW DOG HENDERSON

butter
1 jumbo hot dog
1 sesame seed hot dog bun
French's mustard

coleslaw (stringy with extra mayonnaise)
salt
pepper

In a 10 inch frying pan melt 1 tablespoon of butter on low heat. Add hot dog and increase temperature to medium high. Hot dog must be continuously rolled while in frying pan. Turn oven on broil. Open bun and lightly butter each side. Place open bun on cookie sheet and place in oven. Remove bun when lightly toasted. Apply mustard to your liking. Remove hot dog and place in bun. Apply coleslaw, salt and pepper to taste.

Yield: 1 serving

SLOPPY JOES

2½ cups ground chuck
2 large onions, chopped
¾ cup catsup
2 tablespoons granulated sugar

2 tablespoons prepared mustard
2 tablespoons vinegar
1 teaspoon salt
⅓ teaspoon pepper

Brown meat and onions in a large skillet. Drain well. Add other ingredients and simmer for 1½ hours. Serve on warm hamburger buns.

Fast and easy.

Yield: 6 to 8 servings

SOUVLAKIA II (SHISH-KA-BOB)

2 pounds lamb or beef
2 cloves garlic, minced
½ cup salad oil
1 cup Burgundy wine
juice of 1 lemon
salt and pepper to taste
2 teaspoons oregano

3 tomatoes (optional)
2 onions (optional)
4 strips bacon (optional)
2 bell peppers (optional)
1 can whole mushroom
   buttons or use fresh
   (optional)

Cut meat into 1½ inch cubes. Place meat in large plastic or stainless steel bowl and add garlic, oil, wine, lemon juice, salt, pepper and oregano, and mix well. Cover and refrigerate overnight to marinate. Quarter tomatoes and onion; cube bacon and peppers. Skewer marinated meat alternating it with whichever optional ingredients are preferred. Charcoal over hot coals or broil in oven to desired doneness.

Delightful change.

Yield: 8 servings

VEAL SCALLOPINI WITH TOMATOES

1½ pounds veal, sliced, cut in
   1 inch pieces and pounded
¾ cup all-purpose flour
2 tablespoons butter
1 tablespoon olive oil
½ pound mushrooms, thinly
   sliced
½ - 1 clove garlic, minced

2 tablespoons chopped fresh
   parsley
1 - 2 tablespoons chopped
   fresh basil
½ cup fresh tomatoes, peeled,
   seeded and diced
½ cup Marsala wine
2 tablespoons grated
   Parmesan cheese

Preheat oven to 325 degrees. Dredge veal squares in flour. Brown veal in butter and oil in large frying pan. Add mushrooms and cook 5 minutes. Add garlic, parsley and basil. Cook 1 minute. Add tomatoes and cook 5 minutes. Stir in Marsala. Remove to baking platter. Sprinkle Parmesan on top. Bake for 45 minutes.

Yield: 4 servings

Entrees
...POULTRY

CHICKEN BREASTS WITH ARTICHOKE HEARTS

3 medium whole chicken breasts
½ cup all purpose flour
3 tablespoons salad oil
2 tablespoons melted butter
2 tablespoons all purpose flour
1 teaspoon salt
⅛ teaspoon white pepper

3 tablespoons brandy
2 teaspoons lemon juice
1½ cups water
2 chicken flavored bouillon cubes or 1 teaspoon
1 cup sour cream
2 (9 ounce) packages frozen artichoke hearts, thawed and drained

On a piece of wax paper coat chicken breast with ¼ cup flour. In a 12 inch skillet over medium-high heat in hot salad oil cook chicken until lightly browned on all sides. Place chicken in a 12 x 9 x 2 inch baking dish and set aside. Preheat oven to 350 degrees. In a 2 quart saucepan over low heat combine butter, 2 tablespoons flour, salt and pepper, until smooth. Gradually stir in brandy, lemon juice, water and chicken bouillon. Cook stirring constantly until thickened and smooth. With wire whisk gradually blend in sour cream. Pour mixture over chicken. Cover baking dish tightly with foil and bake chicken 45 minutes. Add artichoke hearts, recovering the baking dish and bake 15 minutes more.

Set for company.

Yield: 6 servings

CHEESY CHICKEN

1 cup Parmesan cheese
2 tablespoons parsley, chopped
2 teaspoons paprika
1 tablespoon oregano

2 teaspoons salt
½ teaspoon pepper
6 chicken breasts
½ cup melted butter

Combine together cheese and seasonings. Dip chicken in butter; then roll in cheese mixture. Bake at 350 degrees for 1 hour and 15 minutes.

Yield: 6 servings

EASY GEORGIA CHICKEN MARSALA

Casserole

4 chicken quarters
4 tablespoons butter
1 pint Marsala wine
½ clove garlic
½ teaspoon marjoram

½ teaspoon basil
½ teaspoon rosemary
3 whole cloves
1½ teaspoons salt
½ teaspoon pepper

Topping

½ teaspoon paprika

4 tablespoons grated Gruyère
or Swiss cheese

Brown chicken in butter and place in casserole dish. Add wine and seasonings. Bake covered, for one hour at 325 degrees, basting frequently. Uncover and brown for 25 to 30 minutes. Top with paprika and cheese and bake until bubbly and brown.

Yield: 4 servings

CHICKEN CASSEROLE

6 chicken breasts
1 (10.75 ounce) can cream of
chicken soup
2 cups celery, diced, cooked
and drained
1 tablespoon onion, grated
⅓ cup slivered almonds

¾ cup mayonnaise
2 tablespoons lemon juice
1 (2 ounce) jar pimentos
2 bay leaves
1 cup crushed potato chips or
1 stack of Ritz crackers
1 cup grated Cheddar cheese

Cook chicken in water with 2 bay leaves until tender. Cool. Take off bone and dice. Combine cooked chicken, celery, almonds, soup, pimentos, onion, and lemon juice. Mix well. Add mayonnaise. Place in casserole dish. Mix potato chips and cheese together. Sprinkle on top of casserole. Bake at 350 degrees for 45 minutes. Serve hot.

Serve with a salad and you have a meal.

Yield: 4 to 6 servings

SUNDAY CHICKEN CASSEROLE

2 to 3 pounds chicken
1 (8 ounce) package vermicelli
 spaghetti
1 large onion, chopped
1 large bell pepper, chopped
½ stick margarine

1 (16 ounce) can tomatoes
 with chilies
½ to 1 pound Velveeta cheese,
 sliced
1 (4 ounce) can mushrooms

Place cut-up chicken in large saucepan. Use 3 to 3½ cups of water or barely cover, add salt. Cook until tender. Remove chicken and debone. Cook spaghetti in chicken broth. Sauté onions and peppers in margarine, add to cooked spaghetti. Add chicken and other ingredients and mix well, until cheese is melted. Place in a 9 x 13 inch casserole dish and bake at 350 degrees for 20 minutes.

Very good.

Yield: 6 servings

CHICKEN PARMESAN

2⅔ tablespoons butter
1 clove garlic, minced
1 cup bread crumb stuffing
1 cup Parmesan cheese

1 teaspoon salt
⅛ teaspoon pepper
1 cut up fryer or 6 chicken
 breasts

Melt butter, add garlic and simmer. Mix crumbs, cheese, and seasonings. Dip chicken in butter mixture, roll in cheese and crumbs. Place in pan. Bake at 350 degrees in oven for 30 minutes, then reduce oven to 300 degrees and cook for another 30 minutes.

May substitute veal.

Yield: 4 to 6 servings

CHICKEN DELIGHT

8 boneless chicken breasts
8 bacon slices
4 ounces chipped beef

1 (10.75 ounce) can
  mushroom soup
1 cup sour cream
paprika

Wrap each chicken breast in bacon. Cover the bottom of a greased 8 x 12 inch baking dish with chipped beef. Arrange chicken on top. Blend soup and sour cream and pour over chicken. Sprinkle with paprika. Bake uncovered at 275 degrees for 3 hours.

A class act.

Yield: 6 to 8 servings

HICKORY SMOKED BARBECUE CHICKEN

¼ cup vinegar
½ cup water
2 tablespoons brown sugar
1 tablespoon prepared
   mustard
1 teaspoon salt
¼ teaspoon cayenne
½ teaspoon black pepper
juice of 1 lemon

1 large onion, chopped
¼ cup butter
½ cup catsup
2 tablespoons Worcestershire
  sauce
1½ teaspoons liquid smoke
1 broiling chicken split or cut
  in pieces

Preheat oven to 325 degrees. Mix first 10 ingredients. Bring to a boil for 20 minutes, uncovered. Add catsup, Worcestershire and liquid smoke. Place chicken in roasting pan. Pour ½ the sauce over chicken. Roast chicken at least an hour, turning and basting with remaining sauce.

Good with green beans, corn on the cob, slaw and cornbread.

Yield: 2 to 4 servings

CHICKEN CRUNCH

1 (10.75 ounce) can cream of
   mushroom soup
¾ cup milk
1 tablespoon finely chopped
   onion
1 tablespoon chopped parsley

2 pounds chicken parts
1 cup herb seasoned stuffing,
   finely crushed
2 tablespoons melted butter
   or margarine

Mix ⅓ cup soup, ¼ cup milk, onion and parsley. Dip chicken in soup mixture; then roll in stuffing. Place in a 12 x 8 x 2 inch baking dish. Drizzle butter on chicken. Bake at 400 degrees for 1 hour. Combine remaining soup and milk; heat, stir occasionally.

Pour over chicken.

Delicious served over hot rice.

Yield: 4 to 6 servings

CHICKEN POT PIE

1 whole chicken, cooked,
   boned and chucked
   (reserve liquid)
1 (16 ounce) can Veg-All,
   minced vegetables
1½ cups chicken broth

1 (10.75 ounce) can cream of
   chicken soup
1 stick margarine, melted
1 cup self-rising flour
1 cup milk

Layer chicken and vegetables in a 9 x 13 inch pan or large casserole dish. Mix chicken broth and soup and pour over vegetables. Combine margarine, flour and milk and pour over casserole. Bake at 350 degrees for 1 hour.

Cook and freeze to serve later.

Delicious.

Yield: 6 servings

CHICKEN CHOP SUEY

2 cups cooked chicken
2 teaspoons salad oil
2 cups thinly sliced celery
1½ sliced onions
⅛ teaspoon pepper
2 teaspoons cornstarch

2 cups chicken broth
1 can mixed Chinese
  vegetables
1 (4 ounce) can mushroom
  caps
3 teaspoons soy sauce

Remove chicken from bone. Cut in bite size pieces. Sauté in oil. Add celery, onions, and pepper. Add drained Chinese vegetables and mushrooms. Heat to boiling. Combine cornstarch and soy sauce. Add to hot mixture, stirring constantly. Simmer 2 minutes, until slightly thickened. Arrange on platter, garnish with scallions, cut lengthwise. Serve with rice and fried noodles.

Use extra soy sauce if desired.

Yield: 6 servings

CHICKEN AND PEPPERS

4 chicken breasts
olive oil
seasoning salt to taste
garlic powder to taste
½ cup red peppers
½ cup onions, diced

1 (4 ounce) can sliced
  mushrooms
crushed black pepper to taste
green parsley to taste
½ cup sherry

Cut chicken breasts in bite size pieces. Brown chicken in olive oil, over low heat about 10 minutes. Season with salt and garlic powder to taste. Stir 3 to 4 minutes. Add red peppers, onions, mushrooms, parsley, and black pepper. Cook an additional 15 to 20 minutes. When cooking is complete, add sherry. Stir and serve.

Serve with hot rolls and tossed salad.

Yield: 4 servings

CURRIED CHICKEN MONONAQUA

5 or 6 whole, boned, cooked
 and sliced chicken breasts
1 stick melted butter
1 rounded tablespoon curry
 powder
1 tablespoon paprika

1 heaping tablespoon
 cornstarch
¼ cup sherry
3 cups half 'n half
2 cups cooked rice
1 (8 ounce) package Swiss
 cheese, shredded

Mix butter, curry powder and paprika and coat each side of chicken slices. In a large flat casserole, combine cornstarch, sherry and cream. Add coated chicken and cooked rice. Top with cheese and bake at 300 degrees for 45 minutes.

Yield: 6 servings

CRESCENT CHICKEN SQUARES

2 (3 ounce) packages cream
 cheese
2 tablespoons margarine,
 melted
2 cups chicken, cubed and
 cooked

¼ teaspoon salt
⅛ teaspoon pepper
1 tablespoon onion, chopped
1 tablespoon pimento
1 (8 ounce) can crescent rolls
seasoned bread crumbs

Blend softened cream cheese with melted margarine. Add chicken, salt, pepper, onion, and pimento. Mix well. Separate crescent rolls into 4 rectangles. Seal perforations. Spoon ½ cup of chicken mixture into each rectangle. Pull 4 corners of dough together and seal. Brush tops with melted margarine and sprinkle with seasoned bread crumbs. Bake on cookie sheet at 350 degrees for 20 to 25 minutes.

Yield: 4 servings

ITALIAN CHICKEN MARINATE

4 to 6 boneless, skinless
  chicken breasts
1 (8 ounce) bottle Italian salad
  dressing

2 to 3 tablespoons regular
  mustard
dash of oregano
salt and pepper to taste

Put chicken breasts in baking dish. Mix dressing and mustard in separate bowl. Add to chicken and cover. Marinate in refrigerator 2 to 3 days. Take out occasionally to stir. The longer you marinate, the better the taste. Broil or grill.

Delicious.

Yield: 4 to 6 servings

CHICKEN CASSEROLE

2 cups cooked chicken
2 cups cooked rice
1 cup onions, chopped
1 cup celery, chopped
½ cup mayonnaise

1 (10.75 ounce) can cream of
  chicken soup
1 tablespoon lemon juice
1 stack of Ritz crackers
¼ cup melted butter

Combine chicken, rice, onion, celery, mayonnaise, soup and juice. Place in ungreased 11 x 7 x 2 inch baking dish. Crush crackers and mix with melted butter. Place cracker mix on top of casserole. Bake at 350 degrees for 45 minutes.

Yield: 4 to 6 servings

CHICKEN ENCHILADAS

1 large fryer
1 package of tortillas
1 (14.5 ounce) can Rotel
  tomatoes
1 (10.75 ounce) can cream of
  mushroom soup

1 (10.75 ounce) can cream of
  chicken soup
1 cup chopped onions
1 pound grated Cheddar
  cheese

Cook, debone and chop chicken. Break tortillas into pieces. Heat soups and tomatoes. In a 11 x 7 x 2 inch baking pan layer tortillas, soup mixture, chicken, onion then cheese. Bake at 325 degrees for 30 minutes.

Yield: 4 to 6 servings

SWEET AND TANGY CHICKEN

1 (8 ounce) Thousand Island
 dressing
1 (6 ounce) jar apricot
 preserves
1 package dry onion soup mix
2 teaspoons soy sauce
salt and pepper, optional
4 chicken breasts

Combine dressing, preserves, dry soup mix, and soy sauce in mixing bowl. Season chicken to taste. Place chicken in single layer at bottom of baking dish. Cover chicken with dressing mixture with spoon. Bake uncovered at 350 degrees for 1 hour.

Serve with mixed vegetables, rolls, and glass of tea.

Yield: 4 servings

CHICKEN IN SECRET SAUCE

4 (8 ounce) cans tomato
 sauce
½ cup vinegar
1 cup dark Karo syrup
1⅛ teaspoons Tabasco sauce
1 teaspoon salt
4 tablespoons prepared
 mustard
4 tablespoons Worcestershire
 sauce
1 cup onion, minced
¼ teaspoon black pepper
1 tablespoon granulated
 sugar
1 large fryer, cut up

Combine all ingredients except chicken in an electric skillet and stir until blended. Bring to boil and boil 2 minutes. Add chicken and cover. Simmer approximately 45 to 60 minutes, turning occasionally. When chicken is done, remove from sauce. Simmer sauce until desired thickness. Serve sauce on the chicken and over white rice as a side dish.

This recipe makes plenty of extra sauce, so be sure to make enough rice.

Yield: 4 to 6 servings

SWISS CHICKEN

8 boneless, skinless chicken
   breasts
4 slices Swiss cheese, cut in
   half

1 (10.75 ounce) can cream of
   mushroom soup
½ soup can white wine
2 cups herb stuffing mix
1 stick butter, melted

Place chicken and Swiss cheese in an 8 x 12 inch baking dish. Mix soup with wine, cover chicken with soup mixture. Mix stuffing with melted butter and place over chicken. Bake at 350 degrees for 45 minutes.

Easy.

Yield: 8 servings

FRIED CHICKEN THE PIGGLY WIGGLY WAY

seasoning salt
2 cups self rising flour
2 teaspoons garlic salt
2 teaspoons black pepper
seasoning to your liking
   (poultry, sage, etc.)

1 egg, beaten
1 cup milk
1½ cups water
1 cut up fryer or chicken
   breasts

Wash and prepare chicken. Coat heavily with seasoning salt and allow to marinate at least 12 hours. Combine mixture of flour, garlic salt, pepper and other seasonings of your choice in a brown paper bag and shake furiously. Separately mix, egg, milk and water. Dip chicken pieces in egg mixture then coat well in flour mixture. Fry at 325 degrees for at least 12 to 14 minutes in vegetable oil. Drain.

Dark meat takes a little longer to cook.

Can't be beat.

Yield: 6 to 8 servings

QUICK AND EASY CHICKEN

6 chicken breasts (bone-in, skinned)
1 (16 ounce) can whole tomatoes
1 (8 ounce) can tomato sauce
⅓ cup minced onion
8 beef bouillon cubes
2 teaspoons onion powder
¾ cup water

Spray Dutch oven with non-stick cooking spray. Brown chicken approximately 5 minutes on each side. Chop whole tomatoes with juice and remaining ingredients. Bring to a boil, cover and cook on low 45 minutes.

Serve over steamed rice.

Yield: 6 servings

COOL RANCH CHICKEN AND RICE

4 to 6 chicken breasts
1 cup low calorie ranch style dressing
2 tablespoons prepared mustard
dash of Worcestershire sauce
1 tablespoon white vinegar, optional
salt and pepper to taste
hot rice

Arrange chicken in a non-stick coated baking dish. Mix all ingredients into a saucepan. Pour sauce over salted and peppered chicken pieces. Bake uncovered at 325 degrees for 1 hour to 1 hour and 15 minutes. Serve over hot rice.

Yield: 4 to 6 servings

GREEK STYLE CORNISH GAME HENS

2 Cornish game hens
2 tablespoons lemon juice
¼ cup olive oil

Greek seasoning
garlic salt

Split hens in half. Wash. Place in microwave safe dish and cover with saran wrap. Cook in microwave for 8 minutes on high. Mix lemon juice and olive oil and baste hens with this mixture. Sprinkle hens lightly with Greek seasoning and garlic salt. Place on grill over medium coals and cook about 5 minutes. Turn, baste with lemon juice mixture, sprinkle with Greek seasoning and garlic and continue cooking for 8 to 10 minutes or until brown.

Yield: 4 servings

TURKEY DIVAN

2 packages frozen broccoli
   spears
2 cups sliced cooked turkey
2 (10.75 ounce) cans cream of
   chicken soup, undiluted
1 cup mayonnaise

1 teaspoon lemon juice
½ cup shredded sharp
   Cheddar cheese
½ cup soft bread crumbs
1 tablespoon melted butter

Cook broccoli in salted boiling water until tender. Drain and arrange in greased 9 x 9 inch baking dish, place turkey on top. Combine soup, mayonnaise, lemon juice, and pour over turkey. Sprinkle with cheese. Combine bread crumbs and butter and sprinkle over top. Bake at 350 degrees for 30 minutes or until thoroughly heated.

Yield: 4 servings

CAJUN FRIED TURKEY

1 (10 to 11 pound) turkey
1 ounce of Cajun spicy
   chicken seasoning
1 ounce of Cajun blackened
   fish seasoning or Creole
   seasoning

3 to 5 gallons of peanut oil
   (depending on size of pot,
   oil should completely
   cover turkey)

Rinse and dry turkey thoroughly, both outside and inside cavity. Trim all fat. Mix spice and sprinkle turkey heavily, both outside and inside cavity. Refrigerate overnight. Heat oil to 350 degrees. Slowly lower turkey into oil. Using a candy thermometer, maintain oil at 350 degrees to 375 degrees while cooking. Cook for 4 minutes per pound.

Do not stuff turkey.

You've heard about it, here's how to do it.

Yield: 6 to 8 servings

Seafood

LOW COUNTRY CASSEROLE

1 (4 ounce) can mushrooms, drained or ½ cup fresh
3 tablespoons chopped onions
3 tablespoons butter
¼ cup flour
½ teaspoon salt
½ teaspoon dry mustard
⅛ teaspoon pepper
dash of celery salt
1½ teaspoons parsley flakes
1½ cups milk
1 cup grated Cheddar cheese
½ pound shrimp, peeled and cooked
½ pound crab meat
1 cup butter bread squares

Cook mushrooms and onion in butter until tender. Add flour, salt, mustard, pepper, celery salt and parsley flakes. Gradually add milk and cook, stirring constantly. Add ¾ of the cheese, stir until melted. Add seafood and pour into well greased casserole dish. Combine remaining cheese and bread squares. Sprinkle over casserole. Bake at 400 degrees for 10 minutes.

Excellent served with herbed rice.

Yield: 4 to 6 servings

COQUILLE ST. JACQUES

6 tablespoons butter
3 tablespoons flour
1 teaspoon salt
⅛ teaspoon white pepper
2 cups light cream
½ pound scallops, sliced
¼ cup onion, finely chopped
½ cup mushrooms, sliced
½ pound shrimp, cooked and cleaned
¼ pound white crab meat
2 tablespoons Madeira or sweet sherry
3 tablespoons bread crumbs

In double boiler top, melt four tablespoons of butter, blend in flour, salt and pepper. Gradually add cream, over direct heat, stirring constantly, to boiling point. Return to double boiler and cook five minutes longer. Melt remaining butter in skillet, add scallops and onions and sauté. Remove scallops and onions, add mushrooms and sauté for three minutes. Combine the sauce, scallops, mushrooms, shrimp, crab meat and wine. Mix lightly and taste for seasoning. Spoon into six scallop shells and sprinkle with bread crumbs. Bake at 400 degrees for 10 minutes or until delicately browned.

Yield: 6 servings

CRISPY BAKED FISH FILLETS

1 pound fish fillets
1 teaspoon herb seasoning
salt and pepper to taste

3 tablespoons of cooking oil
1 to 2 cups crushed corn flake
crumbs

Preheat oven to 500 degrees. Wash and dry fish fillets and cut into serving size. Season, dip in oil, and coat with corn flake crumbs. Arrange in a single layer on a lightly oiled shallow baking dish. Bake 10 minutes without turning or basting.

This is unbelievable. You'll never fry again. Delicious.

Yield: 4 servings

"JACK'S" DEVILED CRABS

3 cups crab meat
¾ cup mayonnaise
5 teaspoons prepared
    mustard
2½ teaspoons Worcestershire
    sauce

1 egg
½ cup bell pepper, diced
1 large onion, diced
2 teaspoons thyme
1 cup saltines, crushed
dash chili pepper

Preheat oven to 350 degrees. Mix all ingredients together, put in crab shells. Bake 15 to 30 minutes until brown on top.

Can be rolled into small balls, and served as appetizers, following same cooking procedure.

Yield: 12 servings

SAUTÉED SCALLOPS WITH TOMATO GARLIC

2½ pounds of scallops
¼ cup olive oil
¼ cup butter

2 teaspoons chopped garlic
½ cup chopped tomato
¼ cup chopped parsley

Heat oil and butter in pan until hot. Before cooking, dredge scallops with flour. Quickly sauté scallops. When scallops are halfway done, add garlic. Add tomato and parsley and sauté a few more seconds.

Exquisite.

Yield: 10 servings

SHRIMP TEMPURA

Shrimp
25 large shrimp   salt and pepper to taste

Batter
1 cup ice cold water   1⅛ cups tempura flour
1 egg

Sauce
½ cup water   1 tablespoon granulated
1 teaspoon hon-dashi   sugar
¼ cup soy sauce

Cut the shrimp on the back part down the middle — not all the way through just so the shrimp will lay open and devein. To make batter stir together water, egg and flour. Do not overstir. Batter should not be completely smooth, it should be lumpy. Add salt and pepper. Salt and pepper shrimp and dip each shrimp in batter. Fry shrimp over medium to medium high heat. Do not overcook. Remove shrimp when golden brown. To prepare sauce bring water and hon-dashi to a boil. Remove from heat and stir in soy sauce and sugar. Put sauce in individual bowls. Dip shrimp in sauce and eat.

Yield: 3 servings

SHRIMP CREOLE

¼ pound bacon   ⅛ teaspoon paprika
1 large onion, chopped   2 teaspoons parsley
1 bell pepper, chopped   1 teaspoon chili powder
1 cup celery, chopped   2 cups canned tomatoes
1 clove of garlic, minced   Tabasco sauce to taste
1 teaspoon salt   2 pounds raw shrimp, shelled
dash pepper   and deveined
⅛ teaspoon rosemary

Fry bacon in saucepan, add onions, garlic, bell peppers and celery. Sauté until tender. Add everything else but shrimp and bring to boil. Reduce heat and simmer. Add shrimp 10 minutes before serving. Serve over hot rice.

Yield: 8 servings

OLD FASHION SHRIMP PIE

2 pounds diced potatoes
3 large onions, chopped
4 celery ribs, sliced
1 teaspoon pepper

1 teaspoon salt
2 pounds fresh shrimp
1 (7 ounce) package Bisquick
  mix

Cook diced potatoes and onions until done. Add celery, seasoning, and shrimp. Cook until shrimp is done. Put liquid and cooked items in 12 x 4 inch pan. Cover with thin layer of mixed Bisquick. Bake at 250 degrees until dough turns light brown. Spoon out with dough. Serve hot.

Garnish with parsley and serve in a shallow bowl.

This is very spicy.

Yield: 4 servings

FISH FOR THE GRILL

2 pounds skinless deep sea
  fish
⅓ cup melted margarine
½ cup vegetable oil
2 tablespoons soy sauce

½ cup Italian seasoning
1 tablespoon Worcestershire
  sauce
2 tablespoons lemon juice

Cut fish into pieces. Combine all other ingredients in a bowl. Place fish in a hinged wire grill basket about 4 inches from hot coals. Make sure basket is well coated with spray. Cook approximately 7 minutes per side. Baste frequently with sauce. Remove when opaque and keep warm till served.

Yield: 4 servings

COMPANY CRAB CASSEROLE

1 pound blue crabmeat, fresh
   or frozen
1 (15 ounce) can artichoke
   hearts, drained and halved
1 (4 ounce) can sliced
   mushrooms, drained
2 tablespoons butter
2½ tablespoons flour

½ teaspoon salt
⅛ teaspoon cayenne
1 cup half and half
2 tablespoons sherry
2 tablespoons cereal crumbs
1 tablespoon grated
   Parmesan cheese
Paprika

Preheat oven to 450 degrees. Place artichoke halves into a greased, shallow 1½ quart casserole dish. Cover with mushrooms and crabmeat. In a small saucepan, melt butter and blend in flour, salt and cayenne. Gradually add half-and-half and cook until thick, stirring constantly. Stir in sherry. Pour sauce over crabmeat mixture. Combine cereal crumbs and cheese and sprinkle over top dish. Sprinkle with paprika. Bake at 450 degrees for 15 minutes or until bubbly.

Great dish for company.

Yield: 6 servings

SALMON CASSEROLE

8 ounces uncooked medium
   noodles
1½ cups creamed cottage
   cheese
1½ cups dairy sour cream
½ cup finely chopped onion
1 clove garlic, minced

1 to 2 teaspoons
   Worcestershire sauce
dash red pepper sauce
½ teaspoon salt
1 (16 ounce) can salmon
   or 2 cans tuna, drained
½ cup shredded sharp
   Cheddar cheese

Preheat oven to 325 degrees. Cook noodles and drain. Mix noodles, cottage cheese, sour cream, onion, garlic, Worcestershire sauce, red pepper sauce, salt and salmon. Place about 1 cup salmon mixture in each of 5 or 6 greased baking shells or individual casseroles. Sprinkle with cheese. Bake uncovered for 20 to 25 minutes.

Yield: 5 to 6 servings

CRAB AND WILD RICE CASSEROLE

½ cup onion, chopped
1 cup celery, chopped
1 cup mushrooms, sliced
margarine
1 (6 ounce) package Uncle
   Ben's wild rice, prepared
   according to directions

1 pound shrimp
1 (1 pound) can crab meat
1 small chopped chili pepper
1 cup mayonnaise
1 tablespoon Worcestershire
   sauce

In a skillet sauté onions, celery, and mushrooms in margarine. In a greased 9 x 13 inch baking dish, combine sautéed vegetables and remaining ingredients. Bake at 350 degrees for 30 minutes.

Yield: 4 servings

SEAFOOD EGGROLLS

2 cups cooked, chopped
   seafood (crab or shrimp or
   both)
1 tablespoon olive oil
2 tablespoons minced celery
2 tablespoons chopped bean
   sprouts
1 tablespoon grated carrot

2 tablespoons grated onion
2 teaspoons sugar
1 teaspoon salt
pepper
24 egg roll wrappers
1 egg, beaten
1 teaspoon water
oil for frying

Sauté vegetables in olive oil in a heavy skillet until crunchy-tender. Add seafood, sugar, salt and pepper. Set aside. Divide seafood mixture evenly among egg roll wrappers, placing some of mixture in center of each wrapper. Fold two sides of wrapper over filling and seal ends. Brush with egg beaten with water. Fry in deep, hot oil until golden brown. Serve with hot mustard or sweet and sour sauce.

The best in town.

Yield: 24 eggrolls

FRIED SHRIMP

1 pound shelled, deveined
  large shrimp
1 egg
2 tablespoons all-purpose
  flour
½ teaspoon salt
dash pepper

½ cup salad oil
⅔ cup minced onions
¾ cup chicken broth
1 tablespoon cornstarch
1 teaspoon soy sauce
hot cooked rice

Blot shrimp well with paper towels to dry. In medium bowl, with fork, beat egg; add flour, salt and pepper; mix well. Add shrimp; stir to coat well. In electric skillet at 370 degrees or in a 10 inch skillet over medium heat, heat salad oil. With fork, lift shrimp, one by one, from batter; drop into oil and fry until golden, 2 to 3 minutes on each side. On paper towels, drain shrimp; remove to warm platter. For sauce: In 2 tablespoons oil left in skillet, cook onions until tender, about 5 minutes. In cup, stir broth into cornstarch until smooth; add soy sauce and stir into onions; cook, stirring, until thickened. Pour over shrimp. Serve with rice.

Delicious.

Yield: 6 servings

QUICK AND EASY SALMON PATTIES

1 (16 ounce) can pink salmon
1 egg
⅓ cup minced onions

½ cup flour
1½ teaspoons baking powder
1½ cups vegetable shortening

Drain salmon, set aside 2 tablespoons of the juice. In a medium mixing bowl, mix salmon, egg, and onion until sticky. Stir in flour. Add baking powder to salmon juice, stir into salmon mixture. Form into small patties and fry until brown (about five minutes) in hot vegetable oil.

Serve with tartar sauce or Caesar salad dressing.

Yield: 4 to 6 servings

LOBSTER NEWBURG

6 tablespoons butter or
   margarine
2 tablespoons all-purpose
   flour
1½ cups light cream
3 beaten egg yolks

1 (5 ounce) can or 1 cup
   lobster, broken in large
   pieces
3 tablespoons dry white wine
2 teaspoons lemon juice
½ teaspoon salt
paprika
pastry petal cups

Melt butter in skillet; blend in flour. Add cream all at once. Cook, stirring constantly, till sauce thickens and bubbles. Stir small amount of hot mixture into egg yolks; return to hot mixture; cook, stirring constantly, till thickened. Add lobster; heat through. Add wine, lemon juice, and salt. Sprinkle with paprika. Serve in cups or seafood shells.

Seafood lovers delight.

Yield: 4 to 5 servings

OYSTER CASSEROLE

1½ cups coarse cracker
   crumbs
8 tablespoons butter, melted
1 pint oysters
½ teaspoon salt
⅛ teaspoon pepper

dash of nutmeg
2 tablespoons parsley,
   chopped (optional)
¼ cup oyster liquor
2 tablespoons milk

Combine cracker crumbs and butter. Put thin layer in bottom of 1 quart casserole dish; alternate layers of oysters and crumb mixture, sprinkling each layer with seasonings. Never use more than 2 layers of oysters. Pour oyster liquor and milk over layers; top with crumbs. Bake at 450 degrees for 30 minutes.

May prepare ahead.

Yield: 4 to 6 servings

CRAB POTATO CAKES

2 cups crab meat
6 medium potatoes
1 egg
½ cup finely chopped shallot
 whites
½ cup chopped shallot greens
½ cup chopped parsley

¼ cup chopped bell peppers
2 cloves chopped garlic
½ teaspoon Creole seasoning
salt and pepper to taste
flour
oil

Steam potatoes until cooked. Mix in a large bowl egg, crab meat, shallots, parsley, bell peppers, garlic, creole seasoning, salt and pepper. Add cooked mashed potatoes and mix well. Form patties to size desired. To cook, coat with flour and fry in slightly oiled heavy gauge skillet, browning on both sides.

Yield: 6 servings

SHRIMP AND WILD RICE CASSEROLE

3 tablespoons chopped green
 pepper
3 tablespoons chopped
 onions
2½ pounds peeled raw shrimp
3 tablespoons melted butter
1 (10.75 ounce) can cream of
 mushroom soup
1½ tablespoons lemon juice

½ teaspoon Worcestershire
 sauce
½ teaspoon dry mustard
½ teaspoon salt
½ teaspoon pepper
1 (6 ounce) package long
 grain and wild rice with
 seasonings, prepared by
 directions
1 cup Monterey Jack cheese

Sauté pepper, onions, and shrimp in butter until shrimp turns pink. Mix with remaining ingredients and pour into casserole dish. Top casserole with cheese. Bake at 350 degrees for 30 minutes.

Yield: 6 servings

SHRIMP SCAMPI

4 tablespoons butter
⅛ teaspoon garlic salt
2 tablespoons parsley flakes

½ cup California Chablis
1 pound raw shrimp, peeled
  and deveined

Melt butter in skillet. Add garlic salt, parsley and wine. Heat to simmer. Add shrimp and cook over low heat until heated thoroughly (about 5 minutes).

You may wish to boil your shrimp first before adding to sauce.

Serve with rice for a delicious main dish.

Yield: 4 to 6 servings

CHAMORRO SHRIMP PATTIES

1 pound shrimp, cleaned,
  deveined and chopped
1 (10 ounce) package frozen
  mixed vegetables
1 medium onion, chopped
1 (7 ounce) can corn
¼ cup celery, chopped
2 eggs

½ cup chopped green bell
  pepper
2 cloves garlic, crushed
½ cup flour
½ cup canned milk
1 teaspoon baking powder
salt and pepper to taste

Mix all ingredients in a bowl. Heat oil to 350 degrees. Drop from spoon into hot fat. Fry until golden.

Chamorro is the true name of the islanders native to Guam. Shrimp patties are one of the essential main dishes of any traditional island village fiesta. Taste and enjoy one of the island's most exotic delicacies.

Yield: 6 servings

CRAB AND SHRIMP BAKE

1 pound boiled shrimp, peeled
1 (7½ ounce) can crab meat,
    drained and flaked
1 cup diced celery
¼ cup chopped green pepper
3 tablespoons finely chopped
    onion

½ teaspoon salt
pepper to taste
1 teaspoon Worcestershire
    sauce
¾ cup mayonnaise
1 cup soft bread crumbs
1 tablespoon melted butter

Combine first 9 ingredients and mix well. Place into 1 quart greased casserole or individual baking dishes. Combine bread crumbs with melted butter and sprinkle on top. Bake at 350 degrees for 30 minutes or until hot.

Yield: 4 servings

TUNA CASSEROLE

6 ounces medium noodles
1 (7 ounce) can tuna
½ cup mayonnaise
1 teaspoon celery salt
1 teaspoon onion powder
1 teaspoon salt

1 (10.75 ounce) can cream of
    celery soup
½ cup milk
1 (4 ounce) package shredded
    sharp cheese
bread crumbs
salt and pepper to taste

Cook noodles until done. Drain and combine noodles, tuna, celery salt, onion powder, salt, soup, and milk, heating thoroughly. Add cheese to mixture. Pour in an ungreased 11 x 7 x 2 inch baking dish. Coat top with bread crumbs. Bake at 425 degrees for 20 minutes.

An old time favorite.

Yield: 4 to 6 servings

JACK'S CRAB CASSEROLE

½ cup celery, chopped
½ large green pepper,
   chopped
½ cup green onion, chopped
¼ cup fresh parsley
   or 1 teaspoon dried
1 pound crab meat

⅓ teaspoon dry mustard
1¼ cups crushed cracker
   crumbs
¼ cup heavy cream
½ cup melted butter
Tabasco sauce to taste

Preheat oven to 350 degrees. Mix all ingredients, but only ½ of cracker crumbs, saving ½ for topping. Pour into a buttered baking dish. Top with remaining cracker crumbs. Bake for 25 to 30 minutes.

Serve with tossed salad and rice pilaf.

Yield: 6 servings

OYSTER STEW

1 pint oysters with juice
1 quart milk, scalded
½ stick margarine

1 cup green onion, chopped
salt and white pepper to taste

Sauté onion in margarine until tender, but not brown. Add oysters and cook for 5 minutes over medium heat. Add scalding milk and seasonings; bring to a near boil. Remove from heat and serve with oyster crackers.

Traditional Lowcountry.

Yield: 2 to 4 servings

SHARK NUGGETTS

2 pounds shark steak
2 teaspoons garlic salt
2 teaspoons pepper
2 teaspoons seasoned salt

Creole seasoning
2 cups self-rising flour in
   double brown paper bag
2 quarts peanut oil

Use fresh cut shark steaks. Remove inside round bone and cut into nuggets. Season heavily; dip in flour and deep fry at 375 until they float to top.

A must after the fishing trip.

Yield: 4 to 6 servings

GRILLED MONKFISH

4 pieces of monkfish
1 bottle Italian dressing
salt and pepper to taste

1 stick butter, melted
¼ cup lemon juice, fresh
   squeezed

Wash and dry pieces of fish. Place in a large glass baking dish and pour dressing evenly over each fish. Sprinkle with salt and freshly ground pepper. Let marinate for at least 1 hour. When coals are very hot, place fish on grill and cover. Cook on each side 6 to 10 minutes, turning only once. Just before fish are done, mix melted butter and lemon juice and drizzle over fish.

This fish tastes a lot like lobster and because it is a thick fish, it grills beautifully.

Yield: 4 servings

SEAFOOD KABOBS

½ pound scallops
½ pound shrimp, peeled
½ pound grouper, cut into
   cubes, or use 1½ pounds
   of shrimp and grouper
   only

1 green pepper, cut into
   chunks
12 cherry tomatoes
¼ cup olive oil
4 minced scallions
¼ cup lemon juice
3 tablespoons soy sauce

Combine olive oil, scallions, lemon juice and soy sauce. Add seafood. Let marinate 1 to 2 hours. Skewer seafood alternately with green peppers and tomatoes. Broil or grill 5 to 6 minutes on each side, basting with reserved marinade. Serve over hot rice.

Easy and makes a colorful and healthy meal.

Yield: 4 to 6 servings

SHRIMP CASSEROLE

2 pounds shrimp, cooked and
    cleaned
1½ cups celery, chopped
1 bell pepper, chopped
1 large onion, chopped

1 (6 ounce) box wild rice,
    prepared by directions
2 (10.75 ounce) cans cream of
    mushroom soup
1 small jar chopped pimentos
3 tablespoons butter

Sauté celery, bell pepper, and onion in butter. Mix rice, soup and pimentos with the rest of the ingredients. Bake at 350 degrees for 1 hour.

May be prepared ahead.

Yield: 6 servings

SEAFOOD CASSEROLE

1 pound white crab meat
1½ pounds fresh or frozen
    shrimp, cleaned
2 to 3 stalks celery, chopped
1 medium onion, chopped
1 green bell pepper, chopped
1¼ cups mayonnaise
¼ cup Durkee's French fried
    onions

2 tablespoons fresh squeezed
    lemon juice
dash Worcestershire sauce
dash Tabasco sauce
salt and pepper to taste (takes
    very little salt)
2 to 3 slices of bread,
    crumbled
¼ stick of butter or margarine

Combine all the ingredients together, but bread crumbs and butter. Place in a greased 3 quart oblong casserole dish. Bake at 400 degrees for 30 minutes. While baking, toast bread crumbs with butter. Sprinkle bread crumbs over top of casserole before serving.

May be prepared ahead, but not cooked.

Yield: 6 to 8 servings

SAUTÉED SCALLOPS

1 pound scallops
¼ cup butter
½ scant teaspoon salt
⅛ teaspoon freshly ground
   black pepper

¼ teaspoon paprika
1 clove garlic, minced
1 tablespoon minced parsley
3 tablespoons lemon juice

Wash scallops and dry thoroughly. If sea scallops are used, cut into thirds or quarters. In large skillet, heat 2 tablespoons of butter and add the salt, pepper, paprika and garlic. Add enough scallops to cover the bottom of the skillet without crowding. Cook quickly over high heat, stirring occasionally until golden brown, 5 to 10 minutes. Transfer the scallops to a heated platter. Repeat the process until all the scallops are cooked. In the same skillet, place the parsley, lemon juice and remaining butter. Heat until the butter melts and pour over scallops.

Yield: 4 servings

CHEESY SHRIMP CASSEROLE

2 tablespoons chopped onion
2 tablespoons butter
1 pound shrimp, peeled and
   deveined
1 (10.75 ounce) can Cheddar
   cheese soup

1 (10.75 ounce) can broccoli
   cheese soup
1 (3 ounce) jar sliced
   mushrooms
3 tablespoons milk
1 tablespoon lemon juice
1 cup white rice, cooked

Sauté onion and shrimp in butter for 5 minutes or until shrimp is done. Add soup, mushrooms, milk and lemon juice. Line bottom of casserole dish with rice and pour mixture over it. Bake at 300 degrees for 20 to 30 minutes.

Yield: 4 to 6 servings

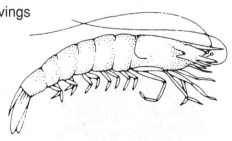

Special
SIDEDISHES

PINEAPPLE AND CHEESE CASSEROLE

2 (15½ ounces) cans
   pineapple, chunk style
1 cup granulated sugar
⅓ cup flour

2 cups grated sharp Cheddar
   cheese
1 stick melted butter
1 stack Ritz crackers

Drain pineapple juice from pineapple chunks into mixing bowl. Stir sugar and flour into juice. Add pineapple chunks. Pour into 9 x 12 inch casserole dish and top with grated cheese. Add melted butter to crushed Ritz crackers and sprinkle on top of cheese. Bake at 350 degrees for 30 minutes.

A great accompaniment for baked ham or pork.

Yield: 8 servings

HASH BROWN POTATO CASSEROLE

1 (2 pound) package frozen
   hash browns
1½ sticks butter, melted and
   divided
½ cup chopped onion
2 cups sour cream

1 (10½ ounce) can cream of
   celery or cream of chicken
   soup
2 cups grated Cheddar cheese
1 teaspoon salt
2 cups crushed corn flakes

Mix hash browns, 1 stick butter, onion, sour cream, soup, cheese and salt. Place in 9 x 13 inch Pyrex dish. Blend remaining ½ stick of butter with corn flake crumbs and place over top of casserole. Bake at 350 degrees for 30 minutes.

Yield: 4 to 6 servings

ESCALLOPED POTATOES

4 cups diced potatoes
1 can creamed soup (chicken,
   celery or mushroom)

1 medium onion, diced
½ stick margarine
¼ cup milk

Cook diced potatoes in salted water until tender. Drain and set aside. Sauté onion in melted margarine. Add soup and milk and stir until smooth and thick. Place potatoes into a greased casserole dish and cover with soup mixture. Bake at 350 degrees uncovered for 30 minutes.

Yield: 6 servings

TASTY POTATOES

6 medium potatoes, peeled,
   cubed and boiled
1 medium onion, chopped
3 tablespoons butter or
   margarine

1 teaspoon paprika
1 teaspoon seasoned salt
½ teaspoon seasoned pepper

Put the margarine in a large skillet on medium heat. Add onions and cook until clear (not brown). Add the potatoes and the seasonings, and cook on medium heat until potatoes are golden on one side, then turn and cook on other side.

Delicious and so easy.

Yield: 4 to 6 servings

POTATO WEDGES

1 teaspoon salt
½ teaspoon garlic salt
½ teaspoon onion salt
½ teaspoon pepper (or to
    taste)
½ cup flour

½ cup Parmesan cheese
7 or 8 medium baking
    potatoes sliced into
    wedges (skin on)
1 stick margarine, melted

Mix the first 6 ingredients together in a zip-loc bag. Shake potatoes in flour mixture a few at a time. Place in a 9 x 13 inch baking dish and pour melted margarine over potatoes. Bake at 375 degrees for 1 hour, stirring occasionally.

Yield: 8 servings

GRILLED POTATO SALAD

1 envelope onion or onion-
    mushroom soup mix
⅓ cup vegetable oil
2 tablespoons red wine
    vinegar
1 teaspoon chopped garlic

2 pounds small red potatoes,
    cut 1 inch pieces
2 medium peppers, (1 red,
    1 green) chopped
2 tablespoons chopped fresh
    basil
⅛ teaspoon ground pepper

Blend soup mix, oil, vinegar and garlic. Stir in potatoes and peppers. Grease a 30 x 18 inch sheet of aluminum foil. Put in potato mixture. Wrap and seal edges all tight with double foil. Grill 40 minutes or until potatoes are tender. Shake pack occasionally and turn once during cooking time. Toss with basil and pepper.

Yield: 8 servings

OLD SMOKEY CHEESE AND POTATO CASSEROLE

2 cups shredded Cheddar
   cheese
6 white medium potatoes,
   sliced
6 smoked sausages, sliced

½ stick melted butter or
   margarine
⅓ diced bell pepper
½ diced medium onion
salt, pepper and garlic, to
   taste

Preheat oven to 400 degrees. In a ½ quart casserole dish, layer sliced sausages, sliced potatoes, diced bell pepper, diced onion, cheese and seasonings (retain enough seasonings to sprinkle over casserole). Pour melted butter or margarine over top of casserole. Sprinkle remaining cheese over top. Bake one hour or until potatoes are tender.

Yield: 6 servings

CANDIED SWEET POTATOES

3 cups yams, baked, boiled or
   canned and cut into pieces
1 cup dark corn syrup
½ cup dark brown sugar

½ stick margarine, melted
1 tablespoon lemon juice
grated rind of one lemon
1 teaspoon cinnamon

Place potatoes into greased casserole dish. Combine other ingredients and pour over potatoes. Bake at 350 degrees uncovered for 30 minutes, basting often.

Traditional.

Yield: 8 to 10 servings

FRENCH FRIED SWEET POTATOES

sweet potatoes   **water**
salt   **vegetable oil**

Peel raw sweet potatoes and cut into ½ to ¾ inch strips. Soak in cold, salted water for a short time; drain and dry between towels. Fry in deep fat (365 degrees) 3 to 5 minutes until brown. Drain on absorbent paper and sprinkle lightly with salt.

Serve with pork chops, steaks, or ham.

Yield: 6 to 8 servings

SWEET POTATO CRUNCH

Casserole
3 cups cooked yams   **1 tablespoon vanilla extract**
2 eggs   **½ cup butter**
1 cup sugar

Topping
1 cup brown sugar   **⅓ cup butter**
1 cup chopped pecans   **⅓ cup self rising flour**

Preheat oven at 350 degrees. Blend yams, eggs, sugar vanilla and butter with an electric mixer until smooth. Pour into greased casserole dish. For topping combine brown sugar, pecans, butter and flour, mixing thoroughly. Sprinkle over top of casserole. Bake for 30 to 35 minutes.

Delicious.

Yield: 4 to 6 servings

YAM AND CRANBERRY CASSEROLE

4 large sweet potatoes, baked
   or boiled
½ cup light brown sugar
2 cups fresh cranberries

½ cup lemon juice
1 teaspoon cinnamon
½ cup melted margarine
chopped pecans

Peel cooked sweet potatoes and cut lengthwise into ¼ inch slices. Place into greased casserole dish, layering alternately with cranberries. Add brown sugar to melted margarine in saucepan and stir in lemon juice and cinnamon. Cook until smooth. Pour over potato and cranberry mixture. Cover and bake at 350 degrees for 40 minutes. Uncover and sprinkle with chopped pecans and return to oven until lightly browned.

Yield: 6 to 8 servings

SWEET POTATO BONBONS

3 pounds sweet potatoes,
   peeled and cooked
¼ cup butter
½ cup brown sugar
1 teaspoon salt

½ teaspoon grated orange
   rind
6 marshmallows, halved
⅓ cup melted butter
4 cups corn flakes, crushed
12 pecan halves

Mash sweet potatoes until light and fluffy. Beat in butter, sugar, salt, and orange rind. Let cool. Divide into 12 portions. Press potatoes around each marshmallow half, being careful to keep marshmallows in center. Shape into oval. Coat each with melted butter. Roll in crushed corn flakes; top with pecan half and place on lightly greased baking sheet. Bake at 450 degrees for 7 to 8 minutes.

Yield: 6 to 8 servings

CAROLINA RED BEANS AND RICE

1 pound red beans (soak in
   water overnight)
½ pound ham hocks or 1
   large, meaty ham bone
5 bay leaves
2 tablespoons sugar
salt, pepper, cayenne to taste
2 tablespoons bacon
   drippings
2 large onion, chopped
2 stalks celery, chopped

1 large bell pepper, chopped
2 cups diced tomatoes, fresh
   or canned with juice
3 cloves garlic, crushed
   or 1 teaspoon garlic salt
1 cup fresh chopped parsley,
   optional
1 pound country sausage,
   cut in 2 inch pieces and
   cooked

Drain beans early on the morning after soaking. In a large cooking pot or kettle, place beans in 1 gallon of water; add ham bone, bay leaves, sugar, salt, pepper and cayenne. Bring to a boil, reduce heat and cover. Simmer four hours. While beans are simmering, fry onion, celery, pepper, garlic and parsley in bacon drippings. Add tomatoes and cook until slightly thick. Add to simmering beans; red beans should really simmer all day. Add water if necessary. Continue cooking. Remove bay leaves and serve over fluffy white rice. Top each bowl with piece of cooked sausage. Adjust seasoning to taste.

Hot French bread and a green salad is great with this.

Double recipe and freeze leftovers.

Yield: 8 servings

BAKED BEAN SPECIAL

1 pound ground beef
1 cup chopped onion
1 (12 ounce) package bacon
1 (28 ounce) can pork-n-beans

1 (16 ounce) can pinto beans
⅓ cup light brown sugar
dash vinegar
1 cup ketchup

Preheat oven to 350 degrees. Brown ground beef and drain well. Sauté onion and bacon together and drain well. Pour beans and ground beef in a 13 x 9 x 2 inch pan or large casserole dish. Crumble bacon and onions in beans and beef. Add remaining ingredients and stir to combine. Bake at 350 degrees for 1½ hours.

Serve with salad and garlic bread to make a complete meal.

Yield: 6 servings

SOUTHERN BAKED BEANS

1 small onion, minced
½ bell pepper, chopped
2 stalks celery, chopped
2 tablespoons bacon
  drippings or butter
1 (20 ounce) can pork and
  beans

4 tablespoons catsup
2 tablespoons molasses
2 tablespoons brown sugar
3 drops Tabasco sauce
salt to taste
3 slices bacon, uncooked

Sauté onion, bell pepper, and celery in bacon drippings. Mix all ingredients except bacon. Put in a greased shallow baking dish. Cut bacon slices in half and put on top of beans. Bake at 375 degrees for 30 minutes.

Yield: 4 servings

STUFFED GREEN BELL PEPPERS

6 green bell peppers
6 cups cooked minced meat
  (chicken, lamb, veal, roast
  pork, or shrimp)
1 onion, minced
1 tablespoon butter, melted

1 tablespoon parsley, minced
1 teaspoon salt
¼ cup bread crumbs or rice
1 egg, beaten
1 cup water or beef bouillon

Cut peppers in half, crosswise, remove seeds and cut off stems. Mix all remaining ingredients together, except water or bouillon. Fill peppers with mixture, stand in pan, and pour water around them. Bake at 350 degrees, basting often, until tops are toasty brown.

Corn may be substituted for meat.

Yield: 6 servings

RICE MUSHROOM MEDLEY

1 (6 ounce) package long
    grain and wild rice mix
1 (10½ ounce) can condensed
    beef broth or (1¼ cups)
1¼ cups water

1 small onion, chopped
½ cup chopped celery
4 tablespoons butter
1 (3 ounce) can sliced
    mushrooms, drained

Prepare rice mix substituting beef broth and water for liquid called for in recipe. Sauté onion and celery in butter until tender, about 3 to 5 minutes. Add onion and celery to rice 5 minutes before end of cooking time. Stir well and continue cooking until all liquid is absorbed.

Yield: 6 to 8 servings

GREEN RICE CASSEROLE

1 stick margarine
1 cup instant rice
1 cup chopped celery
1 cup chopped onion
1 (10 ounce) package
    chopped broccoli

1 (3 ounce) can sliced
    mushrooms
1 pound cheese, chopped
1 (10½ ounce) can cream of
    mushroom soup
¼ cup water

Melt margarine in casserole dish and add rice. Mix in celery, onion, broccoli, mushroom and cheese. Mix soup and water together and pour over casserole. Bake at 350 degrees for 20 minutes. Remove from oven and stir. Bake another 20 minutes.

Yield: 6 servings

BROWN RICE

1 stick butter or margarine
1 cup rice
1 (10½ ounce) can French
    onion soup

1 (10½ ounce) can beef
    consommé
1 (6 ounce) can sliced
    mushrooms
seasonings to taste

Melt butter or margarine in large baking dish. Add rice and stir for a few minutes. Add soups, stir, and top with can of mushrooms. Bake at 350 degrees for 45 minutes.

Yield: 6 servings

BEER RICE

1 cup raw rice
1 (10¾ ounce) can chicken
    broth
1 (6 ounce) can beer
½ small onion, finely chopped

¼ small green pepper,
    chopped
⅓ cup butter or margarine
1 teaspoon salt
dash pepper
¼ teaspoon thyme

Sauté onion and pepper in butter until soft, but not brown. Add all other ingredients. Bring to a boil, stirring occasionally. Cover and simmer over very low heat for about 40 minutes, or until rice is tender.

Yield: 4 servings

OKRA AND RICE

4 pieces of bacon, chopped in
    small pieces
2 small links of hot sausage,
    chopped
1 large onion, chopped
1 cup okra

2 cups water
1 cup of rice
2 bouillon cubes (chicken or
    beef)
salt and pepper

Fry out bacon and sausage, cook onion in drippings. Add okra and stir fry about 5 minutes. In separate heavy pot add water, rice, and bouillon cubes, and seasonings. Stir in bacon, sausage, onions, and drippings. Bring to boil. Keep covered and cook for at least 30 minutes on low.

An okra lover's must.

Yield: 4 to 6 servings

HOPPING JOHN

1 cup raw rice	2½ cups juice from peas
3 slices bacon	1 teaspoon salt
1 smoked ham hock (cooked	pepper to taste
tender in peas)	1 cup cooked drained peas

Prior to making Hoppin John, cook dried field peas or blackeye peas according to directions with smoked ham hock. After cooking you now have the necessary ingredients. Fry bacon, remove from heavy pot and crumble. Sauté onion in bacon grease. Add ham hock, juice, seasoning, peas and rice. Bring to boil then simmer for about 30 minutes. Remove from heat and let stand 15 minutes, then fluff. Keep the extra peas as a side dish, especially for added liquid.

South Carolina was the birthplace of rice in America. Many rice recipes and traditions have been passed from generation to generation and are still enjoyed across the Carolinas today. "Hoppin John" is believed to bring good luck if eaten on New Year's Day. Complete the meal with collard greens (for wealth) and ham hock (for health) - a guaranteed HAPPY NEW YEAR.

Yield: 6 to 8 servings

PERFECT RED RICE

½ pound bacon	1 (64 ounce) tomato juice can
2 large onions, chopped	filled with instant rice
2 large bell peppers, chopped	(always use equal
1 (64 ounce) can tomato juice	amounts of instant rice
salt, pepper, garlic, etc.,	and tomato juice)
to taste	

Chop bacon and fry in large pan until brown. Remove bacon and save drippings. Sauté onions and bell peppers in bacon drippings (3 to 4 minutes). Add bacon, tomato juice, and seasonings and bring to boil. Add instant rice, cover and simmer for 10 minutes.

Add smoked sausage or shrimp for variety. You'll never have gummy or raw rice again.

Perfection with ease.

Yield: 10 to 12 servings

RED RICE CASSEROLE

1 pound sliced smoked
   sausage or 1 pound
   ground beef
4 teaspoons bacon drippings
1 cup long grain rice

2 cups tomato juice
1 green pepper, chopped
2 medium onions, chopped
3 tablespoons margarine
salt and pepper to taste

Brown meat slightly in bacon drippings. Combine all other ingredients. Mix well. Bake covered at 350 degrees for 1 hour in casserole dish.

Yield: 4 servings

CORN PIE

1 (16 ounce) can cream style
   corn
1 tablespoon sugar
1 teaspoon salt
2 tablespoons flour

3 eggs, well beaten
2 tablespoons butter or
   margarine, melted
1 cup milk

Mix in order given above. Pour into well greased casserole dish. Bake at 350 degrees for 1 hour.

Yield: 6 to 8 servings

CORN CASSEROLE

1 (8½ ounce) box Jiffy corn
   muffin mix
2 eggs, beaten
1 (8 ounce) container sour
   cream

1 cup sugar
1 (16 ounce) can whole corn
1 (16 ounce) can cream style
   corn
1 stick margarine, melted

Mix Jiffy mix, eggs, sour cream, sugar and both cans of corn together. Pour melted butter into a 9 x 12 inch casserole dish and add corn mix. Bake at 350 degrees for 35 minutes or until brown and set in middle.

Yield: 6 to 8 servings

SOUTHERN STYLE STEWED CORN

10 ears yellow corn
8 strips fat back, cut thin

1 teaspoon salt
½ cup water

Fry fat back in an iron skillet. Remove meat, leaving grease in skillet. Set aside to cool. Shave thin layers of corn from cob, then scrape cob, making a creamy substance. Place cut corn into skillet with ½ cup water and salt. Mix all together. Let come to a good boil and stir constantly to prevent sticking. Turn heat down and let simmer for 30 minutes, stirring occasionally.

Serve with fried chicken, biscuits, butterbeans, sliced tomatoes and spring onions.

Yield 6 to 8 servings

MASSAQA'S

2 cups tomato sauce
¾ pound ground beef, cooked
salt, pepper, and mixed spices
    to taste

2 medium eggplants
4 medium green peppers
3 tablespoons olive oil

Mix ½ cup tomato sauce with cooked minced beef and season with salt, pepper, and mixed spices. Cook for 7 to 10 minutes. Fry thinly sliced eggplant and green pepper in olive oil until brown. Line bottom of oven dish with one layer of fried eggplant and green pepper, spread with beef/tomato mixture and cover with remaining eggplant and green peppers. Bake in center of a 350 degree oven for 30 minutes.

Yield: 6 servings

ZUCCHINI SOUFFLÉ

3 cups zucchini, unpeeled, grated
½ onion, thinly sliced
3 tablespoons chopped parsley
1 clove garlic, minced
1 cup biscuit mix
½ cup vegetable oil
½ teaspoon seasoned salt
½ teaspoon salt
½ cup grated Parmesan cheese
4 eggs, lightly beaten
2 tablespoons melted butter

In a large bowl, toss together first 9 ingredients. Add eggs and mix well. Place in a greased 9 x 13 inch baking dish and drizzle with melted butter. Bake at 350 degrees for 35 minutes. Cut into squares before serving.

Cut into smaller portions and serve as an appetizer.

Yield: 8 servings

BROCCOLI CASSEROLE

Casserole
2 packages frozen chopped broccoli
1 large onion, minced
1 cup mayonnaise
1 (10.75 ounce) can cream of mushroom soup
1 egg, beaten
½ cup Pepperidge Farm cornbread dressing mix
1 (8 ounce) package sharp Cheddar cheese, grated

Topping
1 cup Pepperidge Farm dressing
½ stick margarine

Cook broccoli according to package directions. Drain. Add onion, mixing well. Add mayonnaise, soup, egg, and dressing mix. Spray a 9 x 13 inch pan with Pam and spread mixture in it. Sprinkle cheese over top. To prepare topping, melt margarine and mix with dressing. Sprinkle evenly over casserole. Bake at 350 degrees for 35 minutes or until top is brown and casserole is bubbly, or microwave on medium for about 15 minutes.

Yield: 6 to 8 servings

ONION BROCCOLI CASSEROLE

1 pound fresh broccoli
  or 1 (10 ounce) package
  frozen broccoli
2 cups onions, quartered
4 tablespoons, butter
1 (3 ounce) package cream
  cheese

2 tablespoons all purpose
  flour
½ cup sharp cheese, grated
1 cup milk
1 cup soft bread crumbs
salt and pepper to taste

Cook broccoli and onions separately in salted water. Set aside. In a saucepan melt 2 tablespoons of butter and blend in flour plus ¼ teaspoon salt. Add milk, cook and stir until thick and bubbly. Reduce heat and blend in cream cheese until smooth. Place vegetables in 1½ quart casserole dish. Pour sauce over all, mix slightly. Top with cheese then bread crumbs, top with remaining 2 tablespoons of butter. Bake at 350 degrees for 30 minutes.

Yield: 4 to 6 servings

COPPER PENNIES

1 pound carrots, sliced
½ medium onion
½ medium bell pepper
1 rib celery
½ cup tomato soup
1½ teaspoons Worcestershire
  sauce

½ cup sugar
⅛ cup vegetable oil
⅓ cup apple cider vinegar
1½ teaspoons dry mustard
½ teaspoon salt
¼ teaspoon pepper

Cook sliced carrots until fork tender. Drain and set aside. Combine finely chop onion, bell pepper and celery with carrots. Mix remaining ingredients in saucepan and bring to a boil. Pour hot mixture over carrots and stir. Refrigerate at least 24 hours before serving.

Can be used as a vegetable dish or add a cup of chopped meat and serve with rice.

Yield: 8 servings

LAZY STUFFED CABBAGE

2 pounds ground beef
1 package dry onion soup mix
1 cup instant rice
2 pounds cabbage, finely
    chopped

2 (10 ounce) cans tomato
    soup
2 soup cans of water

Sauté ground beef and onion soup in skillet. When brown, drain off fat and add rice to meat mixture. Put sliced cabbage into large baking pan or casserole dish. Spread meat and rice mixture over cabbage. Mix soup and water and pour over casserole. Cover and bake at 350 degrees for 1½ hours.

Yield: 8 to 10 servings

OKRA FRITTERS

1 cup okra, thinly sliced
½ teaspoon salt
¼ teaspoon pepper
¼ cup plain flour

⅓ cup cornmeal
½ teaspoon curry powder,
    optional
1 egg, beaten

Combine all ingredients; stir well. Drop by tablespoonful into hot grease; cook until golden brown.

Okra lovers' special.

Yield: 12 to 16 fritters

FRIED OKRA

1 pound tender okra
½ cup milk
1 egg

1 cup cornmeal
seasoning or salt and pepper
cooking oil

Cut tender, young okra in 1 inch rounds and season to taste. In a small bowl beat egg and add milk. Dip okra in mixture and roll in seasoned cornmeal. Fry in deep fat until crisp and brown. Drain on absorbent paper.

Tastes like fried oysters.

Yield: 4 servings

DELUXE SCALLOPED TOMATOES

7 fresh tomatoes	½ teaspoon salt
½ cup butter, melted	½ teaspoon nutmeg
1 cup onion, chopped	3 cups white bread cubes
2 tablespoons brown sugar	

Peel tomatoes, cut 3 slices to reserve for top garnish, and chop rest of tomatoes. Sauté onion in 2 tablespoons of butter. Add all remaining ingredients to onions, except bread cubes and remaining butter. Simmer for 15 minutes. Toss bread with butter to coat. Layer 2 cups bread cubes in a greased 10 inch quiche or pie pan. Cover with tomato mixture and top with remaining bread. Bake at 375 degrees covered for 15 minutes. Uncover, top with reserved tomato slices brushed lightly with vegetable oil and bake uncovered for 15 more minutes.

Can substitute 3½ cups canned tomatoes for fresh tomatoes.
Garnish with parsley.

Yield: 8 servings

FRIED GREEN TOMATOES

5 green tomatoes, sliced	1 teaspoon salt
1 egg, well beaten	⅛ teaspoon pepper
½ cup buttermilk	⅛ teaspoon garlic powder
½ cup cornmeal	½ cup cooking oil
¼ cup all-purpose flour	

Combine egg and buttermilk until well mixed, set aside. Combine dry ingredients. Dip green tomato slice in to egg mixture and then dry mixture. Heat oil in large skillet over medium heat, place coated green tomato slices into hot oil, forming a single layer. Cook until golden brown on each side. Repeat until all are cooked. (Add extra oil, if needed). Drain on paper towels.

For extra flavor, sprinkle with Parmesan cheese.

A favorite.

Yield: 6 servings

FRIED GREEN TOMATOES CHARLESTON STYLE

6 green tomatoes
1 cup self-rising flour
salt and pepper to taste

3 slices bacon
¼ cup peanut oil

Slice tomatoes. Dip each slice in flour, then salt and pepper. Fry bacon and remove from pan. Add peanut oil to bacon grease. Dip each tomato slice in flour again and cook in hot grease until brown on each side.

Good ole southern style.

Yield: 6 servings

TOMATO PIE

1 deep dish pie shell, baked
  and cooled
3 large tomatoes, completely
  ripened
3 green onions, finely
  chopped
salt to taste
pepper to taste

basil to taste
1 cup sharp Cheddar cheese,
  grated
1 cup mayonnaise
4 slices bacon, fried crisp and
  drained well
Parmesan cheese

Place layer of peeled, thick sliced tomatoes in bottom of pie shell. Sprinkle with spices and onion. Place another layer of tomatoes on top of that and sprinkle again with spices and onion. Spread mixture of mayonnaise and grated Cheddar cheese over tomatoes. Top with crumbled bacon and Parmesan cheese. Bake at 350 degrees until lightly browned on top, approximately 30 minutes.

A wonderful addition to any meal and a summertime delight.

Yield: 4 to 6 servings

SPINACH EVEN KIDS LOVE

1 (10 ounce) package frozen spinach, thawed and drained well
1 (4 ounce) can mushrooms, drained
½ cup shredded Cheddar cheese
⅓ cup butter or margarine, melted
1 teaspoon dill
1 teaspoon nutmeg
¼ teaspoon hot pepper sauce
3 slices bacon, cooked and crumbled

Grease an 8 inch square baking dish. Layer spinach, mushrooms and cheese. Blend butter, dill, nutmeg and hot sauce together and pour over casserole. Sprinkle bacon over top. Bake at 350 degrees for approximately 10 minutes.

This same recipe can be used to make Fish Florentine. Place white-fish fillets in bottom of greased baking dish. Pour spinach mixture over the top as directed above. Bake at 350 degrees for 30 minutes.

Yield: 4 to 6 servings

BROCCOLI AND/OR CAULIFLOWER CASSEROLE

1 (10 ounce) package frozen chopped broccoli
1 (10 ounce) package frozen cauliflower
1 teaspoon garlic salt
1 (10 ounce) can mushroom soup, undiluted
1 egg, beaten
1½ cups sharp Cheddar cheese, grated
1 cup Pepperidge Farm stuffing
½ stick butter, melted

Cook broccoli and cauliflower a few minutes, adding garlic salt to the cooking water. Drain vegetables. Add soup, egg and cheese. Put in a greased 2 quart casserole and top with mixture of stuffing tossed with melted butter. Bake at 350 degrees for 30 minutes.

Yield: 4 to 6 servings

SUPER SQUASH CASSEROLE

1 (8 ounce) bag Pepperidge
   Farm cornbread dressing
   mix
1 stick margarine, melted
3 pounds yellow squash,
   sliced

½ cup onion, diced
1 carrot, grated
1 (8 ounce) carton sour cream
1 (10½ ounce) can cream of
   chicken soup
salt and pepper to taste

Mix dressing and melted margarine together and set aside. Cook squash and onion together until tender (approximately 10 minutes). Drain. Mix squash, ½ dressing mix, sour cream, and chicken soup. Place in greased casserole dish and top with remaining dressing mix. Bake, uncovered, at 350 degrees for 30 minutes.

Add zucchini squash for color.

Yield: 6 to 8 servings

COLESLAW

1 medium head cabbage,
   shredded
1 medium green pepper, thinly
   sliced
3 carrots, cut in thin strips
1 tablespoon grated onion

¼ cup granulated sugar
¼ teaspoon salt
¼ cup white vinegar
2 tablespoons vegetable oil
mayonnaise

In a large bowl, toss vegetables, cover and chill. Before serving combine sugar, salt, vinegar and oil. Pour over cabbage. Toss well. Add mayonnaise if desired, a tablespoon at a time, until creamy.

Yield: 4 to 6 servings

ZUCCHINI PIE

3 cups chopped zucchini
   squash (do not peel)
½ cup chopped onion
1 cup shredded Cheddar
   cheese (about 4 ounces)

1½ cups milk
¾ cup Bisquick mix
3 eggs
1 teaspoon salt
¼ teaspoon pepper

Mix zucchini, onion, and cheese in lightly greased 9 x 11 inch dish. Beat together milk, Bisquick, eggs, salt, and pepper and pour into baking dish. Bake 35 to 40 minutes at 400 degrees until golden brown. Let stand 5 minutes before serving.

Yield: 8 to 10 servings

CORNBREAD STUFFING

2 (12 ounce) packages corn
   muffin mix or 2 (10 ounce)
   packages cornbread mix
½ cup butter or margarine
1½ cups chopped celery

1 cup chopped onions
1½ cups orange juice
1 teaspoon seasoned salt
2 hard-boiled eggs, chopped

Bake corn muffin mix as label directs for cornbread; cool in pans on wire rack. In large saucepan over medium heat, in hot butter or margarine, cook celery and onions about 10 minutes or until tender; remove from heat. Crumble cornbread into mixture; stir in remaining ingredients; mix well.

Good any time of year.

Yield: 9 cups

CANS-CAN-BE-GOOD VEGETABLE CASSEROLE

1 (16 ounce) can Veg-All
   mixed vegetables, drained
¼ cup water chestnuts, sliced
¼ cup onion, chopped
½ cup celery, chopped

½ cup sharp Cheddar cheese,
   grated
½ cup mayonnaise
1 tablespoon butter, melted
½ cup Ritz cracker crumbs

Mix all ingredients except butter and cracker crumbs. Combine butter and cracker crumbs and sprinkle on top. Bake at 325 degrees for 25 minutes.

Yield: 4 servings

SAUSAGE GRITS

1 pound bulk pork sausage
3 cups hot cooked grits
2½ cups shredded Cheddar
   cheese
3 tablespoons butter or
   margarine

3 eggs, beaten
1½ cups milk
parsley and pimento strips for
   garnish

Cook sausage until browned in a heavy skillet, drain well. Spoon into a lightly greased 13 x 9 inch baking dish. Combine hot cooked grits, cheese and butter. Stir until cheese and butter melts. Combine eggs and milk, stir into grits. Pour into baking dish over sausage. Bake at 350 degrees for 1 hour. Garnish with pimento strips and parsley, if desired.

Let's do breakfast for supper.

Yield: 15 servings

QUICHE

2 (8 inch) pie shells
1 tablespoon flour
1 cup meat (ham or sausage)
¼ teaspoon salt

1 cup shredded Cheddar
 cheese
¼ teaspoon pepper
6 eggs, beaten
1½ cups milk

Brown meat and drain. Mix flour with small amount of water. Mix remaining ingredients and pour into pie shells. Bake at 400 degrees for 30 minutes.

Great served with hash brown potatoes. You may want to serve for breakfast or brunch.

Yield: 8 to 10 servings

E-Z THREE CHEESE QUICHE

½ cup grated Cheddar cheese
¼ cup grated Parmesan
 cheese
¼ cup grated Swiss cheese
1 pie shell

3 eggs
1½ cups milk
½ teaspoon salt
pinch of pepper
pinch of nutmeg

Mix cheeses together and sprinkle on pie shell. Beat eggs, milk, salt, pepper and nutmeg together. Pour on top of pie shell to within ⅛ inch of top of pie shell. Bake 350 degrees for 30 minutes.

Yield: 4 to 6 servings

SOUTHERN COLLARD GREENS

3 pounds collard greens,
 fresh
2 tablespoon sugar

1 meaty ham hock or ¼ pound
 bacon
salt and pepper to taste

Wash and clean greens. Tear off stems and cut up. Place all in Dutch oven or large heavy pot. Cover with water ¾ full. Cook about 2 hours on medium heat. May drain.

Some say they're even better the following day.

Double your recipe for New Years.

Yield: 6 servings

CRAB MEAT QUICHE

1½ cups crab meat (6½ ounce can)
½ cup mayonnaise
½ teaspoon salt
2 eggs, beaten
¼ cup milk
2 tablespoons white wine

8 ounces Swiss cheese, chopped
2 tablespoons flour
⅓ cup sliced celery
¼ cup sliced green onions
1 (9 inch) unbaked pie shell

Remove any pieces of shell from crab meat. Combine mayonnaise, salt, eggs, milk and wine. Blend well. Toss cheese with flour. Add to mayonnaise mixture. Stir in crab meat, celery and onion. Pour into pie shell. Bake at 425 degrees for 10 minutes, then reduce heat to 325 degrees and bake 30 minutes or until set.

Yield: 6 servings

EGGPLANT PARMESAN

1 (2 pound) eggplant
salt to taste
3 eggs
1½ to 2 cups dried bread crumbs
½ to ¾ cup oil

¾ pound Mozzarella cheese, sliced
3 cups tomato sauce
1 cup Parmesan cheese, grated
4 teaspoons fresh oregano, chopped

Preheat oven to 350 degrees. Peel eggplant and slice into ⅜-inch slices. Salt and let drain for 30 minutes; pat dry. Beat eggs with 2 tablespoons water. Dip the eggplant slices first into the eggs, then into the crumbs. Heat ¼ cup oil in a large frying pan and sauté the eggplant slices until golden brown on both sides. Remove and drain on brown paper. Continue cooking the eggplant, using additional oil if needed. Place half the eggplant slices in a 9 x 13 inch pan. Sprinkle with ⅓ of the Mozzarella cheese. Cover with half the tomato sauce and oregano. Repeat the layers. Top with the last of the Parmesan and Mozzarella cheeses. Bake for 30 minutes.

Yield: 6 to 8 servings

MARINATED VEGETABLES

1 (16 ounce) can whole small
    green beans, drained
1 (16 ounce) can green peas,
    drained
1 cup chopped celery
1 medium onion, chopped

2 cans water chestnuts
1 cup chopped bell pepper
1 cup vinegar
1½ cups water
1 cup sugar
¼ cup salad oil

Marinate the first 6 ingredients in vinegar, water and sugar mixture for 12 hours. Add the salad oil and toss like a salad. It can be served in lettuce cups like a salad or as a cold vegetable.

Yield: 6 to 8 servings

KELLY'S BARBECUE HASH

6 pounds fresh pork
3 pounds fresh chicken
3 pounds potatoes, ground
1½ pounds onions, ground

1 (32 ounce) can tomato purée
salt to taste
pepper to taste
red pepper to taste

In a large pot place pork and chicken, cover with water. Bring to boil, turn down heat and let simmer with lid on pot until meat falls off bone. Let cool. Debone and mash meat. Using same pot and liquid, place meat in pot and let come to a boil. Add potatoes, onions, tomato purée, salt, pepper and red pepper. Cook at a slow boil, constantly stirring. Cook for 1 hour; if too thin cook longer for desired thickness.

To thicken, add more potatoes.

Delicious.

Yield: 15 servings

Pasta

SHELLS STUFFED WITH CHEESE

1 egg, lightly beaten
½ cup grated Parmesan
  cheese
½ cup grated Swiss cheese
½ cup grated Mozzarella
  cheese
1 cup cottage cheese

¼ cup sour cream
1 clove garlic, minced
½ teaspoon dill weed
¼ teaspoon pepper
15 giant pasta sea shells,
  cooked al dente
1 can Italian-style tomatoes

Combine egg, cheeses, sour cream and seasonings in a medium mixing bowl. Spoon into drained pasta shells. Place in a greased 13 x 9 inch baking dish and top with tomatoes. Bake, uncovered, at 350 degrees for 40 to 45 minutes.

Serve lukewarm to enjoy the delicate flavor of the filling.

Yield: 4 servings

FETTUCCINE WITH POPPY SEEDS

6 ounces fettuccine,
  uncooked
⅓ cup butter or margarine,
  melted
¾ teaspoon garlic salt
¾ teaspoon dried parsley
  flakes

½ teaspoon poppy seeds
⅛ teaspoon pepper
½ cup sour cream
½ cup grated Parmesan
  cheese

Cook fettuccine according to package directions; drain. Combine butter and next 4 ingredients; stir in sour cream. Combine fettuccine and sour cream mixture; add cheese, and toss until fettuccine is coated. Serve immediately.

Yield: 6 servings

SHRIMP AND FETTUCINI

3 pounds peeled, raw shrimp
1 stick margarine
1 cup green onion, minced
1 cup fresh sliced mushrooms
1 pint half and half cream

½ cup Romano cheese, grated
salt and white pepper to taste
1 (8 ounce) package spinach
fettucini, cooked and drained

Sauté shrimp and onion and mushrooms in margarine until shrimp are pink and tender, about 8 to 10 minutes. Add cream and cheese; continue simmering, stirring constantly, until cheese melts. Add salt and pepper to taste, cover and simmer 20 minutes. Toss prepared fettucini with sauce and heat throughout. Serve immediately with hot bread or rolls.

Yield: 6 to 8 servings

ERA'S LASAGNA

3 pounds ground chuck
2 onions, chopped
3 (16 ounce) cans tomato
    sauce
1 (1½ ounce) package Italian
    spice mix with mushrooms

garlic salt to taste
5 cups grated sharp cheese
3 cups Mozzarella cheese
1 box lasagna noodles

Brown meat and onions, drain. Add sauce, spices and garlic salt; simmer 2 hours. Cook lasagna noodles according to package. When noodles have been cooked and drained, layer lasagna noodles, meat sauce and cheese alternately. Cover top with Mozzarella cheese. Bake at 300 degrees for 1 hour or until browned lightly on top.

Always a hit.

Yield: 6 to 8 servings

CHEESY LASAGNA

sea shell noodles
2 pounds ground round beef
2 teaspoons minced onions
2 tablespoons Worcestershire
   sauce
2 (16 ounce) cans tomato
   sauce
1 small can tomato paste
1 (8 ounce) container sour
   cream
½ teaspoon basil
½ teaspoon oregano
½ teaspoon pepper
2 teaspoons Italian seasoning
1 (8 ounce) package cream
   cheese
2 large packages shredded
   Mozzarella cheese
Parmesan cheese, optional

Cook noodles in boiling water until tender, drain. Brown ground round, onions, Worcestershire sauce. Add tomato sauce, tomato paste, sour cream, spices, and cream cheese, diced. Simmer until all cream cheese is blended. Layer in a 10 x 13 inch pan; bottom to top layer, meat sauce, noodles, Mozzarella cheese. Repeat until top layer is meat sauce. Bake at 350 degrees for 35 minutes until bubbly. Top with Parmesan cheese after removing from oven, if desired.

1 cup of cottage cheese or ricotta cheese may be added if desired.

Yield: 6 to 8 servings

SHRIMP AND LINGUINE

1 pound fresh or frozen
   shrimp, peeled
1 cup sliced fresh mushrooms
¼ cup chopped green onions
1 clove garlic, minced
⅓ cup butter or margarine
3 tablespoons flour
1 teaspoon salt
¾ cup white wine
2 cups half-and-half
⅓ cup chopped parsley
4 to 6 servings hot cooked
   linguine
grated Parmesan cheese,
   optional

Sauté shrimp, mushrooms, onions, and garlic in butter for 1 to 2 minutes. Blend in flour and salt and mix well. Stir in wine and gradually add half-and-half, stirring constantly to form a smooth sauce. Add chopped parsley. Simmer for three minutes. Toss with linguine and sprinkle with Parmesan cheese, if desired.

A pasta delight.

Yield: 4 to 6 servings

SHRIMP WITH FETA OVER PASTA

1 (9 ounce) package fresh
    angel hair pasta
2 eggs
1 cup plain yogurt
1 cup half-and-half
¾ cup grated Swiss cheese,
    divided
½ cup crumbled feta cheese

⅓ cup chopped fresh parsley
1 teaspoon basil
1 teaspoon oregano
1 (16 ounce) jar thick and
    chunky salsa (mild or hot)
1 pound shrimp, uncooked
    and peeled

Preheat oven to 350 degrees. Boil pasta in salt water for 2 minutes and drain. Combine eggs, yogurt, half-and-half, ½ cup Swiss cheese, feta, parsley, basil and oregano into a mixing bowl. Place half of pasta in bottom of a buttered 8 x 12 inch baking dish. Top with half of egg mixture. Cover salsa and half of shrimp. Top with remaining pasta and egg mixture. Cover with remaining shrimp and sprinkle with remaining ¼ cup Swiss cheese. Bake for 30 minutes. Let stand 10 minutes before serving.

Yield: 6 servings

SOUTHERN MACARONI AND CHEESE

1 cup macaroni noodles
8 to 12 ounces sharp cheese
1 egg

2 cups milk
2 tablespoons butter
salt and pepper to taste

Boil noodles for 10 minutes and shred Cheddar cheese. Mix together milk, salt and pepper. Layer in glass baking dish, noodles, cheese, butter and pour liquid mixture over all. Bake at 350 degrees for 1 hour or until brown and thickened.

Use a big spoon and enjoy.

Yield: 6 to 8 servings

LITE PRAWNS AND PASTA

2 tablespoons low sodium
   and lite soy sauce
1 cup water
¾ pound medium size shrimp,
   peeled and deveined
¼ cup unsalted butter or
   margarine
½ cup thinly sliced green
   onions and tops
3 large garlic cloves, minced
1½ teaspoons cornstarch

4 teaspoons lemon juice
¼ cup finely chopped fresh
   basil leaves, packed
2 tablespoons fresh parsley,
   minced
½ teaspoon crushed red
   pepper
½ pound of vermicelli,
   spaghetti or linguine,
   cooked and drained

Combine soy sauce and 1 cup water in small saucepan; bring to boil. Add shrimp and cook 2 minutes or until shrimp are pink. Reserve liquid. Remove shrimp and keep warm. Heat butter in large skillet over medium heat. Add green onions and garlic, sauté 2 minutes. Combine cornstarch and lemon juice into skillet along with the reserved shrimp liquid base. Bring to boil and simmer 1 minute. Toss sauce, shrimp, parsley and pepper together with hot pasta. Serve immediately.

Best served with crisp garlic bread and fresh tossed green salad.

Yield: 4 servings

MACARONI AND CHEESE SUPREME

1 cup elbow macaroni,
   uncooked
1 pound lean ground beef
½ cup chopped onion
½ cup sliced celery

1 (15 ounce) can Hunt's
   tomato sauce with tomato
   bits
½ teaspoon salt
¼ teaspoon pepper
1 cup shredded Cheddar
   cheese

Cook macaroni according to package directions. Drain. Brown beef, onion, and celery in a skillet. Pour off excess fat and add tomato sauce, salt, and pepper. Combine meat and macaroni mixture and pour into a 2 quart casserole dish. Top with shredded cheese. Bake at 350 degrees for 25 minutes.

Yield: 6 servings

CHARLESTON MACARONI PIE

4 cups water
1 teaspoon salt
1 cup elbow macaroni
¼ cup margarine
2 eggs
1 teaspoon dry mustard

1¼ cups milk
1 (8 ounce) package of
  medium sharp Cheddar
  cheese, cubed
½ teaspoon pepper

Bring water and salt to boil, add macaroni and cook according to package, stirring occasionally. Drain. Add margarine to hot macaroni. In small bowl, beat eggs, dry mustard and milk with whisk and add to macaroni. Stir and add cheese which has been cut into small cubes. Pour into buttered 2 quart casserole dish. Sprinkle pepper on top. Bake uncovered at 350 degrees for 30 to 35 minutes or until lightly browned around edges but still soft in center.

We all grew up with this.

Yield: 6 servings

PRIMAVERA PASTA

1 (16 ounce) package
  vermicelli
1 cup broccoli florets
1½ cups thin carrot strips
1½ cups red pepper slices
1½ cups green pepper slices
¼ cup olive oil
2 cups shredded zucchini

2 garlic cloves, minced
2 teaspoons basil
1 teaspoon oregano
½ teaspoon salt
¼ teaspoon pepper
¼ cup butter
½ cup Parmesan cheese

Cook pasta as directed, drain and set aside. Boil or steam broccoli and carrots until crisp tender (do not over cook). Sauté pepper strips in oil until tender. Add zucchini and garlic; sauté 1 minute. Add carrots, broccoli, pasta and seasonings. Add butter and toss to coat. Sprinkle with cheese.

Makes a great meatless meal.

Yield: 8 servings

MANICOTTI WITH SPINACH

1 (16 ounce) cottage cheese
½ cup Parmesan cheese
½ pound Mozzarella cheese, grated
2 eggs
1 (10 ounce) box frozen spinach, thawed

salt and pepper to taste
1 teaspoon garlic
1 box manicotti shells
1 (32 ounce) jar spaghetti sauce
¼ cup Parmesan cheese

Mix cheeses and egg with spinach, salt, pepper, and garlic until well blended. Cook manicotti shells and fill with mixture. Place on bottom of 9 x 13 inch glass dish and cover with spaghetti sauce and Parmesan cheese. Bake at 350 degrees for 25 to 30 minutes.

Easy and delicious.

Yield: 4 to 6 servings

HOMEMADE RAVIOLI

2 pounds ground beef
1 small onion, finely chopped
1 (32 ounce) jar spaghetti sauce

2 cans biscuits, (10 count)
10 slices of American cheese

Brown ground beef and onions. Drain fat. Return to pan and pour ¾ jar spaghetti sauce in and simmer. Flatten biscuits into 4 inch circles. Spoon 1 tablespoon mixture onto each of the 10 biscuits. Take remaining biscuits and place on top of mixture and seal edges with fork. Pour remaining mixture into a slightly greased 13 x 9 inch baking dish. Place 10 biscuits on mixture. Bake as to biscuit directions until golden brown. Take out and place 1 slice of cheese on each biscuit. Pour remaining spaghetti sauce over top. Return to oven. Bake until cheese melts and sauce is bubbly. Cool and serve.

Yield: 4 to 6 servings

MOSTACCIOLI ALFREDO

1 (16 ounce) package
  mostaccioli
1 cup whipping cream
½ cup butter or margarine
½ cup grated Parmesan
  cheese

½ cup chopped fresh parsley
1 teaspoon salt
¼ teaspoon freshly ground
  pepper
⅛ teaspoon garlic powder

Cook mostaccioli according to package directions; drain. Combine whipping cream and butter in a Dutch oven; heat until butter melts, stirring occasionally (do not boil). Add cheese and remaining ingredients; stir well. Add mostaccioli, and toss well. Serve immediately.

Yield: 8 servings

CHICKEN TETTRAZINI

1 chicken or 5 to 6 chicken
  breasts
1 small onion, diced
1 (4 ounce) jar mushrooms
½ bell pepper, diced
2 tablespoons margarine
1 pound mild Cheddar cheese,
  shredded

2 to 3 tablespoons cornstarch
2 cups milk
1 (8 ounce) box very thin
  spaghetti
seasoning to taste (salt,
  pepper, garlic, Italian
  seasoning)

Boil chicken until done. Remove bones and cut into bite size pieces. Cook thin spaghetti according to package directions. Sauté onions, bell peppers and mushrooms in 2 tablespoons margarine, set aside. In 9 x 13 inch baking dish, layer thin spaghetti and chicken. To make cheese sauce, combine 2 cups milk, 2 to 3 tablespoons cornstarch and 1 cup of shredded cheese. Cook, stirring frequently, over medium heat. Add sautéed onions, bell pepper, mushrooms and seasoning. Cook until sauce reaches smooth, thick consistency. Pour sauce over chicken and thin spaghetti, sprinkle remaining shredded cheese over top. Bake at 350 degrees for 30 to 35 minutes or until cheese is melted.

Yield: 6 servings

THREE PEPPER LINGUINE

1 large red bell pepper,
 coarsely chopped
1 large green bell pepper,
 coarsely chopped
1 large yellow bell pepper,
 coarsely chopped
½ onion, chopped
2 cloves garlic, minced

1 cup canned plum-style
 tomatoes, drained and
 chopped
2 tablespoons olive oil
1 (9 ounce) package spinach
 linguine or angel hair
 pasta
½ cup grated Parmesan
 cheese

Sauté peppers, onion and garlic in olive oil in large skillet until soft, about 6 minutes. Add tomatoes and simmer 7 minutes. Cook linguine and drain. Toss in Parmesan cheese and divide evenly among 4 plates. Spoon bell pepper sauce over pasta and sprinkle additional Parmesan cheese if desired.

A complete meal.

Yield: 4 servings

SPINACH LASAGNA

2 cups chopped spinach,
 thawed and drained
12 lasagna noodles
1 (1 pound) jar thick spaghetti
 sauce

1 pint cottage cheese
2 cups Mozzarella cheese,
 grated
1 cup Cheddar cheese, grated
½ cup Parmesan cheese

Cook lasagna noodles in salted water until tender and drain. In a well greased pan, layer noodles, sauce, spinach, cottage cheese, Mozzarella, Cheddar and Parmesan. Bake at 350 degrees for 30 to 40 minutes, until hot and bubbly. Wait 10 minutes before cutting in squares.

Yield: 6 servings

FETTUCCINE WITH PESTO CHICKEN

4 chicken breast halves,
skinned and boned
1 medium red bell pepper,
thinly sliced
2 cups torn fresh spinach
leaves
1 cup fresh basil leaves
¾ cup chicken broth
3 tablespoons pine nuts

3 tablespoons grated
Parmesan cheese
1 large clove garlic, minced
1 tablespoon olive oil
1 teaspoon grated lemon peel
pepper to taste
1 (8 ounce) package
fettuccine

Cut chicken in ¼ inch strips and sauté in non-stick pan for 5 to 6 minutes or until done. Remove to a plate and set aside. Add red pepper strips to skillet and sauté until tender. Meanwhile, combine spinach, basil, chicken broth, pine nuts, cheese, garlic and oil in food processor and process until smooth. Stir in lemon peel and pepper. Add this mixture to chicken and pepper in skillet and cook, stirring, over medium heat for 2 minutes. Add cooked fettuccine and toss well. Serve immediately.

Yield: 4 servings

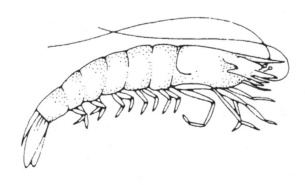

SPAGHETTI MEAT SAUCE

Meat balls

1 pound ground beef
1 cup cracker crumbs
2 eggs
¼ cup Parmesan cheese

1 clove minced garlic
salt and pepper to taste
1 pound sweet Italian sausage

Combine all ingredients together except the Italian sausage. Form into balls. Brown meat balls to remove fat. In drippings, brown sweet Italian sausage. Set aside.

Sauce

1 (16 ounce) can cut up
    tomatoes
1 tablespoon oregano
1 tablespoon basil
1 tablespoon parsley
1 tablespoon garlic salt

2 whole bay leaves
salt and pepper to taste
2 medium size cans tomato
    paste
4 cans water
1 (16 ounce) can tomato purée

In large Dutch oven place tomatoes, spices and simmer for 30 minutes. Add tomato paste, water, purée, meat balls and sausage and simmer for 2½ hours.

Can be divided and frozen.

Yield: 6 to 8 servings

SPAGHETTI WITH TOMATOES AND GARLIC

3 large ripe tomatoes
1 (8 ounce) package of thin
    spaghetti, uncooked
4 cloves garlic, minced
5 ripe olives, sliced
1 Anaheim chili, seeded and
    chopped, or ¼ cup canned
    chopped green chiles

1 tablespoon olive oil
1½ tablespoons lime juice
1 tablespoon chopped cilantro
    or parsley
⅛ teaspoon salt
⅛ teaspoon pepper

Chop tomatoes; drain. Cook spaghetti according to package directions, using 1 teaspoon salt; drain. Combine garlic and remaining ingredients; add tomatoes. Toss with hot spaghetti, and serve immediately.

Yield: 4 servings

SPAGHETTI PIZZA

1 (8 ounce) box of spaghetti
1 cup milk
2 eggs
2 (15 ounce) jars of pizza or
 spaghetti sauce

2 cups Mozzarella cheese
1 pound ground beef,
 browned and drained
Parmesan cheese
seasoning to taste

Cook spaghetti and drain. Mix with milk and eggs. Pour into a greased 9 x 13 inch dish. Pour pizza/spaghetti sauce over spaghetti mixture. Sprinkle with Mozzarella cheese and ground beef. Top with Parmesan cheese. Bake at 350 degrees for 30 minutes.

You can use two small pans and make two. Cook one now and freeze one for later.

Yield: 10 to 12 servings

STACY'S SPAGHETTI CASSEROLE

1 box shell noodles
¾ pound ground beef
1 jar of Hunt's special sauce
1 small can of tomato paste
1 can of stewed tomatoes
1 (8 ounce) package grated
 Cheddar cheese

⅓ cup Parmesan cheese
¼ teaspoon garlic powder
½ teaspoon oregano
1 (8 ounce) package
 Mozzarella cheese
Pepperoni, if desired

Preheat oven to 350 degrees. Boil noodles and set aside. Brown ground beef and drain. In a 9 x 13 inch baking dish combine special sauce, tomato paste, and stewed tomatoes. Add Cheddar cheese, Parmesan cheese, noodles, ground beef, garlic powder, oregano, and ½ of Mozzarella cheese and pepperoni (optional). Top with ½ of Mozzarella cheese and bake for 30 minutes.

Instead of ground beef use turkey, and use no salt, low fat, and low cholesterol products.

Tastes great and dinner within an hour.

Yield: 6 servings

SPAGHETTI AND CRAB SAUCE

¼ cup peanut oil
1 teaspoon chopped celery
1 teaspoon chopped parsley
1 teaspoon chopped garlic
1 cup canned tomatoes
¼ teaspoon paprika
1 (8 ounce) can tomato paste

1 pound crab meat
¼ cup sherry
1 pound spaghetti
1 onion, chopped
1½ cups water
2 teaspoons salt
grated Parmesan cheese

Using oil, sauté celery, onion, and garlic until brown. Add tomatoes, tomato sauce, water and seasonings. Allow to simmer uncovered for 1 hour. Add crab meat and sherry and simmer 10 minutes. Cook spaghetti in salted water until tender, drain. Spoon sauce over spaghetti, sprinkle Parmesan over top.

Yield: 6 servings

TORTELLINI CABONARA

1 (9 ounce) package cheese
  filled tortellini
1 small clove garlic, minced
1½ teaspoons olive oil
½ teaspoon white vinegar
3 slices bacon, cooked and
  crumbled

⅓ cup grated Parmesan
  cheese
¼ cup whipping cream
1 tablespoon minced fresh
  parsley
¼ teaspoon pepper

Cook tortellini according to package directions; drain. Sauté garlic in olive oil; stir in vinegar. Toss mixture with tortellini. Combine bacon and remaining ingredients; toss with tortellini. Serve immediately.

Yield: 3 to 4 servings

Cookies & CANDY

PECAN CRISPIES

½ cup shortening
½ cup butter or margarine
2½ cups brown sugar
2 eggs, beaten

2½ cups all-purpose flour, sifted
½ teaspoon baking soda
¼ teaspoon salt
1 cup chopped pecans

Thoroughly cream shortening, margarine, sugar and eggs. Sift dry ingredients and add to creamed mixture. Add nuts and drop from teaspoon about 2 inches apart onto greased cookie sheet. Bake at 350 degrees for 12 to 15 minutes. Place on wire rack to cool.

Yield: 5 dozen

PEANUT BUTTER OATMEAL COOKIES

¾ cup Butter Crisco or margarine
1½ cups creamy peanut butter
1½ cups firmly packed brown sugar
½ cup honey
¼ cup water

1 egg
1 teaspoon vanilla
3 cups uncooked oatmeal
1½ cups all-purpose flour
½ teaspoon baking soda
granulated sugar

Mix first 4 ingredients until creamy. Beat in water, egg and vanilla. Mix dry ingredients and add to first mixture. Cover and chill for 2 to 3 hours. Heat oven to 350 degrees; shape mixture into 1 inch balls, place on ungreased cookie sheet. Flatten with a fork dipped in sugar. Bake 9 to 11 minutes or till golden brown. Cool on cookie sheet 1 minute. Remove to wire rack or towel. Let sit 2 to 3 hours.

Yield: 6 to 7 dozen

PEANUT BUTTER SURPRISE

1 roll of chocolate chip cookie dough	1 (6 ounce) package of miniature peanut butter cups
	cooking spray

Cut cookie dough in 9 equal slices 1½ inches thick. Cut each slice in fourths. Place quarters in a miniature tart pan sprayed with cooking spray. Bake at 350 degrees for 8 to 10 minutes or until light brown. Remove from oven and immediately push miniature peanut butter cup into the center of each cookie. Cookie will rise around the peanut butter cup. Remove from pan while still warm.

Gourmet with ease.

Yield: 3 dozen

EASY PEANUT BUTTER COOKIES

1 (14 ounce) can Eagle Brand sweetened condensed milk	1 egg
	1 teaspoon vanilla extract
	2 cups biscuit baking mix
¾ to 1 cup peanut butter	granulated sugar

Preheat oven to 350 degrees. In a large mixing bowl, beat sweetened condensed milk, peanut butter, egg and vanilla until smooth. Add biscuit mix and mix well. Chill at least 1 hour. Shape into 1 inch balls. Roll in sugar. Place 2 inches apart on ungreased baking sheets. Flatten with fork. Bake 6 to 8 minutes or until lightly browned.

Yield: makes about 5 dozen

SNICKER DOODLES

3¾ cups all-purpose flour
½ teaspoon baking soda
½ teaspoon cream of tartar
½ teaspoon salt
1 cup butter or margarine
2 cups sugar

2 eggs
¼ cup milk
1 teaspoon vanilla
3 tablespoons sugar
1 teaspoon cinnamon

Grease cookie sheet. Stir together flour, soda, cream of tartar, and ½ teaspoon salt. Beat butter for 30 seconds. Add sugar and beat until fluffy. Add eggs, milk and vanilla. Beat well. Add dry ingredients to mixture, beating until well combined. Form dough in 1 inch balls. Roll in mixture of 3 tablespoons sugar and 1 tablespoon cinnamon. Place on cookie sheet, flatten slightly with bottom of a glass. Bake at 375 degrees for about 8 minutes or until lightly browned.

Yield: 66 doodles

IRIS CHRISTMAS COOKIES

¼ cup margarine
¼ cup butter
½ cup brown sugar
1 cup granulated sugar
4 eggs
1 (16 ounce) package of
   raisins
¼ teaspoon vanilla

3 cups self rising flour
12 dates, chopped
1 cup nuts, chopped (pecans
   or walnuts)
1 teaspoon cinnamon
½ teaspoon of cloves
¼ cup milk

Blend all ingredients thoroughly. Drop on baking sheet. Bake at 325 degrees until lightly brown.

Yield: 2 dozen

FRENCH LACE COOKIES

½ cup corn syrup
½ cup butter
⅔ cup brown sugar, firmly
    packed

1 cup all-purpose flour
1 cup nuts, chopped

Combine corn syrup, butter and brown sugar in saucepan. Bring to boil. Remove from heat. Combine flour and nuts; blend into mixture in saucepan. Drop by rounded teaspoonfuls onto greased cookie sheet. Place 4 inches apart to allow for spreading. Bake at 325 for 8 to 10 minutes until golden brown. Cool 1 minute. Carefully remove from cookie sheet. Reheat in oven for a few minutes to soften.

Cookies may be dipped in chocolate.

Elegant.

Yield: 50 cookies

HOLIDAY BAZAAR COOKIES

½ cup butter
½ cup Crisco
1 cup granulated sugar
1 cup brown sugar, firmly
    packed
1 egg
1 cup salad oil
1 teaspoon vanilla

3½ cups plain flour, sifted
1 teaspoon baking soda
1 teaspoon salt
1 cup rolled oats
1 cup Rice Krispies
½ cup shredded coconut
½ cup nuts, chopped

Preheat oven to 350 degrees. Cream together butter, Crisco and sugars until fluffy. Add egg, salad oil and vanilla, mixing well. Add remaining ingredients. Form into balls the size of walnuts. Place on ungreased cookie sheets and flatten with a fork dipped in water. Bake for 12 to 13 minutes. Allow to cool on cookie sheets for a few minutes before removing.

Freezes well.

Kids of all ages love them.

Yield: 100 plus

CHOCOLATE FILLED COOKIE BALLS

1 cup butter
½ cup sugar
1 teaspoon vanilla
2 cups all-purpose flour,
  sifted

1 (9 ounce) package chocolate
  kisses
confectioner's sugar

Beat together butter, sugar and vanilla until light and fluffy. Add flour, mixing well. Chill dough; then shape dough, about 1 teaspoon, around each chocolate kiss. Bake on ungreased cookie sheet at 375 degrees for 12 minutes or until set, but not brown. Cool slightly, then roll each cookie in confectioner's sugar.

Yield: 3 dozen

SUGAR COOKIES

1 cup granulated sugar
½ cup margarine or
  shortening
1 egg, beaten
4 tablespoons milk

2½ cups flour
3 teaspoons baking powder
½ teaspoon baking soda
½ teaspoon salt
1 teaspoon vanilla

Cream sugar, shortening. Add egg, milk and vanilla. Stir in dry ingredients and mix well. Chill dough for 30 minutes. Roll out and cut as desired. Bake at 325 degrees for 10 to 12 minutes.

A tradition.

Yield: 20 to 25 cookies

SANDS

2 sticks of butter
⅓ cup granulated sugar
2 teaspoons water
2 teaspoons vanilla extract

2 cups all-purpose flour,
  sifted
1 cup chopped pecans
confectioner's sugar

Cream butter and sugar. Add water and vanilla, mixing well. Blend in flour and nuts. Chill 4 hours. Shape into finger shapes (oblong). Bake on ungreased cookie sheet at 325 degrees about 20 minutes. Remove from pan. Cool slightly. Roll in confectioner's sugar.

A must for every occasion.

Yield: 20 to 30 cookies

CHOCOLATE MILLIONAIRES

1 (14 ounce) package
  caramels
2 cups pecan pieces
¼ bar paraffin

3 to 4 teaspoons milk
butter
1 (12 ounce) package semi-
  sweet chocolate morsels

Melt caramels in milk over low heat; add pecans. Drop by teaspoonfuls onto buttered waxed paper. Chill. Melt paraffin and chocolate morsels in heavy saucepan over very low heat. Dip candy into chocolate mixture and return to waxed paper. Chill.

Candy with class.

Yield: 3½ dozen

DOUBLE DECKER FUDGE

2 cups peanut butter chips,
  divided
¼ cup butter, melted
½ cup cocoa
1 teaspoon vanilla
½ cup butter

4½ cups sugar
1 (7 ounce) jar marshmallow
  creme
1½ cups or 1 (12 ounce) can
  Carnation evaporated milk

Line a 13 x 9 x 2 inch pan with foil. Place 1 cup peanut butter chips in medium bowl. Set aside. In second medium bowl blend ½ cup melted butter, cocoa and vanilla until smooth. Add 1 cup peanut butter chips. In heavy saucepan, combine sugar, marshmallow creme, evaporated milk and ¼ cup butter. Cook stirring constantly over medium heat until mixture comes to a rolling boil. Boil and stir 5 minutes. Remove from heat. Immediately add half of hot mixture to bowl with chips only. Pour remainder into cocoa mixture. Stir to blend. Beat peanut butter mixture until chips are melted. Spread evenly in pan. Beat cocoa mixture until chips are melted and it thickens. Spread evenly over peanut butter mixture. Remove from pan, remove foil. Cut in squares.

Yield: 4 pounds

CHOCOLATE FUDGE

⅔ cup evaporated milk
1⅔ cups granulated sugar
½ teaspoon salt
1½ cups marshmallows

1½ cups semi-sweet
   chocolate pieces
1 teaspoon vanilla
1 cup chopped walnuts or
   pecans, optional

Combine milk, sugar and salt in a medium saucepan. Bring to a boil over low heat; boil for 5 minutes. Remove from heat and add marsh-mallows, chocolate pieces, vanilla and nuts. Stir until all is melted. Spread in 11 x 7 x 2 inch pan. Let cool and cut.

Yield: 16 servings

PECAN CLUSTERS

½ cup granulated sugar
½ cup evaporated milk
1 tablespoon corn syrup

1 cup sweet chocolate chips
1 cup nuts

In a heavy 2 quart saucepan combine sugar, milk and corn syrup. Stir over medium heat until mixture is bubbly. Cook 2 minutes longer. Remove from heat. Stir in chocolate chips until melted. Stir in nuts. Drop by teaspoonful on wax paper. Chill until set.

Use any kind of nuts.

Yield: 24 pieces

CHOCOLATE HAYSTACKS

2 cups granulated sugar
1 stick margarine
½ cup milk

½ cup cocoa
2½ cups oatmeal
1 teaspoon vanilla

Mix sugar, margarine, milk and cocoa. Boil 3 minutes, remove from heat and add oatmeal and vanilla. Drop by spoonfuls onto wax paper quickly.

May substitute oatmeal by using Rice Krispies. You may also add raisins, coconut and nuts.

Yield: 24 servings

MICROWAVE BUTTERSCOTCH CRUNCHIES

1 (12 ounce) package
  butterscotch chips
¾ cup chopped walnuts

1 (3 ounce) can chow mein
  noodles

Place chips in microwave-safe bowl. Microwave on high for 2 minutes or until melted. Stir in remaining ingredients, mixing well. Place by teaspoon on waxed paper. Let cool to harden.

Great for after school snacks.

Yield: about 36

FAVORITE PRALINES (MICROWAVE)

2 cups firmly packed light
  brown sugar
¾ cup half-and-half
3 tablespoons butter

1½ cups chopped pecans
⅛ teaspoon ground cinnamon
⅛ teaspoon salt

Combine sugar, half-and-half, and butter in a large mixing bowl. Microwave on high 9 to 12 minutes or until a small quantity dropped in cold water forms a soft ball (235 degrees). Add the chopped pecans, cinnamon, and salt. Cool until creamy smooth. Drop by teaspoonfuls onto waxed paper.

Yield: 20 to 24 pralines

PEANUT BUTTER BALLS

Balls
2 sticks butter
1½ cups graham cracker
  crumbs
½ cup pecans

1 box powdered sugar
1 tablespoon vanilla extract
1 cup peanut butter

Melt butter, add one ingredient at a time. Mix well (add peanut butter last). Roll into balls (any size). Chill one hour in refrigerator.

Chocolate Dip
1 (6 ounce) package chocolate
  bits

¼ cake paraffin wax

Melt chocolate and wax over low heat. Dip balls into chocolate.

Yield: 30 to 50 balls depending on size

TOFFEE CRACKLES

1 cup light brown sugar
1 cup margarine or butter
1 (11 ounce) package of real
    chocolate chips

saltine crackers
1 to 1½ cups chopped pecans

Preheat oven to 350 degrees. Use heavy cookie sheet with edges or jelly roll pan. Pan must be lined with aluminum foil and sprayed well with vegetable non-stick spray. Place saltines edge to edge on pan until covered. Cook sugar and butter until appears foamy. Remove from heat and pour over crackers as evenly as possible. Bake for 10 minutes. Remove and pour chocolate chips over crackers while still hot. Allow to melt for a couple of minutes, then evenly coat by spreading chocolate with spoon. Top with nuts. Cool, then place in refrigerator until hard. Crack up and enjoy.

Gift giving at its best.

PUPPY CHOW

1 cup peanut butter
1 cup chocolate chips
1 stick margarine

8 to 10 cups of toasted oats
    cereal
1½ pounds of powdered sugar

Melt peanut butter, chocolate chips and margarine slowly until well blended and smooth. Pour over 8 to 10 cups of toasted oats cereal. Put all ingredients in paper grocery bag and shake until coated. Store in air tight container at room temperature.

Yield: 10 to 12 servings

THE ULTIMATE CARAMEL APPLE

1 cup water
1 cup granulated sugar
½ cup heavy cream
6 Red Delicious or Golden
   Delicious apples
3 ounces white chocolate,
   finely chopped

3 ounces semi-sweet
   chocolate, finely chopped
¼ cup coarsely chopped
   natural pistachios
red hots or small candy

In a heavy-bottomed saucepan, combine water and sugar. Over low heat, stir mixture gently until sugar is completely dissolved. Increase heat to medium low and cook, without stirring, until mixture is a dark amber color. Remove from heat and carefully stir in heavy cream (mixture will bubble up and spatter a bit, but then subside). Set aside until barely warm and thickened. Insert popsicle sticks or small wooden dowels into bottom center of apples. Have a piece of styrofoam, about 10 inches square, to use as a stand for apples; cover the top of styrofoam with waxed paper to catch any caramel drippings. Dip top half of each apple into thickened caramel; stand caramel-topped apples in styrofoam, allowing caramel to run down sides; refrigerate to harden. Meanwhile, melt white chocolate in top of double boiler of gently simmering water; stir until smooth. Transfer melted chocolate to pastry bag fitted with small writing tip. Drizzle thin, random lines of melted chocolate over each apple. Repeat melting and drizzling with semi-sweet chocolate. Decorate each apple with pistachios and red hot candies. Serve or refrigerate to serve later.

Yield: 6 apples

BIRD NESTS

1 bag butterscotch morsels
½ cup peanut butter
1 can chow mein noodles

1 small can dry roasted
   peanuts

Melt morsels and peanut butter in saucepan. Remove from heat, add noodles and nuts. Spoon out on waxed paper. To make nests, shape with hands.

Add M & M peanuts for bird eggs.

MICROWAVE PRALINES

¾ cup buttermilk
2 cups granulated sugar
2 cups pecan halves

⅛ teaspoon salt
2 tablespoons butter
1 teaspoon baking soda

Combine buttermilk, sugar, pecan halves, salt and butter in glass dish. Microwave on high for 12 minutes, stirring at 4 minute intervals. Stir in baking soda until foamy and cook on high one minute. Beat mixture for 1 to 2 minutes until mixture begins to thicken. Working quickly, drop by rounded teaspoonfuls onto greased waxed paper. Let stand until firm.

Place in pretty tin for gift.

Yield: 5 dozen

MICROWAVE DIVINITY

2 cups granulated sugar
½ cup water
⅓ cup light corn syrup
¼ teaspoon salt

2 egg whites
1 teaspoon vanilla
½ cup chopped pecans or
　walnuts

Combine sugar, water, corn syrup and salt in a 4 cup glass measuring cup. Microwave on high, uncovered for 3 minutes. Stir and insert microwave thermometer. Microwave 6 to 8 minutes, until thermometer reaches 250 degrees. While syrup cooks, beat egg whites until stiff peaks form. Pour hot syrup in a very slow thin stream into egg whites while beating at high speed. Continue beating until candy begins to lose its gloss and holds shape. Beat in vanilla and stir in nuts. Drop by spoonfuls onto waxed paper and allow to set.

Yield: 3 dozen pieces

Special Pleasures ...DESSERTS

AMARETTO BROWNIES

Brownies

1 (23 ounce) package brownie
    mix
¼ cup vegetable oil

3 eggs
1 cup chopped walnuts
6 tablespoons amaretto

Filling

½ cup butter, softened
2 cups powdered sugar

3 tablespoons amaretto

Topping

6 ounces semi-sweet
    chocolate

4 tablespoons butter

Prepare brownie mix according to package directions using ¼ cup oil and eggs and omitting water. Stir in walnuts. Spread in 9 x 13 inch greased baking dish. Bake at 350 degrees for 25 to 30 minutes. Remove from oven and sprinkle with 6 tablespoons of amaretto. Cool completely. To prepare filling combine powdered sugar and 3 tablespoons of amaretto together, stirring well. Spread filling on brownies. Chill at least one hour. For topping, melt chocolate and butter and pour over brownies. Cut and serve.

Scrumptious.

Yield: 32 brownies

MELTAWAYS

1 stick real butter
1 (18.5 ounce) box butter
    recipe golden cake mix
3 eggs

1 (8 ounce) package cream
    cheese
1 (16 ounce) box powdered
    sugar

Melt butter and stir in cake mix. Add one egg and blend until a smooth batter forms. Put evenly into a greased 9 x 13 inch glass baking dish. In a food processor blend cream cheese, add one egg at a time and blend for 2 minutes. Add all but ¼ cup of powdered sugar to cream cheese mixture. Blend for a few more seconds. Pour cream cheese mixture over cake mixture. Bake at 350 degrees for 35 to 40 minutes. Sprinkle with remaining sugar and cut while warm.

Yield: 3½ dozen

CHOCO-MALLOW BROWNIES

Brownies

½ cup butter or margarine, softened
1 cup granulated sugar
2 eggs
¾ cup all-purpose flour
½ teaspoon baking powder

pinch of salt
1 teaspoon vanilla extract
½ cup chopped pecans
2 cups miniature marshmallows

Cream butter gradually. Add sugar, beating at medium speed with an electric mixer. Add eggs, one at a time, beating after each one. Combine flour, baking powder, salt and cocoa; stir into creamed mixture. Stir in vanilla and pecans. Spoon into a greased and floured 9 inch square pan. Bake at 350 degrees for 18 to 20 minutes. Remove from oven: sprinkle top with marshmallows. Cover with foil; let stand until marshmallows melt (or return to oven for a couple of minutes).

Chocolate Frosting

¼ cup butter or margarine, melted
2 cups powdered sugar, sifted

3 tablespoons cocoa
4 to 5 tablespoons half-and-half

Combine butter, sugar and cocoa in a mixing bowl. Gradually add half-and-half, beating at medium speed until frosting reaches spreading consistency. Spread frosting on top of warm brownies. Cool and cut into 1½ inch squares.

Yield: 3 dozen

BLONDE BROWNIES

2⅔ cups plain flour
1 teaspoon salt
2½ teaspoons baking powder
⅔ cup butter

1 (16 ounce) box light brown sugar
3 eggs
1 cup nuts
1 cup chocolate chips

Sift together flour, salt and baking powder and set aside. Melt butter and blend in brown sugar. Beat in eggs one at a time. Add flour mixture, stir well, add chips and nuts. Bake 25 to 30 minutes at 350 degrees. Store in tight container with a piece of bread.

Yield: 24 servings

YUMMY BARS

1 (18.5 ounce) package
  German chocolate cake
  mix
⅓ cup evaporated milk
¾ cup melted butter

50 caramels
⅓ cup evaporated milk
1 (6 ounce) package chocolate
  chips
1 cup nuts

Preheat oven to 350 degrees. Combine cake mix, ⅓ cup evaporated milk and butter until well blended. Pour ⅓ to ½ of mixture into a greased 9 x 13 inch pan. Bake 6 minutes. Melt caramels and ⅓ cup evaporated milk in a double boiler. Cool cake 10 minutes. Sprinkle chocolate chips and nuts over cake. Cover with caramel mixture and cover with remaining cake mixture. Bake 20 minutes or longer if necessary. Cool completely (at least 2 hours) before cutting into bite size bars.

Yields: 32 bars

CHEWIES

1 cup brown sugar
1 stick butter or margarine
2 eggs
1 cup flour

1 cup chopped nuts, pecans
  or walnuts
powdered sugar

Cream together margarine and brown sugar. Add eggs one at a time, making sure ingredients are mixed well. Mix in flour. Batter should be smooth, but stiff. Add nuts. Pour into a greased 8 inch square pan and bake at 350 degrees for 20 to 30 minutes. Remove from oven, cut into squares and dust with powdered sugar.

Do not use the toothpick to test if done. Chewies will be sticky inside and toothpick will not come out clean.

Family favorite.

Yield: 12 servings

NUT BARS

½ cup margarine, melted and cooled
½ cup and 1 teaspoon brown sugar, firmly packed
1 cup all-purpose flour
2 eggs
¼ teaspoon salt

1 cup light brown sugar
1 teaspoon vanilla
1 tablespoon all-purpose flour
1 cup finely chopped nuts
1 (3½ ounce) can coconut
confectioner's sugar

Cream margarine and brown sugar until fluffy. Blend in flour. Spread in a 13 x 9 x 3 inch pan. Bake at 350 degrees for 10 minutes. Combine eggs, salt, light brown sugar, vanilla, 1 teaspoon flour, chopped nuts and coconut. Spread on top and bake an additional 20 minutes. Cool and cut in 2 x 1 inch bars. Sift confectioner's sugar over top. Store in an airtight container.

Yield: 3½ dozen

PUMPKIN PIE SQUARES

Bottom Layer
1 (18.5 ounce) package yellow cake mix, reserve 1 cup for top layer
½ cup margarine
1 egg

Combine cake mix, margarine and egg. Pour into a 13 x 9 x 2 inch greased pan.

Filling
3 cups pumpkin pie mix
2 eggs
⅔ cup milk

Combine all ingredients until smooth and pour over bottom layer.

Topping
1 cup reserved cake mix
1 teaspoon cinnamon
¼ cup margarine, not melted

Combine all ingredients and sprinkle over filling. Bake at 350 degrees for 45 to 50 minutes.

Yield: 12 servings

HELLO DOLLIES

1 stick of margarine
1 cup graham cracker crumbs
1 cup semi-sweet chocolate chips

1 cup chopped nuts
1 cup shredded coconut
1 can condensed milk

Preheat oven to 350 degrees. Melt margarine in a 9 inch square pan. Layer next 4 ingredients in pan, in order as listed. Pour milk over top, being sure to cover evenly. Do not stir ingredients together. Bake for 30 minutes. Allow to cool thoroughly before cutting into 1 inch squares.

Always a hit.

Yield: 2 dozen squares

CREAM CHEESE SQUARES

3 (8 ounce) cans crescent rolls
2 (8 ounce) packages cream cheese

1 cup granulated sugar
1 egg, separated
1 (2 ounce) package slivered almonds

Spread 1½ cans of crescent rolls on cookie sheet. Mix together cream cheese, sugar, vanilla and egg yolk. Pour mixture over crescent rolls. Place remaining 1½ cans of crescent rolls on top over mixture. White wash top with egg white, then top with almonds. Bake at 350 degrees for 15 minutes or until golden. Let cool and cut into squares.

Yield: 16 servings

LEMON SQUARES

1 (18.5 ounce) box lemon cake mix
1 stick butter, melted
1 egg, slightly beaten

1 (8 ounce) package cream cheese
1 (16 ounce) box confectioner's sugar
2 eggs

Combine cake mix, butter, and one egg with fork and press into 9 x 13 inch greased pan. Mix together cream cheese, confectioner's sugar and 2 eggs, beating for 3 to 5 minutes. Pour over other mixture in pan. Bake at 350 degrees for 30 minutes or until brown.

Yield: 24 squares

RICH LEMON BARS

1½ cups and 3 tablespoons unsifted flour
½ cup confectioner's sugar
¾ cup cold margarine or butter
4 eggs, slightly beaten

1½ cups granulated sugar
1 teaspoon baking powder
½ cup ReaLemon lemon juice from concentrate
additional confectioner's sugar

Preheat oven to 350 degrees. In a medium bowl combine 1½ cups flour, ½ cup confectioner's sugar; cut in margarine until crumbly. Press onto bottom of lightly greased 13 x 9 inch baking pan; bake 15 minutes. In a large bowl, combine eggs, granulated sugar, baking powder, lemon juice and 3 tablespoons flour, mixing well. Pour over baked crust and bake 20 to 25 minutes or until lightly browned. Cool. Cut into bars. Sprinkle with additional confectioner's sugar. Store, covered in refrigerator.

Yield: 24 to 36 bars

PEANUT BUTTER "N" JELLY BARS

3 cups all-purpose flour
1 cup granulated sugar
1½ teaspoons baking powder
½ cup margarine, softened

½ cup peanut butter
2 eggs, slightly beaten
1 cup grape jelly

Combine flour, sugar and baking powder. Cut in margarine and peanut butter until mixture resembles coarse meal. Stir in eggs, mixing well. Press half of mixture into a greased 13 x 9 x 2 inch baking pan. Spread grape jelly over peanut butter mixture. Crumble remaining dough over jelly. Bake at 375 degrees for 30 to 35 minutes. Cool and cut into bars.

Add a glass of milk and you're set.

Yield: 2 dozen

GRANDMOMMIE'S POUND CAKE

2 sticks of butter
½ cup shortening
3 cups granulated sugar
5 eggs
1½ cups self-rising flour

1½ cups all-purpose flour, sift
both flours together
1 teaspoon vanilla
1 cup milk

Cream butter, shortening, and sugar for 5 minutes. Add eggs one at a time, beat well after each one. Add 1 cup of flour, ½ cup milk, mixing well. Repeat 1 cup flour, ½ cup milk, mixing well. Combine remaining flour, beat for 3 minutes. In a greased tube pan bake at 325 degrees for 90 minutes. Check to see if cake is done with toothpick or knife.

For chocolate cake add 4 tablespoons of cocoa to flour.

Yield: 12 servings

CAROLINA MUD CAKE

Cake
2 cups sugar
1 cup shortening
4 eggs
1½ cups plain flour
⅓ cup cocoa

1¼ teaspoons salt
3 teaspoons vanilla extract
1 cup chopped pecans
1 package miniature
marshmallows

Frosting for cake
1½ sticks melted margarine
⅓ cup cocoa
1 (16 ounce) box sifted
confectioner's sugar

½ cup evaporated milk
1 teaspoon vanilla extract
1 cup chopped pecans

Cream sugar and shortening, add eggs and beat. Sift flour, cocoa and salt and add to mixture. Add vanilla and 1 cup chopped nuts. Mix well with electric mixer or by hand. Pour mixture into a 9 x 13 x 2 inch greased pan. Bake at 300 degrees for 30 minutes. Remove from oven and spread marshmallows over the top. Return to oven until marshmallows melt (about three minutes). Cool cake for 20 minutes before frosting. Prepare frosting by sifting sugar and cocoa together. Using electric mixer, mix well with melted margarine, add vanilla, milk and chopped nuts.

Great for covered dish dinners.

MR. BULLWINKEL'S WHIPPED CREAM CAKE

2 cups and 2 tablespoons
    granulated sugar
2 whole eggs
4 egg yolks
½ cup skim milk
dash vanilla

¾ teaspoon baking powder
3 cups cake flour
¾ teaspoon salt
1½ quarts whipping cream
¾ cup powdered sugar, sifted
raspberry jelly

With an electric mixer combine granulated sugar, eggs, yolk, milk and vanilla in mixing bowl. Beat at second speed for 45 minutes. (No mistake). Sift together flour, baking powder and salt. Add flour mixture to sugar mixture by hand and mix well. Pour in three 12 inch cake pans. Bake at 390 degrees for about 12 minutes. Cool. Whip cream with mixer until stiff peaks form. Add powdered sugar and vanilla. Spread raspberry jelly on the bottom and middle layer. Spread the whipped topping on the top of the three layers. Stack layers and garnish with a few cherries on top.

Nothing but the freshest ingredients will do.

Mr. George Bullwinkel is 81 years young. He still prepares thousands of his families Whipped Cream Cakes at Piggly Wiggly #1 in Charleston. The prized "Bullwinkels Whipped Cream Cake" has become a holiday tradition for family gatherings. Other Bullwinkle specialties are included in "Cooking for Crowds" section.

Yield: 12 to 16 servings

ICE BOX FRUIT CAKE

1½ pounds marshmallows
1 (16 ounce) box graham
    crackers, crushed
1 can Eagle Brand milk
1 pound pecans, crushed
1 pounds walnuts, crushed

1 pound fruitcake mix
1 small jar maraschino
    cherries
1 cup coconut
1 teaspoon vanilla

Over medium heat melt marshmallows. Mix in remaining ingredients. Pack into a loaf pan and place in freezer for 14 days, thaw, slice and serve.

A delicious no-bake fruitcake.

Yield: 25 servings

RED VELVET CAKE

Cake

½ cup margarine
1½ cups granulated sugar
2 eggs
2½ cups plain flour
1 teaspoon baking soda
1 teaspoon salt

1 teaspoon vinegar
2 tablespoons cocoa
1 cup buttermilk
2 ounces red flood coloring
1 tablespoon vanilla

With electric mixer cream sugar and margarine together and add eggs. In another bowl sift flour, soda, and salt together. Add vinegar and food coloring to sugar and egg mixture mixing well. Add flour mixture and cocoa alternating with buttermilk. Mix in vanilla and beat well. In 3 greased and floured cake pans bake at 350 degrees for 30 minutes.

Frosting

½ cup margarine
1 (8 ounce) package cream
    cheese, softened and
    creamed together

1 (16 ounce) package
    powdered sugar, sifted
1 teaspoon vanilla
1 cup chopped pecans

Mix all ingredients together and frost cake.

Yield: 12 servings

PLUM CAKE

2 cups granulated sugar
1 cup vegetable oil
4 eggs
2 small jars baby food plums

2 cups self-rising flour
1 teaspoon ground cloves
1 cup nuts

Cream sugar and oil. Add eggs, blending well. Add plums, flour, cloves and nuts. Pour in greased and floured tube pan and bake at 350 degrees for 1 hour.

Yield: 16 to 20 servings

PIG-PICKIN CAKE

Cake

1 (18.5 ounce) package yellow cake mix
4 eggs
½ cup oil
1 (11 ounce) can mandarin orange slices, undrained

Mix together the cake mix, eggs, oil and oranges. Pour into 3 greased and floured 9 inch cake pans and bake at 350 degrees for 25 to 30 minutes. Turn layers out to cool.

Frosting

1 (3 ounce) package instant vanilla pudding
1 (15.25 ounce) can crushed pineapple
1 (9 ounce) container non-dairy whipped topping
almonds, if desired

Combine all ingredients and frost cake. May be garnished with almonds.

Light and delicious.

Yield: 16 servings

ITALIAN CREAM CAKE

Cake

1 stick margarine
½ cup shortening
2 cups granulated sugar
5 egg yolks
2 cups cake flour
1 teaspoon baking soda
1 cup buttermilk
1 teaspoon vanilla
1 small can coconut
1 cup chopped nuts
5 egg whites, beaten stiff

Cream butter and sugar. Add shortening and egg yolks, beating well. Combine flour and baking soda, add buttermilk. Stir in vanilla, coconut and nuts. Fold in stiffly beaten egg whites. Pour into 2 or 3 round pans. Bake at 350 degrees for 25 to 30 minutes or until done.

Icing

1 (8 ounce) package cream cheese
½ stick margarine
1 (16 ounce) box powdered sugar
1 teaspoon vanilla

Cream all ingredients together and frost cake.

Yield: 10 to 12 servings

TURTLE CAKE

Cake
1 (18.5 ounce) package
  German chocolate cake
  mix
1 (14 ounce) package
  caramels
¼ cup margarine

½ cup evaporated milk
1 cup chocolate chips
1 cup chopped nuts
1 can Angel Flake coconut,
  optional

Prepare cake mix according to package directions. Pour ½ of batter in a greased 9 x 13 inch baking pan and bake for 15 minutes at 350 degrees. Melt caramels over low heat and add margarine and milk. Spread over cake. Sprinkle chocolate chips, chopped nuts, and coconut over cake and caramel topping. Pour rest of cake batter over cake and bake an additional 30 minutes at 350 degrees.

Icing
1 stick margarine
⅓ cup milk
3½ tablespoons cocoa
dash of salt

1 (16 ounce) box
  confectioner's sugar
1 cup chopped nuts

Bring margarine, milk, cocoa, and salt to a boil over medium heat. Add confectioner's sugar and nuts. Pour over cake while both are hot.

Yield: 12 servings

PUNCH BOWL CAKE

1 (18.5 ounce) box yellow
  cake mix
1 (6 ounce) box vanilla
  pudding mix
1 (15 ounce) can crushed
  pineapple

1 (16 ounce) can cherry pie
  filling
1 (16 ounce) container
  whipped topping
1 cup crushed nuts

Bake cake as directed. Crumble half the cake into the bottom of a punch bowl. Spread ½ of pineapple on top of cake. Spread ½ pie filling, then ½ whipped topping and ½ chopped nuts. Repeat above instructions for second layer. Chill and serve.

Yield: 20 to 25 servings

PORK AND BEAN CAKE

Cake

2 cups granulated sugar
2 teaspoons baking soda
1 teaspoon baking powder
2 cups plain flour
2 teaspoons cinnamon
½ teaspoon salt

4 eggs
1 cup vegetable oil
1 (16 ounce) can pork and
   beans, drained
1 (8 ounce) can crushed
   pineapple, drained

Mix all dry ingredients together. Add eggs and oil to mixture. Mash beans and mix with pineapple. Add this to above ingredients. Pour into a bundt pan and bake at 350 degrees for 40 to 45 minutes.

Icing

1 (8 ounce) package cream
   cheese
2 teaspoons vanilla

¼ cup soft margarine
1 (16 ounce) box 10X sugar
chopped pecans, optional

Cream together all ingredients. Frost cake and sprinkle with chopped pecans if desired.

Surprisingly good.

Yield: 12 servings

JELLO CAKE

1 (18.5 ounce) box white cake
   mix
1 (3 ounce) package
   strawberry gelatin

1 cup boiling water
½ cup cold water
1 (8 ounce) container whipped
   topping, thawed

Prepare cake according to package directions and bake in two 9 inch pans. Cool and remove from pans. Place cooled layers in clean layer pans. Prick each cake with utility fork at ½ inch intervals. Dissolve gelatin in boiling water. Add cold water and pour over cake layers. Chill 3 to 4 hours. Dip one cake pan in warm water for 10 seconds. Turn layer onto serving plate. Top with whipped topping. Unmold second cake layer and place on first layer. Frost top and sides with remaining whipped topping. Chill.

Garnish with strawberries, jelly drops, etc.

Yield: 10 servings

YOGURT APPLE SPICE CAKE

Spice Cake

2¾ cups unsifted all-purpose flour
2¼ cups granulated sugar
2½ teaspoons baking soda
1¼ teaspoons baking powder
1 teaspoon cinnamon
½ teaspoon allspice
1 teaspoon salt
¼ teaspoon cloves
1¾ cups applesauce
1¼ cups plain yogurt
½ cup egg substitute
⅓ cup vegetable oil
1 cup raisins

In a large bowl combine flour, sugar, baking soda, baking powder, cinnamon, allspice, salt and cloves. Add applesauce, yogurt, egg substitute and oil. Blend well using a spoon. Stir in raisins. Pour into a greased and floured bundt pan or 13 x 9 inch pan. Bake at 325 degrees for 1 hour. Cool 15 minutes and invert onto a plate. Cover with foil. Cool completely. Serve with Yogurt Glaze.

Yogurt Glaze

1½ cups plain yogurt
3 tablespoons light brown sugar
1 teaspoon vanilla extract

In a small bowl combine flour, yogurt, brown sugar and vanilla extract. Beat with a fork or whisk until smooth.

Delightful anytime.

Yield: 24 servings

CHOCOLATE, CHOCOLATE CHIP CAKE

1 (18.5 ounce) package devils food cake mix
1 (3 ounce) package instant chocolate pudding mix
4 eggs
2 to 3 tablespoons cocoa
½ cup vegetable oil
½ cup water
1 teaspoon vanilla
1 cup and 2 tablespoons sour cream
1 (12 ounce) package chocolate morsels

Combine all ingredients except chocolate chips. Beat 5 minutes and add chips, mixing well. In a greased and floured bundt pan bake at 350 degrees for an hour.

Yield: 16 servings

MUD IN SNOW TIRE CAKE

1 (18.5 ounce) box German chocolate cake mix
1 can sweetened condensed milk
1 (12 ounce) jar caramel topping
1 (12 ounce) container Cool Whip
3 Heath candy bars, crushed

Prepare cake according to directions in an oblong pan. While cake is warm, punch hole in top of cake and pour heated milk over cake. Pour caramel topping over cake. Let set for 1 hour. Spread Cool Whip over cake and top with crushed Heath candy bars.

Delicious.

Yield: 16 servings

HUNDRED DOLLAR CAKE

Cake
2 cups granulated sugar
½ cup butter
4 squares chocolate
2 eggs
2 cups flour
2 teaspoons baking powder
1½ cups milk
1 cup nuts
1 teaspoon vanilla

Cream sugar and butter. Add melted chocolate and eggs. Sift dry ingredients together and add to chocolate mixture, alternating with milk. Add vanilla and nuts. Bake 375 degrees for 25 to 30 minutes.

Icing
1 cup butter
2 eggs
1 cup nuts
1 teaspoon vanilla
4 squares chocolate
2 teaspoons lemon juice
1 (16 ounce) box powdered sugar

Cream together and spread on cold cake. Refrigerate.

Yield: 12 to 14 servings

COLD OVEN POUND CAKE

1 cup butter	1 cup milk
¼ cup shortening	3 cups all-purpose flour
3 cups granulated sugar	1 teaspoon vanilla
5 large eggs	1 teaspoon lemon extract

Cream butter, shortening and sugar. Add eggs, one at a time, beating well after each one. Add milk and flour alternately to creamed mixture. Add remaining ingredients and beat 5 minutes. Pour into a greased and floured 10 inch tube pan and put in a cold oven. Bake at 325 degrees for 1½ hours.

Easy and delicious.

Yield: 10 to 12 servings

WHIP CREAM POUND CAKE

2 sticks of butter	½ pint whipping cream
3 cups granulated sugar	1 teaspoon vanilla
6 large eggs	½ teaspoon almond extract
3 cups plain flour	½ teaspoon lemon extract

Cream butter, sugar and cream together. Add eggs 1 at a time. Beating each time. Add flour alternately with cream. Add flavoring. Start in a cold oven for 1 hour and 15 minutes at 325 degrees.

Yields: 20 servings

SOUR CREAM POUND CAKE

½ pound butter	3 cups cake flour
3 cups sugar	¼ teaspoon baking soda
6 eggs	1 teaspoon vanilla flavoring
½ pint sour cream	

Cream butter, add sugar (¼ cup at a time), add eggs (1 at a time), add sour cream; sift flour and soda together and add to creamed mixture (½ cup at a time) then add vanilla. Bake at 350 degrees for 1 hour and 20 minutes.

This one never fails.

Yield: 10 to 12 servings

EGG NOG POUND CAKE

2 tablespoons butter or
   margarine, softened
½ cup sliced almonds
1 (18.5 ounce) package yellow
   cake mix
⅛ teaspoon ground nutmeg

2 eggs
1½ cups eggnog
4 tablespoons butter or
   margarine, melted
2 tablespoons rum or ¼
   teaspoon rum flavoring

Grease a 10 inch tube or bundt pan with 2 tablespoons of softened butter; press almonds on sides and bottom of pan; set aside. In a large bowl combine cake mix, nutmeg, eggs, eggnog, melted butter and rum. Using an electric mixer, beat until smooth and creamy (about 4 minutes at medium speed) or beat for about 450 strokes with a wooden spoon. Pour batter into prepared pan. Bake in a 350 degree oven for 45 to 55 minutes or until a wooden pick inserted in center comes out clean. Let cool in pan for 10 minutes; then invert cake onto a rack to cool completely.

A holiday delight.

Yield: 10 to 12 servings

PUMPKIN PIE CAKE

Crust
1 (18.5 ounce) package cake
   mix, reserve 1 cup

1 egg, beaten
½ cup butter, melted

Filling
1 (16 ounce) can pumpkin
1 cup granulated sugar
½ cup milk

2 eggs, beaten
2½ teaspoons pumpkin pie
   spice

Topping
1 cup reserved cake mix
½ cup granulated sugar

¼ cup butter, softened

Mix crust ingredients together and pat dough into a 9 x 13 inch cake pan. Mix filling ingredients and pour over dough. Blend topping ingredients until crumbly and sprinkle evenly over filling. Bake at 350 degrees for 1 hour. Let cake cool and top with whipped cream.

A must for Thanksgiving dinner.

Yield: 6 servings

1-2-3-4 CAKE

Cake

3 cups sifted cake flour
3 teaspoons baking powder
¼ teaspoon salt
1 cup butter

2 cups granulated sugar
1 teaspoon vanilla
4 eggs
1 cup milk

Sift flour, baking powder and salt together. Cream butter with sugar and vanilla until fluffy. Add eggs one at a time. Add sifted dry ingredients and milk. Alternating in small amounts, beating well after each addition. Pour into three 9 inch greased cake pans. Bake at 350 degrees for 30 minutes.

Caramel Frosting

½ cup butter
1 cup firmly packed brown
   sugar

3 to 4 tablespoons milk
3 cups sifted powdered sugar
1 teaspoon vanilla

Melt butter in a medium saucepan. Add brown sugar and cook 1 minute over low heat. Stir in remaining ingredients and beat until smooth. Add more milk if necessary for proper spreading consistency. Frosting will be thin. Frost cake.

Yield: 12 to 16 servings

ALMOST HEAVEN CAKE

1 (18.5 ounce) package yellow
   cake mix
1 (20 ounce) can crushed
   pineapple
1 (3 ounce) package instant
   vanilla pudding

2 cups cold milk
1 (8 ounce) package cream
   cheese
1 (13 ounce) container
   prepared whipped topping

Prepare cake mix according to directions. Bake in a 13 x 9 inch sheet cake pan. After baking cake, prick with fork while cake is still warm. Pour pineapple with juice over hot cake. Blend pudding with milk and beat in cream cheese (small amount at a time). Spread over pineapple. Cover with whipped topping. Garnish with chopped nuts or coconut. Refrigerate until serving time.

The longer the cake is refrigerated, the better the flavor.

Yield: 12 servings

CHOCOLATE POUND CAKE

Pound Cake

½ cup shortening
1 cup margarine, softened
3 cups sugar
5 eggs
3 cups plain flour

½ teaspoon baking powder
½ cup cocoa
1¼ cups milk
1 teaspoon vanilla

Cream together margarine and shortening. Gradually add sugar to shortening, beat until fluffy. Add eggs, one at a time, beat well after each egg. Combine flour, baking powder, salt and cocoa, mix well. Add to creamed mixture alternately with milk, beginning and ending with the flour. Add vanilla. Pour into greased and floured pan and bake at 350 degrees for 1 hour and 15 minutes. Cool in pan for 15 minutes. Let cake cool before adding glaze.

Creamy Chocolate Glaze

2¼ cups confectioner's sugar
3 tablespoons cocoa

2 tablespoons margarine,
   softened
3 to 4 tablespoons milk

Combine sugar and cocoa mixing well. Add remaining ingredients, beat until smooth. Spread on cooled cake.

A chocolate lover's dream.

Yield: 12 servings

APPLE CAKE

1¼ cups vegetable oil
2 cups granulated sugar
3 eggs, beaten well
3 cups flour
1 teaspoon baking powder

½ teaspoon salt
3 teaspoons vanilla
3 cups coarsely chopped
   apples
1 cup chopped nuts

Beat oil, sugar and eggs well. Add flour, baking powder, salt and vanilla. Fold in apples and walnuts. Bake in greased and floured 9 x 13 inch pan at 325 degrees for 40 to 60 minutes until done.

Yield: 10 to 12 servings

CHRISTMAS WHISKEY CAKE

Cake

1 (18.5 ounce) box yellow
  cake mix
1 (3 ounce) package instant
  lemon pudding
4 whole eggs
1 cup water
1 shot whiskey
½ cup vegetable oil
¼ cup chopped walnuts

Combine all ingredients except nuts and blend well. Add nuts and blend well. Pour into a greased and floured bundt pan. Bake at 350 degrees for 45 minutes or until toothpick inserted comes out clean. Let cool 10 minutes and remove from pan. Let completely cool on dish to be served from.

Topping

½ cup water
¾ cup whiskey
1 cup granulated sugar

While cake is cooling, combine water and sugar and bring to a boil. When all sugar is dissolved, let completely cool. Add whiskey. When cake is completely cooled, spoon topping over cake by tablespoonful (gradually). Be sure previous spoonfuls are completely absorbed before adding more. (It will take approximately 4 hours to finish). Store covered for approximately 2 weeks before serving.

Yield: 12 servings

CHRISTMAS NUT CAKE

2 cups sifted granulated sugar
½ cup butter
6 eggs
1 cup of whiskey
4 cups sifted all-purpose flour
2 teaspoons baking powder
pinch of salt
1 teaspoon nutmeg
4 cups chopped nuts
1 pound candied cherries
1 pound candied pineapple

Cream sugar and butter. Add eggs one at a time. Combine whiskey with mixture. Sift flour, baking powder, and salt together. Add nutmeg to dry ingredients. Combine dry mixture, nuts and fruit well. Blend together dry mixture and sugar mixture. Bake at 300 degrees for 1 hour and 20 minutes.

A Christmas must.

Yield: 10 servings

ICE BOX COCONUT CAKE

1 (18.5 ounce) box yellow
  cake mix
2 cups milk
1 cup of sugar

1 teaspoon coconut flavoring
1 (16 ounce) container frozen
  whipped topping
1 large bag frozen coconut

Bake cake according to cake mix package. Bake in a 13 x 9 x 2 inch pan. While cake is baking bring to a boil milk, sugar, coconut flavoring and pour over hot baked cake. Cool completely. Spread thawed whipped topping over cake and cover with coconut. Let stand in refrigerator overnight.

Yield: 10 servings

MAMA'S BLACK WALNUT CAKE

Cake
1 stick butter
½ cup vegetable shortening
2 cups sugar
5 egg yolks
5 egg whites, beaten
1 cup nuts
2 cups cake flour or plain
  flour

1 teaspoon baking soda
½ teaspoon vanilla extract
1 cup buttermilk
1 cup coconut
1 teaspoon black walnut
  extract

Mix all ingredients, folding in beaten egg whites last. Spread batter in 4 greased and floured layer cake pans. Bake at 350 degrees for 25 minutes. Allow to cool.

Icing
1 (8 ounce) package cream
  cheese
1 stick butter
1 (16 ounce) box powdered
  sugar

½ teaspoon vanilla
½ teaspoon black walnut
  extract

Soften cream cheese and butter, adding other ingredients. Mix well. Spread on cooled layers.

Yield: 16 to 20 servings

RUM CAKE

Cake

1 cup chopped walnuts
1 (18.5 ounce) box yellow
   cake mix
1 (3 ounce) package instant
   vanilla pudding

4 eggs
½ cup cold water
½ cup vegetable oil
½ cup rum (dark 80 proof)

Preheat oven at 325 degrees. Grease and flour bundt pan. Sprinkle nuts over bottom of pan. In mixing bowl combine remaining ingredients, mixing well. Pour batter over nuts and bake for 1 hour. Cool and invert on serving plate.

Glaze

¼ pound butter
¼ cup water

1 cup granulated sugar
½ cup rum

Melt butter in saucepan, stir in water and sugar. Boil 5 minutes, stirring constantly. Remove from heat and stir in rum.

Prick top of cake. Spoon glaze evenly over top and sides. Allow cake to absorb glaze and repeat until all is gone.

If using yellow cake mix with pudding already in mix, omit instant pudding, use 3 eggs instead of 4 and ⅓ cup oil instead of ½ cup.

Yield: 15 servings

CHEWY CAKE

1½ cups self-rising flour,
   sifted
1 stick margarine, melted
3 eggs

1 teaspoon vanilla
1 (16 ounce) box light brown
   sugar
1 cup nuts, chopped

Mix all ingredients until well blended. Pour into a greased 9 x 13 inch pan. Bake at 325 degrees for 35 minutes. Cut into squares while warm. They won't look done, but they are. Remove from pan after cooled.

Deliciously rich and easy. Great for get-togethers.

Yield: 24 servings

CARROT CAKE

Cake

2 cups all-purpose flour
2 cups granulated sugar
1 teaspoon baking powder
1 teaspoon baking soda

1 teaspoon ground cinnamon
3 cups finely shredded carrot
1 cup cooking oil
4 eggs

In a mixing bowl combine flour, sugar, baking powder, baking soda and cinnamon. Add carrots, oil and eggs. Beat with electric mixer until combined. Pour into 2 greased and floured 9 x 1½ inch round baking pans. Bake at 350 degrees for 30 to 35 minutes. Cool on wire racks for 10 minutes. Remove cakes from pans. Cool thoroughly on racks.

Cream Cheese Frosting

1 (16 ounce) box powdered
   sugar, sifted
½ cup butter
2 teaspoons vanilla

1 (8 ounce) package cream
   cheese
1 cup pecans, chopped

Cream together butter and cream cheese. Add sugar, vanilla and pecans. Spread on cake.

Yield: 12 to 15 servings

BLACK FOREST CAKE

1 (18.5 ounce) box chocolate
   cake mix
2 (8 ounce) packages Baker's
   semi-sweet chocolate
   squares (reserving 2
   squares for decorating top
   of cake)

1 cup butter or margarine
1 (16 ounce) package of sliced
   almonds
2 quarts strawberries, fresh or
   frozen
2 (16 ounce) containers of
   Cool Whip

Prepare cake mix according to directions. Divide cake into four even layers and bake. Cool completely. Melt butter and chocolate together and add sliced almonds, keep warm. First layer, spread chocolate and almond mixture. Let cool 2 or 3 minutes. Add a thin layer of strawberries. Add a layer of Cool Whip approximately 1 inch thick. Repeat layers, ending with Cool Whip. Decorate with chocolate curls or shavings.

Yield: 12 servings

HUMMINGBIRD CAKE

Cake

3 cups all-purpose flour
2 cups granulated sugar
1 teaspoon baking soda
1 teaspoon salt
1 teaspoon ground cinnamon
3 eggs, beaten

1 cup vegetable oil
1½ teaspoons vanilla extract
1 (8 ounce) can crushed
  pineapple, undrained
1 cup chopped pecans
2 cups chopped bananas

Combine first 5 ingredients in large mixing bowl, add eggs and oil, stirring until ingredients are moistened. Stir in vanilla, pineapple, pecans and bananas. Spoon batter into 3 greased and floured 9 inch cake pans. Bake at 350 degrees for 25 to 30 minutes. Cool in pans for 10 minutes, remove and cool completely.

Cream Cheese Frosting

1 (8 ounce) package cream
  cheese, softened
½ cup margarine, softened

1 (16 ounce) package
  powdered sugar, sifted
1 teaspoon vanilla extract
½ cup chopped pecans

Combine cream cheese and margarine until smooth. Add powdered sugar and vanilla, beat until light and fluffy. Spread frosting between layers, sides and top. Sprinkle top with chopped pecans.

Delicious.

Yield: 12 servings

LEMON CHEESECAKE

1 (9 inch) graham cracker
  crumb crust
1 (8 ounce) package cream
  cheese

2 cups milk
1 (3 ounce) package lemon
  instant pudding mix

Beat 1 package cream cheese until very soft. Blend in ½ cup milk until smooth. Add 1½ cups milk and pudding mix. Beat at lowest speed of electric mixer until blended (about 1 minute). Pour at once into 9 inch crumb crust. Chill until firm, at least 2 hours. Garnish with whipped cream, cherries or strawberries.

Yield: 6 to 8 servings

STRAWBERRY SMOOTHE CHEESE CAKE

Crust

1 cup graham cracker crumbs
3 tablespoons granulated
   sugar

3 tablespoons margarine,
   melted

Preheat oven to 325 degrees. Mix crumbs, sugar and margarine. Press mixture onto bottom of a 9 inch pie pan. Bake 10 minutes.

Filling

1 (3 ounce) package
   strawberry gelatin
½ cup cold water
1 (8 ounce) package cream
   cheese

½ cup powdered sugar
1 (10 ounce) package
   strawberries
milk
1 cup whipping cream

Soften gelatin in water, stir until dissolved over low heat. Beat cream cheese and powdered sugar at medium speed with an electric mixer, until well blended. Drain strawberries reserving liquid. Add enough milk to liquid to measure 1 cup. Gradually add mixture and gelatin to cream cheese mixture and strawberries. Pour over pie crust and refrigerate until firm. Garnish with whip cream and sliced strawberries and fresh mint if desired.

Yield: 8 to 10 servings

FLOWER POT (DIRT) CAKE

1¼ pounds Oreos
2 (3½ ounce) packages vanilla
   or chocolate instant
   pudding
3½ cups milk

1 (8 ounce) package cream
   cheese
½ stick butter
1 (12 ounce) container Cool
   Whip
1 cup powdered sugar

Other items needed: artificial flower, trowel, gummy worms, flower pot 6 inch in diameter. Crumb Oreos in food processor. Mix pudding and milk, put in refrigerator. Combine cream cheese, butter and powdered sugar. Mix pudding with Cool Whip, then cream cheese mixture. Layer Oreos, pudding, worms, Oreos, pudding and Oreos in flower pot. Arrange extra worms on top. Refrigerate until served. To serve put flower in pot.

Decorative.

Yield: 6 to 8 servings

DICK'S MOM'S CHEESE CAKE

Crust

1 package graham crackers
¼ cup granulated sugar

¼ cup melted butter

Combine all ingredients and press in an aluminum 13 x 9 x 2 inch pie pan.

Filling

1 cup granulated sugar
3 (8 ounce) packages cream
   cheese

3 eggs
½ teaspoon vanilla

Soften cream cheese and beat vigorously until real creamy, adding sugar gradually. Add eggs, one at a time and vanilla. Beat and pour into graham cracker crust. Bake at 375 degrees for 17 minutes.

Topping

1 pint sour cream
3 tablespoons granulated
   sugar

½ teaspoon vanilla

Combine all ingredients and beat well. Remove cheese cake from oven and add topping. Bake 5 minutes more. Cool and store in refrigerator.

Yield: 10 to 12 servings

CREAMY BAKED CHEESECAKE (N. Y. STYLE)

1¼ cups graham cracker
   crumbs
¼ cup granulated sugar
⅓ cup margarine or butter,
   melted
2 (8 ounce) packages cream
   cheese, softened

1 (14 ounce) can sweetened
   condensed milk
3 eggs
¼ cup lemon juice
1 (8 ounce) container sour
   cream, optional

Preheat oven to 300 degrees. Combine crumbs, sugar and margarine. Press firmly on bottom of 9 inch pie pan. In a large bowl beat cream cheese until fluffy. Gradually beat in condensed milk until smooth. Add eggs and lemon juice, mix well. Pour into prepared pan and bake for 50 to 55 minutes or until center is set. Top with sour cream. Bake 5 minutes longer. Cool and chill.

Something good from the North.

Yield: 8 servings

CHEESECAKE SUPREME

1 box graham cracker crust
5 (8 ounce) packages cream
  cheese, softened
1¾ cups granulated sugar
3 tablespoons flour
1 grated lemon rind
½ grated orange rind
½ cup heavy cream
5 whole eggs

2 egg yolks
canned apricots, pineapple,
  and maraschino cherries,
  halved
pineapple and apricot syrups
  to make ¾ cup
1 tablespoon cornstarch
2 tablespoons cold water
1 tablespoon lemon juice

Prepare crust according to directions. Butter a 10 x 2¼ inch or 9 x 3 inch springform pan. Press crumb mixture on bottom and sides of pan. Beat cream cheese until fluffy; blend in sugar mixed with flour. Add grated rinds and cream. Beat until smooth. Add eggs and yolks, one at a time, beating well after each one. Turn into crust. Bake at 500 degrees for 10 minutes. Turn oven down to 200 degrees. Do not open oven door. Bake 1 hour longer. Remove sides of pan and put on serving plate. Keep chilled. Fruit and glaze should be put on the day the cake is served. Reserve fruit syrups for glaze. Arrange 4 to 5 apricot halves around center of cake. Set quarter slices of pineapple around them; border cake with 7 to 8 maraschino cherry halves. Mound ⅓ cup cherries in very center of apricot ring. In a saucepan combine ¾ cup pineapple and apricot syrups, cornstarch, and 2 tablespoons cold water. Add 1 tablespoon lemon juice, stirring until thickened. Add a drop of yellow food coloring if desired. Spoon over fruit and chill.

Yield: 12 servings

JAPANESE FRUIT PIE

4 eggs
1 cup frozen coconut
1 cup chopped pecans
1 cup golden raisins
2 sticks butter

2 cups granulated sugar
½ teaspoon vinegar
2 teaspoons vanilla
3 small pie shells or 2 large
  pie shells, browned

Beat eggs with fork, add other ingredients. Pour into 3 small or 2 large browned pie shells. Bake at 300 degrees for 50 to 55 minutes.

A family favorite.

Yield: 8 servings

LUSCIOUS PEACH PIE

1 graham cracker pie crust
shell
1 (8 ounce) package cream
cheese, softened
1 cup powdered sugar
½ teaspoon almond extract

1½ cups whipped topping,
thawed
1 (16 ounce) can sliced
peaches, drained and
chopped

In large mixing bowl, combine cream cheese, powdered sugar and extract. Beat until smooth. Gently fold in whipped topping and peaches. Pour into graham crust. Chill until firm, about 3 hours.

Yield: 6 servings

PUMPKIN PIE

1½ cups or 1 (16 ounce) can
pumpkin
1 cup sugar
2 eggs
1 tablespoon flour
½ teaspoon salt
½ teaspoon nutmeg
½ teaspoon allspice

½ teaspoon ginger
½ teaspoon cinnamon
¼ teaspoon cloves, ground
1⅔ cups or 1 (13 ounce) can
evaporated milk
1 (10 inch) regular
or 1 (9 inch) deep dish
unbaked pie shell

Mix all ingredients, adding milk last. Pour into pie shell. Bake at 425 degrees for 10 minutes, decrease oven temperature to 350 degrees and bake for 35 minutes or until firm.

Edge of crust may need to be covered with foil until last 10 minutes of baking to prevent over-browning.

A Thanksgiving dinner must.

Yield: 6 to 8 servings

SWEET POTATO PIE

Pie

3¾ cups mashed sweet
   potatoes
1 cup granulated sugar
1 tablespoon plain flour
¼ cup margarine, melted
⅓ cup Carnation milk

½ cup milk
⅛ teaspoon lemon extract
1½ teaspoons vanilla
3 egg yolks
1 (10 inch) unbaked pie crust

Combine sweet potatoes, sugar, flour, margarine, cream, milk, lemon extract, vanilla, and egg yolks and mix well. Pour mixture into unbaked pie crust. Bake at 400 degrees for 10 minutes, reduce heat to 350 degrees and bake for 30 minutes or until set.

Meringue

3 egg whites
¼ teaspoon cream of tartar

6 tablespoons granulated
   sugar

Beat egg whites until frothy. Add cream of tartar and beat until stiff enough to hold a point. Add sugar and beat until stiff and glossy. Spread on cooked pie and brown.

Yield: 6 to 8 servings

LEMON PIE

2 (9 ounce) containers
   prepared whipped topping
2 cans sweetened condensed
   milk

2 (6 ounce) cans frozen
   lemonade
2 graham cracker crusts

Mix all ingredients together. Pour into graham cracker crusts. Freeze for several hours.

Easy and delightful.

Yield: 12 to 16 servings

LEMON MERINGUE PIE

Filling

1½ cups granulated sugar
9 tablespoons self-rising flour
1½ cups warm water
⅓ cup fresh lemon juice
3 egg yolks, well beaten

½ stick margarine
1 tablespoon grated lemon
   peel
1 (9 inch) pie shell

In a medium size saucepan mix sugar and flour until you can't see the flour. (This keeps filling from being lumpy.) Add warm water and lemon juice, mixing well. Add egg yolks and melted margarine. Cook over low heat until mixture comes to a boil and begins to thicken. Beat until smooth and continue to cook until thick. Pour into a 9 inch pie shell. Cool to room temperature.

Meringue

3 egg whites
6 tablespoons granulated
   sugar

1 teaspoon vanilla
pinch of cream of tartar

Beat egg whites until stiff, adding sugar as you beat with electric mixer. Combine vanilla and cream of tartar. Beat until it forms stiff peaks. Pour on pie and be sure to seal the edges. (This keeps meringue from shrinking.) Bake at 350 degrees for 15 minutes. Sprinkle lemon peel on meringue after you take it out of oven.

Yield: 6 servings

PEANUT BUTTER PIE

1 (8 ounce) package cream
   cheese, warm
¾ cup peanut butter
1 cup powdered sugar

½ cup milk
1 (8 ounce) container Cool
   Whip
2 graham cracker crusts

Cream together cream cheese, peanut butter and powdered sugar. Add milk and mix with mixer. Fold in Cool Whip and pour into graham cracker crusts. Decorate with a sprinkle of chocolate chips. Served chilled.

Can omit ½ cup milk for a thicker pie.

Yield: 16 servings

MILE-HIGH APPLE PIE

Pastry

2¼ cups unsifted all-purpose
   flour
½ teaspoon salt

½ cup vegetable shortening
5 tablespoons butter, chilled
4 to 5 tablespoons cold water

In a large bowl, combine flour and salt. Cut vegetable shortening and butter into flour mixture until coarsely blended. Gradually add water, stirring gently, until dough binds when pressed between fingers. Form dough into two balls, one slightly larger than the other, wrap and refrigerate for 1 hour. Roll out smaller piece of dough to an 11 inch round; transfer to 9 inch pie plate and line bottom and sides. Roll out large piece of dough to a 12 inch round and keep for top of pie.

Apple Filling

12 Granny Smith apples,
   peeled, cored and thinly
   sliced
1 cup sugar

2 teaspoons ground
   cinnamon
½ teaspoon ground nutmeg
1 teaspoon vanilla extract

In a large pot, medium-low heat, cover and cook apple slices, stirring occasionally, until barely tender, about 10 minutes. Drain apple slices completely. Transfer to large bowl and add sugar, cinnamon, nutmeg, and vanilla; stir gently to blend. Pour filling into pie shell, mounding in center. Place larger piece of dough over pie, covering filling. Trim and pinch edges of bottom and top crusts.

Butter-Pecan Crumb

1 cup unsifted all-purpose
   flour
⅓ cup sugar
¼ teaspoon salt

½ cup butter, softened
½ cup chopped pecans
confectioner's sugar

Preheat oven to 400 degrees. In a medium size bowl, combine flour, sugar, and salt. Cut butter into flour mixture until coarsely blended. Add pecans rub mixture briefly between fingers to form crumbs. Brush top of pie crust lightly with water and gently press crumb topping to crust. Make several slits in top crust of pie to vent steam. Bake 45 to 50 minutes or until crust is golden brown. Cool at least 25 minutes, sift confectioner's sugar over top and serve.

A family tradition.

Yield: 12 servings

STRAWBERRY PIE

1½ cups granulated sugar
4 tablespoons cornstarch
1 (3 ounce) package
   strawberry gelatin

2 cups strawberries
1½ cups water
Cool Whip, optional
2 baked pie shells

Combine sugar, cornstarch and gelatin. Add water and cook, stirring until it thickens and remove from heat. Prepare strawberries and add into filling. Pour filling into 2 baked pie shells and place in the refrigerator.

Can top with Cool Whip if desired.

Yield: 12 servings

FRENCH SILK PIE

3 egg whites
⅛ teaspoon salt
¼ teaspoon cream of tartar
¾ cup granulated sugar
½ cup pecans or black
   walnuts, finely chopped

½ teaspoon vanilla extract
1 (4 ounce) package sweet
   cooking chocolate
3 tablespoons water
1 tablespoon brandy (extract)
2 cups heavy cream

Preheat oven to 300 degrees. In mixing bowl blend together egg whites until foamy. Add salt and cream of tartar. Add sugar gradually and continue beating until very stiff peaks form. Fold in nuts and vanilla extract. Pile into lightly greased 8 inch pie pan forming a nest by building up a half inch rim around the edge of the pie pan. Do not extend over the rim. Bake for 50 minutes. Let cool. In a double boiler, place chocolate and water. Stir until melted. Cool. Add brandy to chocolate mixture. Whip 1 cup of heavy cream. Fold into chocolate mixture. Pile into meringue shell and chill 2 to 3 hours before serving. Whip rest of heavy cream piling high on top of pie. Garnish with bits of shaved chocolate and serve.

You can't eat just one piece.

Yield: 8 servings

SURPRISE PIE

1 (16 ounce) container Cool
    Whip
1 (16 ounce) can crushed
    pineapple, drained

½ cup nuts
1 can condensed milk
juice of one lemon
2 graham cracker crusts

Combine all ingredients and pour into 2 pie crusts. Chill and serve.

Quick and easy.

Yield: 16 servings

PECAN PIE

2 eggs, slightly beaten
½ cup dark corn syrup
½ cup granulated sugar
1 tablespoon margarine,
    melted

½ teaspoon vanilla
3 cups pecans
1 (9 inch) pie crust

Combine eggs, syrup, sugar, margarine and vanilla. Mix well. Stir in pecans. Pour into pie crust and bake at 350 degrees for 50 to 55 minutes. Cool before slicing.

A Christmas tradition.

Yield: 6 to 8 servings

NO CRUST PECAN PIE

1 stick butter, melted
1 (16 ounce) box light brown
    sugar
3 tablespoons flour

1 cup milk
1 teaspoon vanilla
2 eggs
1 cup pecans

Combine all ingredients in bowl. Mix well and add pecans. Bake at 325 degrees for 45 minutes.

Yield: 6 servings

WALNUT COOKIE PIE

½ cup butter or margarine, softened
¾ cup brown sugar, finely packed
2 eggs
1 teaspoon vanilla
½ cup all-purpose flour
1 (6 ounce) package semi-sweet chocolate pieces
1 cup walnuts, chopped
1 (9 inch) unbaked pie shell

In a large bowl, cream butter, brown sugar, eggs and vanilla until light and fluffy. Blend in flour. Stir in chocolate pieces and walnuts. Pour mixture into unbaked pie shell. Bake below oven center at 325 degrees for 50 to 55 minutes or until top is golden brown. Serve warm with vanilla ice cream or Cool Whip.

So much faster than making individual cookies.

Yield: 8 servings

NO CRUST COCONUT PIE

4 eggs, beaten
2 cups sugar
2 cups milk
½ cup plain flour
½ teaspoon baking powder
pinch salt
½ stick margarine, melted
1 teaspoon vanilla
1 can flaked or 1½ cups packaged coconut

Mix all ingredients together. Pour into 2 greased pie plates. Bake at 350 degrees for 30 to 40 minutes or until coconut is nicely browned.

Yield: 16 servings

COCONUT CUSTARD PIE

3 eggs
¾ cup sugar
½ teaspoon salt
dash nutmeg
2 cups milk
½ cup coconut
vanilla flavoring

Beat eggs slightly; add remaining ingredients and mix well. Pour into 2 unbaked pie shells. Bake at 400 degrees for 35 to 45 minutes.

Light and luscious.

Yield: 12 to 16 servings

CHOCOLATE PECAN PIE

1½ cups coarsely chopped
   pecans
1 (6 ounce) package semi-
   sweet chocolate chips
1 (8 inch) pie shell, partially
   baked

½ cup light corn syrup
½ cup granulated sugar
2 extra large eggs
¼ cup butter, melted and
   cooled
whipped cream

Sprinkle pecans and chocolate chips evenly into pie shell. Blend syrup, sugar, and eggs in medium bowl. Mix in melted butter. Pour mixture slowly and evenly into pie shell. Bake at 325 degrees for about an hour or until firm. Serve slightly warm or at room temperature. Garnish with whipped cream.

Very rich and indescribably delicious.

Yield: 8 servings

KEY LIME PIE

1 (10 inch) pie shell, baked
1 envelope unflavored gelatin
½ cup granulated sugar
¼ teaspoon salt
4 egg yolks
½ cup fresh lime juice

¼ cup water
1 teaspoon grated lime peel
green food coloring
4 egg whites
½ cup sugar
1 cup heavy cream, whipped

Combine gelatin, sugar and salt in a saucepan. Beat together yolks, lime juice and water. Stir into gelatin mixture. Cook and stir over medium heat until mixture comes to a boil. Remove from heat, stir in grated peel. Add food coloring to green tint (pale). Chill, stirring occasionally until mounds form when dropped from a spoon. Beat egg whites until soft peaks form. Add sugar, beating to stiff peaks. Fold in gelatin mix. Fold in whipped cream. Place filling into baked shell. Refrigerate until served.

Yield: 6 to 8 servings

LEMON CHESS PIE

2 cups sugar
4 eggs
½ cup butter
2 tablespoons cornstarch

juice and rind of 2 lemons,
  grated
1 unbaked pie shell

Combine ingredients and mix well. Pour into pie shell and bake in a 350 degree oven for 45 minutes or until done.

Great for any occasion.

Yield: 6 to 8 servings

PEACHES AND CREAM PIE

1 (9 inch) frozen pie crust,
  regular
1 (9 inch) frozen pie crust,
  deep
5 to 6 fresh peaches, sliced,
  or 1 (2 pound) can
  peaches, drained

1 cup granulated sugar
5 teaspoons self-rising flour
⅛ teaspoon salt
½ cup dairy sour cream
¼ teaspoon cinnamon

Thaw pie shells. Place peaches in deep pie crust. In bowl, by hand, mix flour, salt, sour cream and sugar (except 2 teaspoons).

Blend until smooth. Pour mixture over peaches. Take 2 teaspoons sugar and mix with cinnamon and set aside. Cover mixture with regular pie shell and crimp edges. Sprinkle with cinnamon and sugar mixture. Cut 4 slits in top crust. Bake at 350 degrees for 40 to 45 minutes or until crust is golden brown.

A Southern tradition.

Yield: 6 to 8 servings

SUGARED PECAN HALVES

3 tablespoons of cold water
¾ cup granulated sugar
¾ teaspoon salt

½ teaspoon cinnamon
2 egg whites, unbeaten
2 cups whole pecan halves

Preheat oven to 250 degrees. Mix all ingredients except pecans in a bowl. Pour pecans into mixture. Spread pecans on a greased cookie sheet. Bake for 1 hour. Remove to another greased cookie sheet to cool at room temperature.

This is great served with your favorite ice cream.

Great for holidays.

Yield: 2 cups

CLASSY CHEEZ-ITS

Cheez-It crackers
peanut butter

white or dark chocolate

Spread peanut butter between 2 crackers (sandwich style). Place chocolate in microwave-safe bowl, then place that bowl in a shallow microwave-safe bowl with a small amount of water in it. Heat until melted. Coat sandwich in chocolate and place on waxed paper to cool.

Will freeze.

A simple treat made special.

BREAD PUDDING

2 cups milk
4 cups bread crumbs
¼ cup melted margarine
2 eggs, beaten

½ cup granulated sugar
½ teaspoon salt
1 teaspoon cinnamon
½ cup raisins

Mix all ingredients and place in a 13 x 9 x 2 inch baking dish. Dot with butter and bake at 350 degrees for 40 to 50 minutes.

Yield: 8 servings

BANANA PUDDING

2 (3 ounce) packages instant
    vanilla pudding
4 cups of milk
1 (8 ounce) container sour
    cream

1 (8 ounce) container Whip
    Cream
8 to 10 bananas
1 box vanilla wafers

Mix pudding and 4 cups of milk. Blend in ⅔ of sour cream and ⅔ of whipped cream. Blend until no lumps remain. In a large bowl, layer half box of cookies, 4 to 5 bananas, cut up, and half pudding mixture. Layer cookies, bananas and remaining pudding mixture. If desired, use remaining whipped topping to decorate.

Family favorite.

Yield: 12 to 15 servings

CHEWY BREAD

½ cup finely chopped pecans
¼ cup butter, melted
1½ cups self-rising flour

1 teaspoon vanilla
2 cups dark brown sugar
2 eggs

Combine all ingredients together. Fold into a lightly greased 9 x 13 x 2 inch pan and bake at 350 degrees for 25 minutes. Cut while warm.

Yield: 18 to 24 squares

ALL BRAN MUFFINS

2 cups All Bran
1 egg
1 cup sour milk (1 teaspoon
    vinegar in 1 cup milk)
1 cup flour
1 cup granulated sugar

1 teaspoon soda
1½ teaspoons baking powder
dash of salt
1 cup dates or raisins
½ cup vegetable oil

Combine All Bran, egg, and sour milk and let stand a few minutes. Combine flour, sugar, soda, baking powder, salt, dates or raisins and vegetable oil and add to All Bran mixture. Bake 350 degrees for 20 minutes.

Yield: 16 muffins

PEAR BREAD

1 cup granulated sugar
¾ cup salad oil
2 eggs
1½ cups plain flour
¼ teaspoon salt

1 teaspoon cinnamon
1 teaspoon soda
1 teaspoon baking powder
1 cup grated pears
½ cup chopped nuts

Cream sugar, oil and eggs together. Add dry ingredients. Mix in pears and nuts. Pour into greased loaf pan. Bake at 375 degrees for 55 minutes.

May prepare ahead, freezes well.

Yield: 1 loaf

BANANA NUT BREAD

½ cup vegetable oil
1 cup granulated sugar
2 eggs, beaten
3 ripe bananas, mashed
2 cups all-purpose flour,
  sifted

1 teaspoon baking soda
½ teaspoon baking powder
½ teaspoon salt
3 tablespoons milk
½ teaspoon vanilla extract
½ cup chopped nuts, optional

Beat oil, and sugar together. Add eggs and bananas beating well. Sift flour, soda, baking powder and salt together. Add to oil and sugar mixture alternately with milk and vanilla, beat well. Stir in nuts. Bake in one large loaf pan or 3 small ones. Bake at 350 degrees for 45 minutes to 1 hour.

Freezes well.

Yield: 16 servings

PUMPKIN ROLL

3 eggs
1 cup granulated sugar
1 teaspoon lemon juice
⅔ cup cooked pumpkin, mashed
¾ cup flour
2 teaspoons cinnamon
½ teaspoon nutmeg
2 teaspoons baking powder
1 teaspoon ginger
½ cup pecans, chopped
¼ cup confectioner's sugar
1 (8 ounce) package cream cheese
4 tablespoons butter, melted
1 teaspoon vanilla

Beat eggs until light and lemon-colored (about 10 minutes). Slowly add sugar and lemon juice. Fold in pumpkin. Sift flour, cinnamon, nutmeg, baking powder and ginger together and fold into egg mixture. Prepare an 11 x 16 inch jelly roll pan by greasing bottom, covering bottom with waxed paper and buttering the waxed paper. Pour in mixture. Sprinkle with pecans. Bake at 350 degrees for 15 minutes. Turn out on damp dishcloth that has been sprinkled with ¼ cup confectioner's sugar. Roll up and cool. Prepare filling by beating together cream cheese, butter, vanilla and 1 cup confectioner's sugar. Unroll pumpkin roll and spread with cream cheese mixture. Reroll and wrap in aluminum foil. Refrigerate several hours. Dust with confectioner's sugar, slice to serve.

Variation, substitute cooked sweet potatoes for pumpkin.

Yield: 6 to 8 servings

PERFECT PEACH COBBLER

1 stick margarine
1 cup flour
1 cup granulated sugar
1½ teaspoons baking powder
¾ cup milk
lots of peaches

Melt margarine in baking dish. Mix flour, sugar, baking powder and milk well. Pour batter over melted butter. (Do not stir.) Pour sweetened peaches over batter. Bake at 325 degrees for 1 hour.

May use any fruit.

Every southern family must have a cobbler recipe.

Yield: 8 servings

CRANBERRY POP

1 pound fresh cranberries
1 medium jar orange
   marmalade

2 cups granulated sugar
2 cups English walnuts,
   broken

Combine all ingredients and pour in deep casserole dish. Bake at 300 degrees until berries pop (about 45 minutes). Will be thin until it cools.

Yield: 8 servings

PINEAPPLE NOODLE KUGEL

1 (8 ounce) broad noodles
1 (16 ounce) container cottage
   cheese
¼ pint sour cream
3 eggs

½ cup sugar
1 stick margarine, melted
1 (16 ounce) can crushed
   pineapple, drained, save
   juice

Cook noodles and drain. Mix cottage cheese, sour cream, beaten eggs, sugar, melted margarine and pineapple with noodles. Spread evenly in a 12½ x 9½ inch casserole dish. Pour pineapple juice over casserole and bake at 350 degrees for 1 hour.

Yield: 6 to 8 servings

CHERRY YUM-YUM

½ cup granulated sugar
1 (8 ounce) package cream
   cheese
½ teaspoon vanilla
2 packages whipped topping

1 stick margarine
2 cups graham cracker
   crumbs
1 (16 ounce) can cherry pie
   filling

Cream sugar, cream cheese and vanilla. Mix whipped topping according to instructions on package and combine with cream cheese mixture. Mix margarine with crumbs. Alternate, using crumbs as first layer, second layer of cream cheese mixture, next layer a can of cherry pie filling, then other half of cream cheese mixture. Top with graham cracker crumbs. Refrigerate.

May substitute blueberry pie filling for cherry pie filling.

Yield: 8 servings

BANANA SPLIT PIE

Crust

2 cups graham cracker
   crumbs

1 stick margarine, melted
¼ cup granulated sugar

Combine butter, sugar, and crumbs. Pour into a 13 x 9 x 2 inch oblong baking pan. Pat down firmly on bottom only. Bake at 325 degrees for 12 minutes and remove from oven.

Filling

1 (8 ounce) package cream
   cheese, softened
2 cups confectioner's sugar
4 sliced bananas
1 (20 ounce) can crushed
   pineapple, drained

1 (12 ounce) container non-
   dairy whipped topping
8 to 10 cherries
½ cup pecans, chopped
3 tablespoons chocolate
   syrup

With an electric mixer combine cream cheese and confectioner's sugar. Spread over graham crust. Slice bananas over cream cheese mixture. Spread pineapple over bananas. Spread whipped topping over pineapple and top with cherries. Sprinkle pecans and drizzle chocolate syrup in thin lines over top. Cover with plastic wrap and refrigerate 1 hour. Cut in 8 to 10 slices and serve. Store in refrigerator.

Yield: 8 to 10 servings

FUDGE SUNDAE PIE

1 pie crust shell
3 cups slightly softened
   vanilla ice cream
¾ cup chocolate fudge ice
   cream topping

1½ cups thawed whipped
   topping
7 maraschino cherries
2 tablespoons chopped
   pecans
1 banana

Prepare pie crust according to package directions for empty baked crust; cool. Spread one-half of the ice cream into baked pie crust. Cover with chocolate topping; top remaining ice cream. Freeze until firm. Remove from freezer and garnish with whipped topping, cherries, pecans and banana spears.

Allow to defrost 20 to 30 minutes before slicing.

Yield: 6 servings

CHOCOLATE DELIGHT

graham cracker crumbs
1 stick of margarine
1 (8 ounce) package cream
 cheese
½ cup confectioner's sugar
2 (8 ounce) containers of Cool
 Whip

2 (3 ounce) packages of
 instant chocolate pudding
3 cups milk
1 small package of pecan
 pieces

In a 9 x 13 inch glass dish spread mixture of graham cracker crumbs and stick of margarine on bottom, covering completely. In a bowl mix cream cheese, confectioner's sugar and 1 (8 ounce) container Cool Whip until smooth. Spread over crumbs evenly. In another bowl mix 2 packages of instant chocolate pudding mix with 3 cups of milk. Mix following directions on box of pudding. Pour over cream cheese mixture. Take remaining Cool Whip and spread on top completely. Sprinkle pecan pieces on top and chill for 15 minutes. Cut into even squares and serve.

Cool and rich.

Yield: 16 servings

ORANGE OR LIME DELIGHT

1 (3 ounce) package orange or
 lime gelatin
1 (8 ounce) can crushed
 pineapple, drained, keep
 juice
1 cup miniature
 marshmallows

1 (8 ounce) package cream
 cheese
½ cup granulated sugar
1 (5 ounce) can evaporated
 milk
nuts, if desired

Add enough water to pineapple juice to make 1 cup. Pour into medium size saucepan and bring to a boil. Dissolve gelatin and marshmallows in liquid. Set aside to cool. With an electric mixer beat cream cheese with sugar. Put evaporated milk in large mixing bowl and place in freezer until crystals form. Beat cream until it is like whipped cream. Add cream cheese, cooled gelatin mixture, pineapple and nuts, if desired. Place in refrigerator.

Yield: 8 to 10 servings

APPLE DUMPLINGS

Dumplings

4 medium apples, peeled and
cored
1 teaspoon cinnamon

4 tablespoons sugar
4 teaspoons margarine
4 canned biscuits

Fill holes in apples with cinnamon and sugar. Top with 1 teaspoon margarine. Roll out biscuit dough and wrap each apple with dough and bring ends together at top and secure with toothpick. Bake at 300 degrees for 30 minutes.

Butter Sauce

¼ cup margarine
2 tablespoons all-purpose
flour

2 tablespoons granulated
sugar
1 cup hot water
½ teaspoon vanilla

Melt margarine, add flour and sugar. Add hot water and boil until thick. Add vanilla and pour over apples.

Serve warm, delicious.

Yield: 4 servings

ICE CREAM SALAD

1 (6 ounce) package lemon
gelatin
1 cup hot water
1 (20 ounce) can crushed
pineapple
1 cup reserved pineapple
juice

1 (8 ounce) package cream
cheese
1 quart vanilla ice cream,
softened
1 (10 ounce) jar maraschino
cherries

Dissolve gelatin in hot water. Combine one cup juice and cream cheese in a large bowl. Add gelatin mixture and ice cream, mixing well. Add pineapple, cherries and pecans. Pour into a 9 x 13 inch pan and freeze for 6 hours. Cut into squares and serve.

Summer treat.

Yield: 10 to 12 servings

CHOCOLATE TRUFFLE

1 (18.5 ounce) box chocolate
   cake mix
2 (3 ounce) package instant
   chocolate pudding mix

3 to 4 Skor candy bars
1 (12 ounce) container Cool
   Whip
¼ cup Kahlúa

Prepare cake according to directions on package. Bake in a 9 x 13 inch pan. Let cool and cut into 1 inch squares. Layer cake, cut edge up, in bottom of truffle bowl. Sprinkle with ⅛ cup of Kahlúa. Make 1 box of pudding according to package directions and pour over cake. Top with ½ of Cool Whip and sprinkle with ½ crushed Skor bars. Repeat layers.

Freeze Skor bars before crushing them. Make pudding 1 box at a time so it won't set.

Yield: 16 servings

FRESH FRUIT CUP

4 apples, cored and cut in
   slices
4 oranges, divided into
   sections

2 cups grapes
4 bananas
½ cup maraschino cherries
1 cup orange juice

Mix all fruits together and pour orange juice over the mixture. Chill overnight. Garnish with maraschino cherries.

Always appealing.

Yield: 12 servings

KIWI FRUIT PIZZA

1 (14 ounce) can sweetened
   condensed milk
½ cup sour cream
¼ cup lemon juice
1 teaspoon vanilla
½ cup butter, softened
½ cup brown sugar

1 cup all-purpose flour
¼ cup regular oats
¼ cup chopped walnuts
3 to 4 kiwi, peeled and sliced
1 (8 ounce) can sliced
   pineapple, drained
6 strawberries, halved

Combine first 4 ingredients in a bowl and chill. Cream butter and sugar with electric mixer. Add flour, oats and walnuts and mix well. Press mixture into a greased 12 inch pizza pan. Prick dough with a fork and bake at 350 degrees for 12 minutes or until crust is browned. Cool. Spread condensed milk mixture evenly over crust. Arrange fruit on top.

Unique and delicious.

Fresh and canned fruit of any variety may be used.

Yield: 8 servings

Cooking
FOR CROWDS

COOKING FOR CROWDS

Large gatherings of family and friends have always been a cherished form of hospitality and tradition in the South. We now offer you excellent recipes designed especially in larger quantities for your easy preparation.

Expertise by professionals at Piggly Wiggly have eliminated guesswork for increased quantities. So be prepared for your next Fund Raiser, Party, Reception, Barbecue or Catering with "Cooking for Crowds".

ARTICHOKE DIP

¾ cup mayonnaise
1 cup canned artichoke
   hearts, drained and
   chopped

1 cup Parmesan cheese,
   grated
⅛ teaspoon garlic salt
¼ teaspoon hot sauce

Place all ingredients in mixing bowl and blend until smooth. Chill. Serve with assorted raw vegetables or crackers.

Yield: 30 servings

SPINACH DIP

4 (10 ounce) packages frozen
   chopped spinach
3 cups mayonnaise
3 cups sour cream
¼ cup chopped green onions

¼ cup chopped fresh parsley
½ teaspoon seasoned salt
½ teaspoon white pepper
1 teaspoon Beau Monde
   seasoning

Thaw and drain spinach. Mix with remaining ingredients. Serve with bread or crackers.

Yield: 100 servings

BAKED BRIE IN CHAFING DISH

1 (3 pound) wheel of Brie
¾ stick butter

½ cup slivered almonds or
   toasted pecans

Trim top crust of Brie. Cut butter in cubes and place over cheese. Sprinkle with almonds. Bake at 325 degrees for 10 to 15 minutes or until soft. Let stand 10 minutes before serving. Serve with crackers.

Yield: 25 to 30 servings

BAKED BRIE WITH PASTRY

**3 pounds Brie or White Saga
(whole wheel)
1 sheet frozen puff pastry**

**1 egg yolk
4 tablespoons heavy cream**

Trim top crust of cheese wheel. Place cheese in center of puff pastry. Bring dough up to a point on top of wheel. Twist dough together then peel down to look like a bow. Mix egg yolk and cream. Brush on pastry and bake at 350 degrees until golden brown, approximately 25 to 30 minutes. Remove from oven and let stand about 20 minutes before serving. Garnish with parsley or other fresh herbs. Serve with crackers.

Yield: 25 to 30 servings

SHRIMP DIP

**1 pound popcorn shrimp,
cooked and peeled
1 (8 ounce) container sour
cream
1 (8 ounce) container cream
cheese**

**½ cup celery, finely chopped
½ cup onion, finely chopped
juice of 1 lemon
red pepper to taste
dash of salt
dash of pepper**

Chop shrimp and mix with remaining ingredients. Chill before serving. Serve with crackers.

Yield: 25 servings

SHRIMP PASTE

**1½ pounds small shrimp,
cooked and peeled
¼ pound butter
dash of mace
½ teaspoon dry mustard**

**dash of salt
dash of white pepper
10 drops onion juice
1 tablespoon sherry wine**

Grind shrimp and mix with remaining ingredients. Chill for several hours. Serve with crackers.

Yield: serves 18 to 20 people

MRS. P'S FAMOUS HOT CRAB DIP

1 pound white crab meat,
   picked over
8 ounces cream cheese,
   softened

1 stick butter, softened
1 cup Parmesan cheese,
   grated

Place crab meat in greased chafing dish. Warm cream cheese and butter until of pouring consistency and add to crab meat. Sprinkle Parmesan cheese over the top. Heat until warm, then serve with tart shells or crusty bread.

Yield: 20 servings

BRENDA'S CRAB DIP

5 (6 ounce) cans crab meat
   or 2 pounds fresh
5 pounds sour cream
1 (16 ounce) jar Kraft
   mayonnaise
4 tablespoons garlic salt
1 package dry beefy onion
   soup mix

¼ cup lemon juice
¼ cup Worcestershire sauce
1 (5 ounce) jar horseradish
   sauce
1 teaspoon red pepper
2 pounds Cheddar cheese,
   shredded

Place all ingredients in a bowl and mix well. Chill overnight. Garnish with parsley and serve with crackers.

Yield: 50 servings

STUFFED MUSHROOMS

2 pounds large mushrooms
¼ pound Roquefort cheese,
   crumbled
2 tablespoons butter

3 ounces cream cheese,
   softened
1 tablespoon grated onion
1 tablespoon Worcestershire
   sauce

Wipe mushrooms to clean and remove stems. Finely chop stems and add remaining ingredients. Mix well. Fill mushroom cups with filling. Chill until ready to serve.

Yield: 50 servings

PUFF PASTRY SHELLS

5 cups beer, room
   temperature
2½ cups butter or margarine
5 cups all-purpose flour

2½ teaspoons salt
20 eggs
10 tablespoons Parmesan
   cheese

In saucepan bring beer to boil and add butter and stir until melted. Stir in flour and salt. Cook until mixture dries and forms a ball. Remove from heat. Add eggs, 1 or 2 at a time, beating into batter until smooth. Place batter in pastry bag fitted with a large writing tip. Using a swirling motion place puff on baking sheet (allow room for expansion). Bake at 450 degrees for 10 minutes. Reduce heat to 350 degrees for an additional 10 minutes or until lightly browned. Cool. Slice and fill with choice of ham salad, tuna salad, chicken salad or shrimp salad.

Yield: 10 dozen

FRENCH STYLE EGGS

50 eggs, hard-boiled
1½ cups mayonnaise
3½ teaspoons Dijon mustard
2½ teaspoons onion salt
2½ teaspoons crushed red
   pepper

½ teaspoon white pepper
½ teaspoon Worcestershire
   sauce
5 green onions, finely
   chopped

Peel eggs and cut in half lengthwise. Remove yolks and add remaining ingredients except green onions. Fill egg shells with yolk mixture and top with green onions.

Yield: 100 servings

SHE CRAB SOUP

2 tablespoons butter
½ cup flour
2 drops onion juice
⅛ teaspoon mace
⅛ teaspoon pepper
½ teaspoon salt

½ teaspoon Worcestershire
   sauce
2 cups crab meat
2 cups milk
2 cups half and half

Heat butter in large skillet over low heat. Add flour and stir until it pulls away from edges and looks brown. Add remaining ingredients and mix well. Simmer for 8 to 10 minutes and serve immediately.

Yield: 10 to 12 servings

SHRIMP COCKTAIL

2¾ gallons water
1 (3 ounce) box seafood
   seasoning
3 tablespoons salt

12 pounds shrimp, peeled and
   deveined
3 quarts catsup
1½ cups horseradish sauce
1 tablespoon hot sauce

Bring water to a boil, add seafood seasoning and salt. Add shrimp and simmer for 5 minutes. Drain and chill. Combine catsup, horseradish and hot sauce and chill. To serve, place sauce in parfait glass and arrange 10 shrimp around glass.

Yield: 40 servings

STEAMSHIP ROUND

25 pounds bone-in beef
   rounds

pepper

Rub beef rounds with pepper to coat. Place on roasting pans, do not cover. Roast in 300 degrees oven for 8 hours or until done. Let stand 20 minutes before slicing.

Yield: 100 servings

BEEF WELLINGTON

47 pounds beef tenderloin	3 pounds and 9 ounces
6 pounds flour	shortening
3 ounces salt	water

Place tenderloins in pans and grill at 400 degrees - 3½ minutes for rare, 4 minutes for medium, 5 minutes for well done. Remove from oven and set aside. Mix flour and salt together in mixing bowl. Cut in shortening until granular in appearance. Add enough cold water to make dough form a ball. Chill 1 hour for easy handling. Roll out dough on floured pastry cloth. Roll into rectangle shape about ¼ inch thick. Place tenderloin in center and roll dough around meat sealing edges with egg wash (1 beaten egg mixed with 2 tablespoons water). Bake at 350 degrees for 20 minutes or until golden brown. Slice and serve.

Yield: 100 servings

BARBECUED BABY BEEF RIBS

25 pounds baby beef ribs	1 cup Dijon mustard
1 pound butter or margarine	1½ gallons beef broth
2 bunches green onions, chopped	16 ounces lemon juice
	24 ounces chili sauce
1 cup flour	2 tablespoons black pepper

Place ribs in roasting pan. Roast at 450 degrees for 20 minutes. Drain fat. Sauté onions in butter until tender. Blend in flour and mustard. Cook 1 to 2 minutes. Stir in beef broth and remaining ingredients. Cook 5 to 7 minutes, stirring until smooth and thickened. Brush over ribs and return ribs to oven and bake an additional 30 minutes or until tender.

Yield: 50 servings

SEAFOOD NEWBURG

Stew

4 gallons water
4 tablespoons seafood boil
14 pounds fish fillets, cut in
    pieces
8 pounds scallops

8 pounds shrimp, peeled and
    deveined
1 pound and 13 ounces
    powdered milk
2 pints half and half, optional

Bring water to a boil and add seafood seasoning. Add fish, scallops, and shrimp. Reduce heat and simmer for 5 minutes. Drain and save liquid. Mix 1 pound, 13 ounces of powdered milk with 8½ quarts of fish stock (can use part half and half for richer broth). Heat, but do not boil.

Sauce

2 pounds butter
1 pound flour
1¼ ounces salt

1 ounce paprika
2 teaspoons nutmeg
15 egg yolks, beaten

Blend melted butter with flour, salt, paprika and nutmeg in a large skillet. Cook for 3 to 5 minutes to blend and brown. Add reserved liquid and milk. Simmer for 10 to 15 minutes or until thickened. Remove from heat and slowly add egg yolks, stirring constantly. Divide seafood into several casseroles. Pour sauce over seafood and keep warm. Serve in tart shells or over toast.

Yield: 100 servings

FROGMORE STEW

water to fill 4 large pots (approximately 20 quart size)
4 (3 ounce) boxes seafood seasoning (1 box in each pot)
½ cup salt (2 tablespoons in each pot)
¼ cup pepper (1 tablespoon in each pot)
2 (5 ounce) bottles Worcestershire sauce (½ bottle in each pot)
1 (⅛ ounce) jar bay leaves (6 leaves in each pot)
4 tablespoons cloves (1 teaspoon in each pot)
8 lemons, sliced (2 in each pot)
20 pounds smoked sausage, divided
100 ears corn, (cut in 3 pieces) divided
50 pounds shrimp, divided

Bring water to boil. Add seafood seasoning, salt, pepper, Worcestershire sauce, bay leaves, cloves and lemon slices. Add sausage, divide among the pots, and cook for 10 minutes. Add corn, divide among pots, and cook for 10 minutes. Add shrimp, divide among pots, and cook for 5 minutes. Remove from heat and drain. Serve immediately.

Yield: 100 servings

SAUERBRATEN

40 pounds boneless beef chuck roast
7½ quarts water
4½ quarts vinegar
1 pound and 14 ounces brown sugar
3 ounces salt
2 ounces cloves
1½ teaspoons black pepper
1 teaspoon garlic powder
12 bay leaves
4 pounds onions, sliced thin
3 pounds carrots, sliced thin
2½ pounds celery, sliced thin
2 pounds ginger snap cookies, crushed

Combine water, vinegar and remaining ingredients except ginger snaps. Pour over roasts in large pans. Simmer on top of stove for 3½ to 4 hours. Remove beef and bay leave. Reserve 3¼ cups of marinade and set aside. Let beef rest for 20 minutes before slicing. Slice ⅛ inch thick and place in serving pan. Bring marinade to a boil, add crushed ginger snap crumbs and stir until dissolved. Pour over beef and serve.

Yield: 100 servings

SUKIYAK

25 pounds beef round, sliced ⅛ inch thick and cut into strips 2 inches long and ½ inch wide.
4 cups soy sauce
1 cup sugar
1 tablespoon black pepper
6 (8 ounce) cans sliced mushrooms
1 cup shortening
8 pounds celery, cut ⅛ inch thick diagonally
5 pounds onions, chopped
3 pounds green peppers, chopped
3 bunches spring onions, chopped
2 packages bean sprouts

Slice beef and set aside. Combine soy sauce, sugar, black pepper and mushrooms, set aside. Melt shortening and sauté celery 1½ minutes, stirring constantly. Add beef strips and fry until brown, about 1½ minutes Add onions and sauté for 2 minutes. Add green peppers and cook for 2 minutes. Add soy sauce and mushroom mixture and stir well. Add green onions and bean sprouts, stir fry for 1 minutes. Serve over rice.

Yield: 100 servings

JAEGERSCHNITZAL
(VEAL STEAK WITH MUSHROOM SAUCE)

10 ounces butter
1 pound, 4 ounces sweet peppers, chopped
3½ pounds fresh mushrooms, wiped and sliced
10¼ ounces canned pimentos
1¼ teaspoons garlic salt
2½ teaspoons black pepper
⅔ cup parsley, chopped
1¼ gallons brown gravy (make your own or use commercially packaged gravy mix)
35 pounds breaded veal steaks (approximately 100 steaks)
vegetable shortening

Sauté peppers mushrooms, pimentos and garlic salt in butter for 3 minutes. Add black pepper and parsley. Set aside. Prepare gravy and add tomato paste, bring to a boil. Add sautéed vegetables and keep warm. Deep fry veal steaks until golden brown, about 5 minutes. Serve with sauce over top.

Yield: 100 servings

BAKED BEANS

2 pounds bacon, chopped
1½ pounds onions, chopped
4 (#10 size) cans pork and
   beans

2 cups catsup
1½ pounds brown sugar
½ cup mustard

Cook bacon until crisp. Remove from pan and place on paper towels. Drain all but ½ cup bacon fat and use to sauté onions. Add remaining ingredients and place in casserole dishes. Bake at 350 degrees, uncovered, for 1½ to 2 hours.

Yield: 100 servings

HOT SPICED BEETS

4 (#10 size) cans beets
3 quarts liquid (use beet juice
   plus water)
2 quarts vinegar
1 tablespoon cinnamon
2 tablespoons cloves, ground

3 tablespoons salt
2 teaspoons black pepper
1 pound granulated sugar
2 pounds brown sugar
1 pound butter

Drain liquid from beets and add enough water to make 3 quarts. Place liquid in large container and add all other ingredients except beets and butter. Bring to a boil, reduce heat and simmer for 10 to 15 minutes. Add beets and butter. Stir well.

Yield: 100 servings

CARROT CELERY ALMONDINE

6 pounds carrots
8 pounds celery
1½ pounds butter

12 ounces sliced almonds
1 cup lemon juice

Cut carrots and celery in ½ inch diagonal slices. Place in saucepan and add enough water to steam (approximately 4 to 6 cups). Bring to a boil and reduce heat and simmer for 20 minutes. Drain. Melt butter, add almonds and toast for about 10 minutes. Stir constantly. Remove from heat and pour over vegetables. Add lemon juice and stir.

Yield: 100 servings

CALICO CORN

2 pounds bacon, cooked crisp
4 (#10 size) cans corn
1 ounce salt
1½ teaspoons pepper
7 ounces pimentos

Drain corn, mix with salt, pepper and pimentos. Place in large stock pot and heat until hot. Crumble bacon and add to corn. Stir lightly.

Yield: 100 servings

SPANISH STYLE LIMA BEANS

8 pounds dry lima beans
enough water to cover beans
4 ounces salt
1 pound onions, chopped
3 quarts stewed tomatoes
1 pound sugar
2 tablespoons mustard
½ teaspoon cloves
1 teaspoon black pepper

Bring lima beans and water to a boil. Remove from heat and let sit for 1 hour. Drain and add more water to cover. Add remaining ingredients and cook for 1 hour. Add remaining ingredients and simmer for 15 to 20 minutes.

Yield: 100 servings

O'BRIEN POTATOES

3 pounds green peppers,
  chopped fine
1 pound and 5 ounces
  pimentos
4 ounces butter
31 pounds potatoes, cubed
3 tablespoons salt
1 teaspoon pepper

Sauté peppers and pimentos for 3 to 5 minutes in butter. Deep fry potatoes until golden brown. Remove from fryer and add peppers and pimentos. Stir lightly, Add salt and pepper.

Yield: 100 servings

BULLWINKEL'S BENNE COOKIES

2 pounds brown sugar
1 cup granulated sugar
1 tablespoon plus 1 teaspoon
   salt
2 tablespoons baking powder

3 sticks margarine
1½ cups Crisco
10 eggs
8 cups flour
1 pound toasted benne seeds

Cream butter and Crisco until light. Add sugar and mix well. Add eggs in 3 parts. Add flour and benne seeds. Place in pastry bag with plain or star tip. Place on greased cookie sheet. Bake at 350 degrees for 10 to 12 minutes. Half way through baking time take cookies out of oven and drop on table to flatten cookies. Return to oven and complete baking.

Yield: approximately 12 dozen

BULLWINKEL'S APPLESAUCE CUPCAKES

1¾ cups granulated sugar
¾ stick margarine or butter
4 eggs
3 cups plus 2 tablespoons
   all-purpose flour
2 teaspoons baking soda
2 teaspoons salt
1 tablespoon cinnamon

1 teaspoon allspice
2 (16 ounce) cans apple pie
   filling
1 pound cake crumbs
2 cups English walnuts
1 pound light brown sugar
1 cup light corn syrup

Cream sugar and butter until light. Add eggs and beat. Sift flour, baking soda, salt, cinnamon and allspice together and add to creamed mixture. Mix in apple pie filling and cake crumbs. Divide walnuts between 4 dozen muffin pans. Mix brown sugar and corn syrup and pour over walnuts, just a tablespoon for each muffin cup. Fill each cup ¾ full with cupcake mix. Bake at 350 degrees for 25 minutes. Remove from oven and turn upside down while still hot.

Yield: 4 dozen

THE FOLLOWING SEGMENT, "*Especially* LIGHT"
IS OFFERED TO APPEAL TO THOSE WHO
ARE NUTRITION CONSCIOUS AND PREFER
RECIPES WITH LOWER FAT AND
CHOLESTEROL LEVELS THAN TRADITIONAL
RECIPES. WE ARE INDEBTED TO DOTTIE
HARDIN, DIRECTOR OF CONSUMER
AFFAIRS, AND EILEEN STELLEFSON, M.P.H.,
R.D., PIGGLY WIGGLY NUTRITIONIST, FOR
COMPILING THE GUIDELINES WHICH CAN
BE USED TO MODIFY CONVENTIONAL
RECIPES TO YOUR NUTRITIONAL NEEDS.
THE EDITORS OF BY *Special* REQUEST HAVE
MADE EVERY EFFORT TO INCLUDE A
VARIETY OF RECIPES TO FIT THE NEEDS OF
EVERYONE AND EVERY TASTE.
Enjoy!

Especially
LIGHT

*In the 1990's, more and more people are concerned with "health" and "diet". Although this **"Especially Light"** section contains recipes lower in fat and cholesterol than similar traditional recipes, most recipes can now be modified to meet the dietary guidelines for health using the following substitutions.*

Ingredient Substitutions To Make Foods More Healthful

TO REDUCE SODIUM: INSTEAD OF...

use...

Fresh, frozen or low sodium canned vegetables.	Canned vegetables, sauerkraut, pickles, olives, vegetables in brine.
Fresh Meats, Poultry, Fish and Shellfish.	Cured, salted or smoked meat or fish such as: corned beef, bacon, cold cuts, canned tuna, smoked salmon, caviar, marinated herring or anchovies in oil.
Unsalted homemade soups and stocks, low sodium bases.	Canned soups and stock, bouillon powder.
Vegetable oil, unsalted butter, vegetable shortening, and fresh peanut butter.	Bacon fat, salt pork, salted peanut butter.
Fresh or dried herbs and spices, horseradish, vinegar, dry mustard, lemon juice, and Worcestershire sauce.	Salt, MSG, soy sauce, meat tenderizers, capers, and chili sauce.

TO REDUCE FAT AND CHOLESTEROL: INSTEAD OF...

use...

Egg whites.	*Whole eggs or yolks.
Plain no-fat yogurt.	*Sour cream.
Milk or skim milk.	*Cream.
Rice, wild rice, pasta, bulgar, couscous and buckwheat.	*Egg noodles.
Wheat, pumpernickel and rye bread, pita, hard rolls.	*Egg breads, brioche, biscuits, croissants, popovers, cheese bread, hush puppies, most muffins and quick breads.
Fresh, frozen, canned or dried fruits, fruit ice, angel food cake and meringues.	*Ice cream, frosted cakes, whipped cream, custard, pastry cream.

MEAT GUIDELINES

The process of eating healthier begins with the foods we purchase. In buying and preparing meats, keep the following in mind.

Beef:

For lower fat choose the following...

Flank Steaks
Tenderloin
Sirloin
Eye of the Round
Ground Round

Additionally...

Trim all visible fat before cooking.
Use meat rack to drain fat.
Baste with broth, tomato juice or wine.

Pork:

For lower fat choose the following...

Tenderloin
Center Loin Chops
Top Loin Chops
Boneless Sirloin Chops
Boneless Loin Roast

Additionally...

Trim all visible fat before cooking.
Baste with broth, tomato juice or wine.

Poultry...

For lower fat, choose breast over dark meat.

Additionally...

Remove skin and trim visible fat before cooking.
Bake, broil, poach, grill or microwave.
Use meat rack to drain fat.
Baste with broth, wine or juices.

Seafood:

Choose fresh fish and canned fish packed in water.

Additionally...

Bake, broil, poach or steam.
Although fish varies in cholesterol and fat content, all are excellent choices in a healthy diet.

SEVEN DIETARY GUIDELINES FOR HEALTH ARE AS FOLLOWS:

(1)
Eat a Variety of Foods.

(2)
Maintain Ideal Weight.

(3)
Avoid too much fat, saturated fat and cholesterol.

(4)
Eat food with adequate starch and fiber.

(5)
Avoid too much sugar.

(6)
Avoid too much sodium.

(7)
If you drink alcohol, do so in moderation.

To help simplify the dietary guidelines, the U.S. Department of Agriculture has prepared the food guideline pyramid. This pyramid, as illustrated, helps us to know the servings we should consume in each food group.

Food Guide Pyramid

A Guide to Daily Food Choices

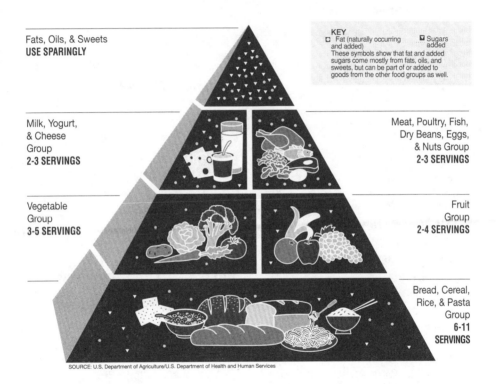

Fats, Oils, & Sweets
USE SPARINGLY

KEY
◻ Fat (naturally occurring and added) 🞂 Sugars added
These symbols show that fat and added sugars come mostly from fats, oils, and sweets, but can be part of or added to goods from the other food groups as well.

Milk, Yogurt, & Cheese Group
2-3 SERVINGS

Meat, Poultry, Fish, Dry Beans, Eggs, & Nuts Group
2-3 SERVINGS

Vegetable Group
3-5 SERVINGS

Fruit Group
2-4 SERVINGS

Bread, Cereal, Rice, & Pasta Group
6-11 SERVINGS

SOURCE: U.S. Department of Agriculture/U.S. Department of Health and Human Services

Use the Food Guide Pyramid to help you eat better every day. . .the Dietary Guidelines way. Start with plenty of Breads, Cereals, Rice, and Pasta; Vegetables; and Fruits. Add two to three servings from the Milk group and two to three servings from the Meat group.

Each of these food groups provides some, but not all, of the nutrients you need. No one food group is more important than another — for good health you need them all. Go easy on fats, oils, and sweets, the foods in the small tip of the Pyramid.

To order a copy of "The Food Guide Pyramid" booklet, send a $1.00 check or money order made out to the Superintendent of Documents to: Comsumer Infromation Center, Department 159-Y, Pueblo, Colorado 81009

U.S. Department of Agriculture, Human Nutrition Information Service, August 1992, Leaflet No. 572

CREAM CHEESE AND PINEAPPLE SPREAD

1 (16 ounce) container fat free
  cream cheese

1 (15 ounce) can crushed
  pineapple, drained
¼ cup powdered sugar

Combine cream cheese and pineapple. Add powdered sugar, mixing well. Serve with low fat crackers.

Yield: 16 servings

Nutrition Information Per Serving:

Calories 61

Fat 0 grams

Cholesterol 0 milligrams

Sodium 85 milligrams

SPINACH DIP

1 (10 ounce) package frozen
  chopped spinach
1 package dry vegetable soup
  mix
1 pint non-fat plain yogurt
1 cup non-fat Miracle Whip
  dressing

1 onion, minced
1 (2½ ounce) jar dried beef,
  chopped fine
1 (8 ounce) can sliced water
  chestnuts

Thaw spinach, squeeze dry and add remaining ingredients. Mix well and chill in refrigerator for 3 to 4 hours. Serve with crackers.

Yield: 16 servings

Nutrition Information Per Serving:

Calories 70

Fat 1 gram

Cholesterol 5 grams

Sodium 408 milligrams

CHILLED STRAWBERRY SOUP

2 pints strawberries, cleaned
and without stems
2 cups watermelon, seeded

1 small cantaloupe, peeled
and seeded
1½ cups apple cider
½ cup honey

Purée strawberries, watermelon and cantaloupe. Adjust soup texture with apple cider and season with honey. Keep chilled.

Yield: 10 servings

Nutrition Information Per Serving:

Calories 108

Fat 0 grams

Cholesterol 0 milligrams

Sodium 8 milligrams

BOK CHOY SOUP

4 chicken breasts
1 bunch bok choy, sliced
diagonally
4 stalks celery, sliced
diagonally

2 (10.5 ounce) cans chicken
broth
4 tablespoons cornstarch
salt and pepper to taste

Boil chicken in a 5 quart pot until tender and falling off bone. Remove skin and bones. Dice into small pieces. Return to pot. Reserve liquid. Add bok choy and celery, reserving half of leafy section of bok choy for garnish. Add chicken broth. Fill with water. Cook over medium heat for one hour. Mix cornstarch with water to make a paste. Add slowly to soup to thicken.

Yield: 12 to 15 servings

Nutrition Information Per Serving:

Calories 150

Fat 4 grams

Cholesterol 48 milligrams

Sodium 173 milligrams

CUCUMBER SALAD WITH MINT

1 cup plain yogurt
2 tablespoons finely snipped
   fresh mint leaves
   or ½ teaspoon dried mint
   leaves

1 tablespoon lemon juice
1 clove garlic, finely chopped
dash white pepper
1 medium cucumber, thinly
   sliced

Mix together all ingredients except cucumber. Cover and refrigerate. Just before serving, stir in cucumbers. Place in a serving dish. Garnish with additional mint if desired.

Yield: 4 servings

Nutrition Information Per Serving:

Calories 42

Fat 0 grams

Cholesterol 1 milligram

Sodium 46 milligrams

GOURMET CATFISH

2 (4 to 5 ounce) fresh, skinned
   catfish fillets
½ teaspoon tarragon
⅛ teaspoon lemon pepper
1 tablespoon butter

1 carrot, cut into matchstick
   size pieces
1 zucchini, cut into matchstick
   size pieces

Prepare carrots and zucchini by covering with plastic wrap and microwaving 3 minutes on high. Fold 12 to 14 inch squares of heavy brown or parchment paper in half. Fold fillets in half and insert in center against the fold of paper. Sprinkle on tarragon, pepper and top with butter. Add the cooked vegetables. Fold paper over and crimp edges all around to seal tightly. Microwave each packet on high for 2 minutes or until fish is barely done. Serve still wrapped with parsley potatoes.

Yield: 4 servings

Nutrition Information Per Serving:

Calories 144

Fat 7 grams

Cholesterol 58 milligrams

Sodium 87 milligrams

GRILLED FISH

2 pounds swordfish or
    dolphin, separated into
    ½ pound pieces
1 tomato, sliced

1 medium onion, sliced
dash of salt
dash of pepper
1 tablespoon melted butter

Place each piece of fish on a sheet of aluminum foil. Sprinkle with salt and pepper. Add slice of tomato and onion. Dot with butter. Seal foil and grill for 10 minutes.

Yield: 4 servings

Nutrition Information Per Serving:

Calories 384

Fat 14.6 grams

Cholesterol 122 milligrams

Sodium 293 milligrams

SHRIMP CREOLE

3 tablespoons oil
½ cup chopped celery
½ cup chopped onion
½ cup chopped bell pepper
1 clove garlic, minced
1 (16 ounce) can tomatoes

1 (8 ounce) can tomato sauce
1 teaspoon chili powder
1 tablespoon Worcestershire
    sauce
dash Texas Pete
12 ounces raw peeled shrimp

Cook celery, onion, pepper and garlic in oil until tender. Add tomatoes, tomato sauce and seasonings. Simmer 45 minutes. Add shrimp for about 5 minutes. Serve on white rice.

Yield: 4 servings

Nutrition Information Per Serving:

Calories 212

Fat 11 grams

Cholesterol 166 milligrams

Sodium 524 milligrams

ZESTY SHRIMP WITH GINGER ROOT

1 pound medium shrimp,
   peeled and deveined
1 teaspoon freshly chopped
   garlic
½ teaspoon freshly shredded
   ginger root

1 tablespoon butter
1 package Ramen noodles
   (without seasoning)
¼ pound fresh snow peas

Sauté garlic and ginger root for one minute in butter. Boil and drain noodles; set aside. Sauté shrimp in butter and herb mixture approximately 3 minutes. Add snow peas and noodles. Cook all ingredients together over medium-high heat until peas are slightly tender.

Yield: 4 to 6 servings

Nutrition Information Per Serving:

Calories 189

Fat 6 grams

Cholesterol 229 milligrams

Sodium 490 milligrams

SWEET AND TANGY CHICKEN STIR FRY

2 tablespoons vegetable oil
1 pound boneless, skinless
   chicken breasts, cut into
   strips
2 cups frozen Oriental-style
   vegetables, thawed

1 cup chicken broth
¼ cup Worcestershire sauce
2 tablespoons brown sugar
1 tablespoon red hot cayenne
   pepper sauce
1 tablespoon cornstarch

Heat oil in a large skillet or wok. Add chicken; stir-fry until golden. Add vegetables; cook 2 minutes until crisp-tender. Combine remaining ingredients; mix well. Pour into skillet. Bring to a boil. Reduce heat; simmer until thickened, stirring occasionally. Serve over rice.

Yield: 4 servings

Nutrition Information Per Serving:

Calories 356

Fat 11 grams

Cholesterol 97 milligrams

Sodium 458 milligrams

CHICKEN SQUASH DELIGHT

4 boneless chicken breasts,
    cut into small pieces
4 small yellow squash, thinly
    sliced

2 medium zucchini squash,
    thinly sliced
½ bell pepper, chopped
1 small onion, sliced
vegetable cooking spray

Spray frying pan with vegetable cooking spray. Place chicken in the pan. Cook under low heat for 20 to 30 minutes. In another frying pan sprayed with cooking spray, combine squash, zucchini, bell pepper, and onion. Cover and let cook on low heat for 15 minutes, stirring every 3 to 4 minutes. Combine chicken and vegetables. Serve over rice.

Yield: 6 servings

Nutrition Information Per Serving:

Calories 201

Fat 4 grams

Cholesterol 97 milligrams

Sodium 86 milligrams

PANAMANIAN CHICKEN

6 chicken breasts
garlic salt to taste
pepper to taste
2 tablespoons oil

1 medium onion, chopped
1 green pepper, chopped
2 (14.5 ounce) cans whole
    tomatoes

Brown chicken seasoned with garlic salt and pepper in oil until cooked. Add onion and green pepper; cooking until brown and soft. Add tomatoes with juice. Simmer 20 minutes. Serve over rice.

Yield: 6 servings

Nutrition Information Per Serving:

Calories 342

Fat 11 grams

Cholesterol 146 milligrams

Sodium 244 milligrams

GINGER CHICKEN

⅓ cup honey
⅓ cup soy sauce
⅓ cup catsup

1 teaspoon grated fresh
　ginger
2 chicken breasts

Mix honey, soy sauce, catsup and ginger. Pour over chicken. Cover and microwave on high for 10 minutes. Turn and cook another 5 to 11 minutes.

Yield: 4 servings

Nutrition Information Per Serving:

Calories 269

Cholesterol 73 milligrams

Fat 3 grams

Sodium 1723 milligrams

CHICKEN MARENGO

1 (3 pound) chicken
12 pearl onions, peeled
½ pound fresh mushrooms,
　sliced
2 tablespoons butter or
　margarine
2 tablespoons all-purpose
　flour

1 cup white wine
¾ cup water
1 chicken bouillon cube
3 tomatoes, peeled and cut
　into wedges
2 cloves garlic, minced
½ teaspoon salt
dash of black pepper

Rinse chicken. Cut into serving pieces. In a skillet, heat butter. Add chicken pieces and sauté until well browned on all sides. Transfer to a Dutch oven. Sauté mushrooms and onions in skillet until lightly browned. Sprinkle with flour and stir well to combine. Add wine, water, and crumbled bouillon cube. Bring to a boil, stirring. Pour over chicken. Cover with lid. Cook for 20 minutes. Add tomatoes and garlic and stir. Season with salt and pepper. Cook covered 5 to 10 minutes. Serve with steamed rice, greens or broccoli.

Yield: 4 servings

Nutrition Information Per Serving:

Calories 536

Cholesterol 193 milligrams

Fat 15 grams

Sodium 476 milligrams

STIR FRY BEEF AND PEA PODS

¾ pound boneless sirloin
    steak
½ cup water
1 tablespoon cornstarch
1½ teaspoons sugar
¼ cup plus 1 tablespoon soy
    sauce
½ to 2 tablespoons oyster
    flavored sauce
3 tablespoons peanut oil
¼ teaspoon salt

1 large onion, thinly sliced
    and separated into rings
3 stalks celery, diagonally
    sliced
4 ounces fresh mushrooms,
    sliced
½ cup coarsely chopped
    water chestnuts
1 (6 ounce) package frozen
    Chinese pea pods, thawed
    and drained
hot cooked rice

Partially freeze steak. Slice across grain into 2 by ¼ inch strips. Set aside. Combine water, cornstarch, sugar, soy sauce, and oyster sauce; set aside. Pour oil around top of preheated wok, coating sides; allow to heat at medium high (325 degrees) for 2 minutes. Add steak and salt; stir fry about 3 minutes. Push meat up sides of wok, forming a well in center. Place onion, celery, mushrooms, and water chestnuts in well; stir fry 2 to 3 minutes. Add pea pods; cover and reduce heat to medium (275 degrees). Simmer 2 to 3 minutes. Stir in soy sauce mixture. Cook on medium-high heat (325 degrees) stirring constantly until thickened and bubbly. Serve over rice.

Yield: 6 servings

Nutrition Information Per Serving:

Calories 275

Fat 10 grams

Cholesterol 51 milligrams

Sodium 1000 milligrams

WOK YOUR VEGGIES

One of the most healthful ways to enjoy produce is in an easy stir-fry. A wok helps, but it's not essential. Follow these basic steps: 1. Have everything ready, to go. 2. You'll need vegetable oil (not olive; it may burn) as well as any sauce (simplest: equal parts soy sauce, sherry, corn starch; stir before adding). 3. Cut all veggies bite-size with each type in separate dish. 4. Heat oil over high heat. 5. When sizzling, add hardest vegetables (carrots, broccoli) stir-frying until barely tender. Add tender vegetables (celery, pepper strips); continue cooking. Add most tender stuff (sprouts, mushrooms). 6. Drizzle in soy-cornstarch mixture. Toss until liquid thickens. 7. Serve over hot steamed brown rice.

SWISS STEAK

2 tablespoons flour
¾ teaspoon salt
½ teaspoon fresh ground
  pepper

1½ pounds boneless round
  steak
2 tablespoons oil
1 cup sliced onions
1½ cups stewing tomatoes

Preheat Dutch oven to 375 degrees. Combine flour, salt and pepper. Sprinkle half of the mixture on one side of meat; pound in with a mallet. Turn meat over and repeat flouring and pounding. Heat oil in a Dutch oven. Add meat and brown on both sides. Add onions and tomatoes; Cover and bake for 3 hours or until tender.

Yield: 6 servings

Nutrition Information Per Serving:

Calories 239

Fat 7 grams

Cholesterol 82 milligrams

Sodium 430 milligrams

CROCKPOT CHILI

1½ pounds ground chuck
2 medium onions, diced
2 (15 ounce) cans kidney
  beans, drained
2 (8 ounce) cans stewed
  tomatoes
2 (8 ounce) cans tomato
  sauce

1 (6 ounce) can tomato paste
2 tablespoons brown sugar
2 tablespoons parsley
1 teaspoon oregano
1 teaspoon garlic powder
1 teaspoon dry mustard
1 tablespoon Tabasco sauce

Crumble ground chuck in the bottom of a crockpot. Layer remaining ingredients in order listed. Set crockpot on low. After cooking 3 hours, stir all ingredients and cook 3 more hours.

Yield: 6 servings

Nutrition Information Per Serving:

Calories 358

Fat 10 grams

Cholesterol 66 milligrams

Sodium 664 milligrams

EASY GOULASH

2 pounds ground round
2 teaspoons minced onion
4 tablespoons Worcestershire
sauce
2 (15 ounce) cans light red
kidney beans

2 (15 ounce) cans whole
potatoes, diced
2 (15 ounce) cans tomato
sauce
1 (6 ounce) can tomato paste

Brown ground round and onions. Add remaining ingredients and simmer until potatoes are tender. May be served over rice.

Yield: 8 servings

Nutrition Information Per Serving:

Calories 353

Fat 10 grams

Cholesterol 65 milligrams

Sodium 685 milligrams

TERIYAKI BEEF

2 pounds beef sirloin tips, cut
into ½ inch cubes
2 teaspoons powdered ginger
2 cloves garlic, chopped fine

2 tablespoons granulated
sugar
1 cup soy sauce
½ cup sherry

Combine ginger, garlic, sugar, soy sauce and sherry. Pour over beef cubes, and let stand 12 or more hours. Put beef cubes on skewers and cook over charcoal grill. Serve hot.

Yield: 8 servings

Nutrition Information Per Serving:

Calories 218

Fat 9 grams

Cholesterol 89 milligrams

Sodium 532 milligrams

VEAL MARSALA

6 ounces veal cutlets
2 tablespoons all-purpose flour
olive oil flavored cooking spray
⅓ cup Marsala wine
1 cup sliced fresh mushrooms
½ cup sweet red pepper strips
½ cup sliced red onion, separated into rings
⅔ cup no-salt added chicken broth
1 teaspoon lemon juice
¼ teaspoon salt
¼ teaspoon pepper
1 cup hot cooked fettuccine (cooked without salt or fat)

Place veal cutlets between 2 sheets of heavy duty plastic wrap, and flatten to ¼ inch thickness using a meat mallet or rolling pin. Cut veal into 1 inch squares; dredge in flour. Coat a non-stick skillet with cooking spray; place over medium-high heat until hot. Add veal; cook on both sides until browned. Transfer veal to a lightly greased 1 quart casserole. Deglaze pan by pouring wine into skillet; pour pan drippings over veal, and then set aside. Combine the mushrooms and next 6 ingredients in skillet; cook until vegetables are tender. Spoon the vegetables and pan drippings over veal and bake at 400 degrees for 15 to 20 minutes, or until bubbly. Serve over ½ cup cooked fettuccine.

Yield: 2 servings

Nutrition Information Per Serving:

Calories 429

Fat 10.7 grams

Cholesterol 163 milligrams

Sodium 430 milligrams

PORK CHOPS WITH APPLES

4 (4 ounce) lean center-cut
pork chops, trimmed
1 medium onion, chopped
vegetable cooking spray
1¼ cups water

1 teaspoon chicken flavored
bouillon granules
¼ teaspoon pepper
3 medium size cooking
apples, peeled and sliced
½ teaspoon ground cinnamon

Brown pork chops and onion in a large skillet coated with cooking spray. Combine water, bouillon granules, and pepper, stirring to dissolve; add to skillet. Cover and bring to a boil. Reduce heat, and simmer 20 minutes. Skim off fat. Add apple slices and cinnamon to mixture in skillet. Cover and simmer an additional 15 minutes. Transfer to a serving platter, and serve hot. (1 chop with ¾ cup apples.)

Yield: 4 servings

Nutrition Information Per Serving:

Calories 264

Fat 8.6 grams

Cholesterol 83 milligrams

sodium 507 milligrams

PORK TENDERLOIN WITH ROSEMARY AND THYME

vegetable cooking spray
2 (½ pound) pork tenderloins
2 tablespoons Dijon mustard
1 tablespoon honey

1 teaspoon chopped fresh
rosemary
½ teaspoon chopped fresh
thyme
¼ teaspoon pepper

Trim fat from tenderloins. Place on a rack coated with cooking spray; place rack in a shallow roasting pan. Combine Dijon mustard and next 4 ingredients in a small bowl; brush over tenderloins. Insert a meat thermometer into thickest part of tenderloin. Bake at 350 degrees for 50 minutes or until meat thermometer registers 160 degrees, basting frequently with Dijon mustard mixture.

Yield: 4 servings

Nutrition Information Per Serving:

Calories 169

Fat 4.8 grams

Cholesterol 79 milligrams

Sodium 280 milligrams

MICROWAVED SESAME PORK

non-stick vegetable cooking
   spray
2 tablespoons sesame seed
1 tablespoon cornstarch
1 tablespoon packed brown
   sugar
¼ teaspoon ground ginger
¼ cup low-sodium soy sauce
2 tablespoons white wine
   vinegar

1 tablespoon vegetable oil
¾ pound pork tenderloin,
   trimmed and cut into
   strips (2 x ¼ inch)
1½ cups thinly sliced carrots
1 medium onion, cut into
   8 wedges
1½ cups frozen peas
3 cups hot cooked rice

Spray 10 inch skillet with non-stick vegetable cooking spray. Heat skillet conventionally over medium heat. Add sesame seed. Cook for 1 to 4 minutes or until golden brown, stirring constantly. Set aside. In 2 quart casserole, combine cornstarch, sugar, and ginger. Mix well. Blend in soy sauce, vinegar and oil. Add pork strips, carrots and onion. Toss to coat. Microwave at high for 9 to 11 minutes, or until pork is no longer pink and sauce is thickened and translucent, stirring 3 times. Add peas and sesame seed. Mix well. Cover. Microwave at high for 2 to 4 minutes, or until mixture is hot, stirring once. Serve over rice.

Yield: 6 servings

Nutrition Information Per Serving:

Calories 292

Fat 6 grams

Cholesterol 43 milligrams

Sodium 511 milligrams

DUTCH CABBAGE

1 large head of cabbage,
   chopped into small slices
2 large onions, chopped

2 teaspoons margarine
8 ounces water

Mix cabbage and onion. Add water and margarine. Cook for 20 minutes in an electric skillet, or until desired tenderness.

Yield: 8 servings

Nutrition Information Per Serving:

Calories 17

Fat 1 gram

Cholesterol 0 milligrams

Sodium 17 milligrams

TORTILLA - BEAN CASSEROLE

2 cups chopped onion
1½ cups chopped green
    pepper
1 (14½ ounce) can tomatoes
¾ cup picante sauce
2 cloves garlic, minced
2 teaspoons ground cumin
2 (15 ounce) cans black
    beans, drained

12 (6 inch) tortillas
2 cups shredded low-fat
    Monterey Jack cheese
2 medium tomatoes, sliced
2 cups shredded lettuce
1 green onion, sliced
½ cup plain yogurt

In a large skillet combine onion, green pepper, undrained tomatoes, picante sauce, garlic and cumin. Bring to a boil. Reduce heat. Simmer uncovered for 10 minutes. Stir in beans. In a 13 x 9 x 2 inch baking dish spread ⅓ bean mixture over bottom. Top with half the tortillas and half of the cheese. Add another ⅓ of bean mixture, then tortillas, then bean mixture. Cover and bake at 350 degrees for 30 to 35 minutes or until heated thoroughly. Sprinkle with remaining cheese and let stand 10 minutes. Top with tomato slices, green onions and yogurt.

Yield: 6 servings

Nutrition Information Per Serving:

Calories 428

Fat 11 grams

Cholesterol 20 milligrams

Sodium 470 milligrams

YELLOW RICE WITH CORN

1½ cups water
½ teaspoon salt
½ teaspoon ground cumin
¼ teaspoon ground cinnamon

¼ teaspoon ground turmeric
1 cup frozen corn kernels,
    thawed
1½ cups instant rice

Combine water, salt, cumin, cinnamon, and turmeric in a medium size saucepan. Bring to a boil. Add corn. Reheat to boiling. Stir in rice. Cover; remove from heat. Let stand 10 minutes before serving.

Yield: 4 servings

Nutrition Information Per Serving:

Calories 133

Fat 0 grams

Cholesterol 0 milligrams

Sodium 270 milligrams

SESAME BROCCOLI

1½ pounds broccoli	1 tablespoon lemon juice
1 teaspoon vegetable oil	1 tablespoon soy sauce
1 tablespoon sesame seeds	1 tablespoon sugar

Trim off leaves and hard stalk of broccoli. Wash broccoli; separate into individual spears. Arrange broccoli spears in a steamer. Cover and steam until fork tender. Drain and place in a serving dish. Heat oil in a small pan. Add sesame seeds, lemon juice, soy sauce and sugar. Bring to boil and remove from heat. Pour over broccoli and toss gently to coat.

Yield: 4 servings

Nutrition Information Per Serving:

Calories 112	Cholesterol 0 milligrams
Fat 7 grams	Sodium 304 milligrams

ZUCCHINI APEATS OLÉ

¾ to 1 pound zucchini (2 to 3 small)	¼ teaspoon ground red pepper
¾ cup oat bran hot cereal, uncooked	2 egg whites
1 teaspoon chili powder	1 tablespoon margarine, melted
¾ teaspoon ground cumin	½ cup salsa

Preheat oven to 450 degrees. Lightly spray a 15 x 10 inch baking pan with cooking oil spray. Cut off ends of zucchini; cut in half crosswise; slice each piece in half lengthwise, then again in half. In a plastic bag, combine oat bran, chili powder, cumin and red pepper. In a shallow dish, lightly beat egg whites. Coat zucchini with oat bran mixture; shake off excess. Dip into egg mixture; then coat again with oat bran mixture. Place in prepared pan. Lightly brush with margarine. Bake 20 minutes or until zucchini is crisp-tender. Serve with salsa.

Yield: 6 servings

Nutrition Information Per Serving:

Calories 56	Cholesterol 0 milligrams
Fat 3 grams	Sodium 188 milligrams

ONION ROASTED POTATOES

1 envelope onion soup mix
2 pounds all-purpose
   potatoes, cut into large
   chunks

3 tablespoons water

Preheat oven to 450 degrees. Mix all ingredients in a large plastic bag. Close bag and shake until potatoes are evenly coated. Empty potatoes into a shallow baking or roasting pan, sprayed with vegetable cooking spray. Bake 40 minutes, stirring occasionally. Garnish with chopped parsley.

Yield: 8 servings

Nutrition Information Per Serving:

Calories 114

Fat 5 milligrams

Cholesterol 0 milligrams

Sodium 442 milligrams

LOW FAT PASTA SALAD

1 (16 ounce) box tricolor pasta
   twists
1 (16 ounce) bottle fat free
   Italian salad dressing

3 hard-boiled egg whites,
   chopped
1 cucumber, sliced
1 tomato, chopped
1 small onion, thinly sliced

Cook pasta according to package directions. Drain. Pour salad dressing over pasta while still warm. Refrigerate. Add egg whites and vegetables before serving. Mix well.

Yield: 8 servings

Nutrition Information Per Serving:

Calories 122

Fat 1 gram

Cholesterol 0 milligrams

Sodium 498 milligrams

FRIED RICE

**1 pound boneless, skinless
  chicken breast, cubed
1 large onion, chopped**

**2 tablespoons soy sauce
½ cup egg substitute
4 cups cooked white rice**

Cook chicken and onion in a large skillet or wok using soy sauce as marinade. In a separate pan, scramble egg lightly. Add rice to skillet with chicken and onion. Stir until well blended. Cook, stirring frequently until warmed through. Add cooked egg and green onion. Mix well. Serve warm.

Yield: 4 servings

Nutrition Information Per Serving:

Calories 557

Fat 6 grams

Cholesterol 97 milligrams

Sodium 657 milligrams

LOW FAT CAKE

**1 (18.5 ounce) package yellow
  or white cake mix
3 egg whites**

**1¼ cups water
⅓ cup applesauce**

Blend all of the above ingredients. Pour into a cake pan sprayed with vegetable cooking spray. Bake according to package directions. Use cut up fresh fruit as frosting.

Yield: 12 servings

Nutrition Information Per Serving:

Calories 195

Fat 4 grams

Cholesterol 0 milligrams

Sodium 205 milligrams

LOW CALORIE REESE CUP PIE

1½ cups graham cracker
  crumbs
3 packets sugar substitute
⅓ cup reduced calorie
  margarine, melted

1 (4⅛ ounce) package sugar-
  free chocolate instant
  pudding mix
2 cups skim milk
2 tablespoons peanut butter

Mix cracker crumbs, sugar substitute, and margarine. Press in pie pan. Bake at 350 degrees for 8 minutes. Mix pudding and milk for 1 minute. Add peanut butter and mix well. Pour into pie pan. Refrigerate until well chilled. Garnish with low fat whipped topping.

Yield: 6 servings

Nutrition Information Per Serving:

Calories 282

Fat 11 grams

Cholesterol 1.7 milligrams

Sodium 515 milligrams

LOW FAT BROWNIES

1 (21.5 ounce) package
  brownie mix
½ cup applesauce

½ cup water
2 egg whites

Preheat oven to 350 degrees. Spray bottom of a 13 x 9 inch pan with vegetable cooking spray. Mix all ingredients. Spread in pan and bake for 30 to 35 minutes. Cool completely before slicing.

Yield: 16 servings

Nutrition Information Per Serving:

Calories 160

Fat 6 grams

Cholesterol 6 milligrams

Sodium 104 milligrams

BAKED APPLES

4 baking apples, cored
4 dates, pitted

1 cup water

Place apples in a deep baking dish. Stuff center of each apple with one date. Pour water around apples and bake covered in moderate oven (375 degrees) for 45 minutes or until tender.

Yield: 4 servings

Nutrition Information Per Serving:

Calories 104

Fat 5 grams

Cholesterol 0 milligrams

Sodium 1.2 milligrams

FRESH FRUIT CUP

4 apples, cored and sliced
4 oranges, peeled and
   sectioned
2 cups grapes

4 bananas, sliced
½ cup maraschino cherries
1 cup orange juice

Mix all fruit together. Pour orange juice over the mixture. Chill over-night. Garnish with maraschino cherries.

Yield: 12 servings

Nutrition Information Per Serving:

Calories 106

Fat 0 grams

Cholesterol 0 milligrams

Sodium 1.3 milligrams

BANANA MILK SHAKE

2 bananas, over-ripe, peeled
   and frozen
1½ cups skim milk

1½ tablespoons dark maple
   syrup

Cut up bananas while still frozen. Add to blender with skim milk and syrup. Blend for 30 seconds.

Yield: 2 servings

Nutrition Information Per Serving:

Calories 214

Fat 0 grams

Cholesterol 3 milligrams

Sodium 122 milligrams

Potpourri

DURHAM'S BEANLESS CHILI

1 pound extra lean ground
  beef
½ cup catsup

⅓ cup water
1½ tablespoons chili powder
salt to taste

Place all ingredients in saucepan and stir, making sure the ground beef is not lumpy. Bring to a boil stirring several times. Simmer for 20 minutes, stirring occasionally. Salt to taste after the chili is done.

Yield: 6 servings

VEGETABLE BATTER

¾ cup cornstarch
¼ cup plain flour
1 teaspoon baking powder
½ teaspoon salt

¼ teaspoon pepper
½ cup cold water
1 egg, slightly beaten

Combine all ingredients whisking very well. Let set while chopping vegetables. Use onions, squash, okra, mushrooms, zucchini, bell peppers, etc. Heat oil at 350 degrees. Dip vegetables in batter and fry until golden brown. Drain and serve hot.

Yield: 6 servings

LOW COUNTRY PEPPER JELLY

1 cup green pepper, minced
½ cup hot pepper, minced
1½ cups cider vinegar
6½ cups granulated sugar

1 bottle Certo
3 to 4 drops red or green food
  color

Place peppers and vinegar in blender and blend for a few seconds. In a 6 quart saucepan, mix peppers and sugar together. Bring to a rolling boil that cannot be stirred down. Remove from heat for 10 minutes. Skim off froth. Stir in certo and food color. Pour into sterilized jars and seal with paraffin.

Serve with cream cheese and crackers.

This is a Charleston favorite.

Yield: 6 half-pint jars

PEPPER RELISH

12 red peppers
12 green peppers
12 medium onions

3 cups granulated sugar
1½ pints red vinegar
3 teaspoons salt

Chop up peppers and onion in blender. Drain well. In a saucepan combine sugar, vinegar and salt, let come to a boil. Add peppers and onions. Let boil for 5 minutes. Pour into sterilized jars and seal.

HOME MADE BARBECUE SAUCE

1½ cups ketchup
½ cup sugar
1 teaspoon basil
1 teaspoon chili powder

1 medium onion, chopped
1 teaspoon dry mustard
1 teaspoon pepper

Mix all ingredients together and place on meat.

May use with pork, beef or chicken.

Yield: 2½ cups

T.O.P. RELISH

2 quarts chopped green
tomatoes
2 hot green peppers, chopped
2 cups chopped onions
2 cups white vinegar

¼ cup salt
3 cups sugar
½ cup pickling spice (tied in cheesecloth)

Mix all ingredients and bring to a boil. Simmer for 30 minutes, stirring occasionally. Remove spice bag and pour into sterilized jars and seal.

Great served with pork, fish or country style steak.

Yield: 6 pints

ERIC'S HOT DOG CHILI

1 pound ground beef
1 (16 ounce) bottle ketchup
1 cup of water

1 small onion, finely chopped
salt and pepper to taste

Brown ground beef and onions and drain. Add ketchup, water, salt and pepper. Let simmer over medium heat 30 minutes stirring occasionally.

Add cheese to chili for an even better taste.

Yield: 6 servings

GRANDMA'S DRESSING

1 pound pork sausage
2 eggs, beaten
1 cup milk, scalded
7 cups coarse, dry bread crumbs

2 tablespoons diced onion
1 cup diced celery
2 tablespoons minced fresh parsley
½ teaspoon salt

Brown sausage in skillet, drain. In large mixing bowl, combine sausage with other ingredients, mix well. Pour in sausage skillet, bake, covered, at 350 degrees for 30 minutes, uncover and bake 10 minutes more or until lightly browned.

Makes enough to stuff a big turkey.

Yield: 6 to 8 servings

CRAB MEAT STUFFING

1½ cups crab meat
½ cup onion, chopped
½ cup celery, chopped
1 cup bread crumbs

3 eggs, beaten
2 tablespoons melted butter
seasoning to taste

Combine all ingredients together and mix well.

This is excellent to stuff flounder.

ACKNOWLEDGEMENTS

The committee of *"By Special Request"* wishes to express our sincere appreciation to the hundreds of employees, families, and friends who contributed over 1,300 recipes in this united effort of community support.

This has been a remarkable employee project and represents unselfish contributions of untiring employees who have labored to make this dream a reality.

Due to an overwhelming response, duplications and similarities, coupled with cost limitations, we were unable to publish every single recipe submitted. We do hope everyone will understand our necessary compromise and share in the excitement and camaraderie generated by our finished product, *"By Special Request"*.

CONTRIBUTORS

Ideas, recipes, proofing, testing, tasting, typing, professional expertise and personal time.

Angelia M Abdur-Rahim
Robin Ackerman
Joyce Adams
Sherif Amer
Sonja J. Anderson
Mildred Axson
William E. Baggett
Betty Jo Bagwell
Irma Baisden
Frances Barfield
Earl Barnwell
Ann Barrett
Scott Bartlett
Rachel Basinger
Tammy R. Bass
Frances Bastian
Juanita Baxley
Brenda Kay Bazemore
Heather Beck
Dianne Bell
Lori Bell
Linda Bellamy
Rounette Belue
Wendell Beverly
Theresa M. Blacklocke
Cindy Blackstock
Jana M. Blackwell
Robert Blake
Cheri L. Bledsoe
Gary Blewer

Cassie S. Booker
Lynn S. Bowers
Brenda Branham
Barbara Branton
Betty Jean Brazell
Alan Brooks
Donnie Brown
Elnora M. Brown
Marion E. Brown
Jennifer Browne
Tommy Browne
Galen Brownell
Sarah Bryant
George H. Bullwinkel
Jeanette Bundrick
Walter Burkett
George J. Busuttil
Mike Cade
Betty Cain
Carol Campbell
Tony Campbell
Denise Cannon
Linda L. Cantrell
Quindelia D. Capers
Ronnie Caraviello
Betsy Carpenter
Larry Carroll
Richard Casey
John Caughman
Adrene J. Chassereau

Rosanne Christo
Kelly C. Clements
Rosemary Cockrell
Rose Colley
Jessie L. Cooper
Melinda J. Cooper
Margaret Corbin
Charlotte Cordeiro
Sherri Coulter
Joan Craven
Jan Crawford
Janice Crawford
Carl H. Crews
Lisa Cribb
Susan D. Crites
Lisa Lynn Crossley
Kathy Crumpton
Richard Cuban
Charlotte H. Culpepper
Corrine Cummings
Vickie Curtis
Allene Dabbs
Merry Lynn Dallas
Anice Davis
Iyonda L. Davis
Joyce Davis
Ginger S. Dearth
Joseph DeChateauveri
Cheryl DeForrest
Idalia Delgado

Rosemary DeLoache
Kathleen Dempsey
Julia Dickson
Jennifer Dingler
Beverly C. Driggers
Kathy Driggers
Phil Driggers
JoAnn H. DuBose
Lorraine DuBose
David Duggar
Jean Dunn
Jerry Durham
Kay Dydek
Amy S. Eade
Albert J. Eclavea
Denny C. Edenfield
Jack Edwards
Leslie Edwards
Margaret Edwards
Lisa S. Elliot
Mona Lee Emily
Charlie Estes
Joan Faison
Charlie Mae Faust
Elizabeth Fields
Dolly Fingar
Dale Flanigan
Faye Fletcher
Renee Fletcher
Christina G. Flowers
Charlie Man Foust
Debbie Fowler
Lorraine C. Frazier
Jeffrey French
Ron Frye
Dawn Fulton
Barbara Furman
Maja G. Fickett
Dori Gann
Avery Gardner
Lisa Tipps Germanoff
Charlene Godbee
Carroll Godwin
Miriam Godwin
Lori L. Goforth
Keith Gore
Terry Goss
Virginia F. Goude
Linda Ann Gowan
Joey Grace
Darlene Green
Wendy L. Greene
Wayne Greer
JoAnn Grezek

Carol Ray Grooms
Dawn E. Guindon
Joyce B. Hair
Berri Hall
Cherri Hall
Tammy Hall
Terrie Hall
Donna Hamrick
Jack Hamrick
Henry Hard
Dottie Hardin
Kelly Harris
Lisa Harris
Mary Harrison
Shirley Hartley
Denise Hayes
Kathy Hazinakis
Valerie Heath
Theresa G. Hedgecock
Jill Marie Helmly
Barney Henderson
Betty S. Henderson
True Henderson
Doris Hendrick
Lisa Marie Herndon
Frankie Herrington
Tammy Hester
Alethea Hicks
Janice Hines
Shirley Hipp
Jackie Hodge
Mary F. Holloman
Lavon E. Hood
Tracy L. Hooks
Sarah J. Horton
Letha Howard
Tena Howard
Earline Hucks
Nikki Hudspeth
Deresa Hunter
Jackie Hunter
Nancy Hunter
Paula J. Hutto
Peggy D. Hutto
Joseph L. Broughton, III
Jocelyne R. Immell
Stephen Inglis
Brenda P. Jackson
Heather Jacob
Clara Jenkins
Florence Jenkins
Gloria Jernigan
Amanda Johnson
Ann Johnson

Connie Johnson
Heide A. Johnson
Teresa S. Johnson
Carol L. Jones
Michele Jones
Jill Joyner
Graddy L. Lewis, Jr.
James Lewis, Jr.
Joseph J. Edwards, Jr.
Phillip J. Lemmon, Jr.
Tommy E. Waddell, Jr.
Steve Kay
Bonnie Keister
Charles C. Kelly
Michael Kennedy
Patricia Kennedy
Carol Kennerty
Nicholas C. Kentopp
Richard King
Cynthia Ann Kirby
Dottie Kirton
Marilyn Knight
Monica Knight
Rebecca Lake
Theresa Lang
Jacqueline D. Lazarus
Mary Lee
Michelle K. Lee
Margaret Lingerfelt
Billie R. Lutes
Melissa Madison
Mike Mankin
R. J. Marti
Nancy W. Martin
Edna Maxwell
Chris Mayes
Brinkley McArver
Debbie McClam
Renee McCormick
Michell McCracken
Jessie C. McDaniel
Karen McGowan
Theresa McKenzie
Cheryl McPherson
Debra Mechling
Jeanette Meggett
Dutch Meyer
Dinah Miles
Homer Miles
Lyn Miller
Michell Miller
Patricia A. Miranda
Joyce Mitchell
Mike Mock

Paula R. Mole
Dallas Moody
Robert Bryan Moody
Marcia Moore
Kenneth R. Morgan
Ardith T. Morris
James Moses
Bert Motley
Raymond Moultrie
Jacklyn Mundy
John Nakon
Amy Nelson
Donna Nesbitt
Joseph T. Newton, Jr.
Joseph T. Newton, III
Tradd Newton
Patricia Oberg
Iris Orbach
Keith W. Owen
Crystal Parker
Juanita Parker
Linda Parker
Sandy Parker
Irvin Parkman
Gracie Parsons
Jack Peeples
Ted O. Peeples
Nippie Penneston
Judy Perry
Teresa R. Phillips
Nell Piedmont
Anthony Pitchers
William Player
Lyndal Plummer
Stacy E. Pope
Angela Postell
Rita Postell
Nora M. Potter
Linda Powell
Wanda Frances Pruitt
Donna Quigley
Renee Ramsey
Bryan Raver
Anne Reddick
Audrey Denise Register
Scott Reynolds
Nancy Rich
Lillie Richardson
Jayne Riley
Gladys Rimer
Judy L. Roberts
Ross Robertson

Nancy E. Roch
Henry Rodgers
Rose Mary Rogers
Lisa Dianne Ross
Cleo Roton
Mitchell G. Rowe
Donald Rowland
Jan Sarvis
Bonita Saxton
Debra Schaer
Burton R. Schools
David Schools
Nichole Scott
Susan M. Scott
Betty M. Settle
Sandra O. Sexton
Lynn L. Seymour
Wendy Lee Shumpert
James Simmons
Donna C. Skipper
Linda Slane
Kevin Smalls
Barbara Smith
Eleanor Smith
Lori Smith
Rodger Smith
Brenda Snipes
Shirley Sonenshine
Nestorio A. Sosa
John H. Spear
Eric A. Spell
Lane Spell
Betty Sprague
Jeanette Stancil
Barbara Staton
Eileen Stellefson
Beth Stepp
Dewayne Stewart
Shawn Still
Barbara Stone
Melissa B. Straughan
Brenda Sullivan
Terry Sullivan
Kimie Sutton
Dorothy Sweat
Betty Syfrett
Sharon Takach
Tommy Takach
Dottie Tanner
Lacy Tarver
Leona Taylor
Lovonia Terry

Mary Rose Terry
Ann Marie Thomas
James C. Thomas
Jenny Thomas
Mychael Thomas
Rhonda Thomas
Louise Thompson
Annie Pearl Tillman
Willie Tisdale
P. J. Tobias
Mary Frances Todd
Bessie Tucker
Bill Utter
Joann Dawn Valdez
Teresa Vance
Barbara VanThullenar
Julie VanThullenar
Leigh Vaughn
Betty B. Walker
Marty Wallace
Nancy Wallace
William M. Wallace
Clara Ann Walters
Sarah S. Wanamaker
John Ward
Chester Washington
Wanda Watford
Cynthia R. Welch
Lisa Welch
Carolyn Sue Wells
Donna Wells
Peter C. Werner
Julia West
Debra White
Lisa White
Robert White
Donna Widener
Brenda Williams
Carolyn Williams
Irene Williams
Margaret L. Williams
Sharon S. Williams
Brenda Williamson
Dorothy H. Wilson
Vicky Windham
Diane Wood
Cobina D. Wright
Eula Mae Wright
Andi Wyndham
Pat Yandle
Carrie Zimmerman

In the following pages of this publication, we proudly list our stores and subsidiaries who service the people of South Carolina and Savannah with typical Piggly Wiggly Carolina pride.

We invite you to take advantage of our convenient locations and enjoy shopping the most unique privately owned and operated grocery business in the Southeast.

PIGGLY WIGGLY CAROLINA COMPANY, INC.

4401 Piggly Wiggly Drive, P. O. Box 118047, Charleston, SC 29423

*Piggly Wiggly #1
445 Meeting Street
Charleston, SC 29403
803 722-2767

*Piggly Wiggly #2
5060 Dorchester Road
Charleston, SC 29418
803 552-9421

*Piggly Wiggly #3
1948 East Godbold Street
Marion, SC 29571
803 423-9912

Piggly Wiggly #4
1620 High Market Street
Georgetown, SC 29440

~ *Piggly Wiggly #5
Florence Shopping Mall
Florence, SC 29501
803 661-5323

Piggly Wiggly #6
1700 Kings Highway
Myrtle Beach, SC 29577
803 448-4813

*Piggly Wiggly #7
4310 Rivers Avenue
Charleston, SC 29405
803 554-7451

~ *Piggly Wiggly #8
630 Skylark Drive
Charleston, SC 29407
803 556-7522

*Piggly Wiggly #9
680 Bacons Bridge Road
Summerville, SC 29485

*Piggly Wiggly #10
1260 Ben Sawyer Blvd.
Mt. Pleasant, SC 29464
803 884-4489

Piggly Wiggly # 11
404 North Cedar Street
Summerville, SC 29483
803 873-9180

Piggly Wiggly #12
Main Street
Moncks Corner, SC 29461
803 761-8610

~ *Piggly Wiggly #14
1739 Maybank Highway
James Island, SC 29412
803 795-9091

Piggly Wiggly #15
645 Russel Street
Orangeburg, SC 29115
803 534-7708

*Piggly Wiggly #16
15 W. Ashland Street
Andrews, SC 29510
803 264-5251

Piggly Wiggly #17
W. Broadway - Hwy. 501
Myrtle Beach, SC 29577
803 448-3537

~ *Piggly Wiggly #18
251-A Bells Highway
Walterboro, SC 29488
803 549-8519

*Piggly Wiggly #19
Highway 162
Hollywood, SC 29449
803 889-2267

*Piggly Wiggly #20
1110 East Palmetto
Florence, SC 29501
803 669-5705

*Piggly Wiggly #21
206 McIntyre
Mullins, SC 29574
803 464-7271

~ *Piggly Wiggly #22
8780-A Rivers Avenue
N. Charleston, SC 29418
803 764-3039

*Piggly Wiggly #23
1511 4th Street
Conway, SC 29526
803 248-9112

*Piggly Wiggly #24
1015 King Street
Charleston, SC 29403
803 723-5226

*Piggly Wiggly #26
1005 Harborview Road
James Island, SC 29412

Piggly Wiggly #27
1097 State Street
Holly Hill, SC 29059
803 496-3315

*Piggly Wiggly #28
2571 Ashley River Road
Charleston, SC 29414
803 556-1245

~ *Piggly Wiggly #29
1501 Highway 17 North
Mt. Pleasant, SC 29464
803 881-7921

Piggly Wiggly #30
1270 Yeamans Hall Road
Charleston, SC 29406
803 747-6373

Piggly Wiggly # 31
Highway 15 - Church Street
Summerton, SC 29148
803 485-4445

Piggly Wiggly #32
Sunset Drive - Mill Street
Manning, SC 29102
803 435-2118

*Piggly Wiggly #33
2000 Boundary Road
Beaufort, SC 29902
803 524-2932

Piggly Wiggly #35
842 South 5th Street
Hartsville, SC 29550
803 332-8241

Piggly Wiggly #36
7 Main Street
Hardeeville, SC 29927
803 784-3201

*Piggly Wiggly #37
Highway 17 - Wilson Street
Ridgeland, SC 29936
803 726-8626

Piggly Wiggly #38
2002 Marlboro Avenue
Barnwell, SC 29812
803 258-1117

*Piggly Wiggly #39
602 Ribaut Road
Beaufort, SC 29901
803 524-2750

~ *Piggly Wiggly #40
5101 Ashley Phosphate Rd.
North Charleston, SC 29418
803 552-3353

*Piggly Wiggly #41
119 College Park Road
Ladson, SC 29456
803 572-3936

*Piggly Wiggly #42
613 Johnny Dodds Blvd.
Mt. Pleasant, SC 29464
803 884-5118

~ *Piggly Wiggly #43
14 Sumar Street
Highway 7 - Northbridge
Charleston, SC 29407
803 571-0960

Piggly Wiggly #44
Highway 321 North
Estill, SC 29918

Piggly Wiggly #45
802 Elm Street East
Hampton, SC 29924
803 943-2556

*Piggly Wiggly #46
512 South Main Street
Bamberg, SC 29003
803 245-5151

*Piggly Wiggly #47
32 Shelter Cover Lane Z
Hilton Head, SC 29928
803 842-4090

Piggly Wiggly #48
Lake City Plaza
Lake City, SC 29560
803 394-8517

*Piggly Wiggly #49
7360 Skidaway Road
Savannah, GA 31406
912 354-6263

Piggly Wiggly #50
Johnny Mercer Blvd.
Savannah, GA 31410
912 897-1241

Piggly Wiggly #51
401 West Memorial Blvd.
St. George, SC 29477
803 563-4555

*Piggly Wiggly #52
206 East Main Street
Kingstree, SC 29556
803 354-9632

Piggly Wiggly #53
501 Pearl Street
Darlington, SC 29532
803 393-2872

Piggly Wiggly #54
1404 North Main Street
Marion, SC 29571
803 423-1106

*Piggly Wiggly #55
500 2nd Loop Road
Florence, SC 29505
803 662-0195

*Piggly Wiggly #56
221 Cherokee Road
Florence, SC 29501
803 662-5605

~ *Piggly Wiggly #57
4415 Augusta Street
Garden City, GA 31408
912 964-7324

*Piggly Wiggly #58
2142 Victory Drive
Savannah, GA 31404
912 233-8207

*Piggly Wiggly #62
9940 Two Notch Road
Columbia, SC 29223
803 736-9174

*Piggly Wiggly #65
2001 Rosewood Drive
Columbia, SC 29205
803 799-1448

*Piggly Wiggly #66
326 Dearborn Street
Great Falls, SC 29055
803 482-2560

*Piggly Wiggly #67
210 S. Jefferson Street
Saluda, SC 29138
803 445-2955

Piggly Wiggly #68
110 South Main Street
Bishopville, SC 29010
803 484-6315

Piggly Wiggly #70
3818 Devine Street
Columbia, SC 29205
803 256-3434

Piggly Wiggly #72
Park - Earl Streets
Wagner, SC 29164
803 564-3174

*Piggly Wiggly #74
2023 Platt Springs Road
West Columbia, SC 29169
803 796-2545

*Piggly Wiggly #75
2060 Columbia Road
Orangeburg, SC 29115
803 531-1810

Piggly Wiggly #76
Great Falls Highway
Lancaster, SC 29720
803 285-5339

Piggly Wiggly #77
522 York Street
Aiken, SC 29802
803 649-4521

Piggly Wiggly #78
East Dekalb
Camden, SC 29020
803 432-7011

~ *Piggly Wiggly #79
2702 Emanuel Church Rd.
W. Columbia, SC 29170
803 359-1433

Piggly Wiggly #80
Main Street
Bethune, SC 29009
803 334-6227

*Piggly Wiggly #81
1034 West Highway 80
Pooler, GA 31322
912 748-5302

*Piggly Wiggly #82
1160 South Main Street
Greenwood, SC 29646
803 229-1178

Piggly Wiggly #83
Greenwood Avenue
Ware Shoals, SC 29692
803 456-2613

Piggly Wiggly #84
343 Pinewood Road
Sumter, SC 29150
803 773-2370

Piggly Wiggly #85
Wateree Plaza
Lugoff, SC 29078
803 438-3781

*Piggly Wiggly #87
2053 Chesnee Highway
Spartanburg, SC 29305
803 582-2322

~ *Piggly Wiggly #88
1600 Reidville Road
Spartanburg, SC 29301
803 574-8220

Piggly Wiggly #89
Broad Street
Prosperity, SC 29127
803 364-2307

Piggly Wiggly #90
1003 Broad Street
Sumter, SC 29150
803 773-6011

Piggly Wiggly #91
114 East Calhoun Street
Sumter, SC 29150
803 775-4712

Piggly Wiggly #92
674 West Liberty Street
Sumter, SC 29150
803 775-1312

Piggly Wiggly #95
438 West Railroad Av.
Batesburg, SC 29006
803 532-6808

Piggly Wiggly #96
204 North Cambridge
Ninety Six, SC 29666
803 543-2429

*Piggly Wiggly #97
7412 Garners Ferry Road
Columbia, SC 29209
803 776-4830

Piggly Wiggly #98
3724 Covenant Road
Columbia, SC 29204
803 782-4172

*Piggly Wiggly #100
11605 Abercorn Drive
Savannah, GA 31419
912 925-5953

*Piggly Wiggly #102
655 St. Andrews Boulevard
Columbia, SC 29210
803 772-0927

*Piggly Wiggly #103
3775 Maybank Highway
Johns Island, SC 29457
803 559-5542

*Piggly Wiggly #104
74 Folly Road
Charleston, SC 29407
803 571-1522

*Piggly Wiggly #106
43 W. Montgomery
  Crossroads
Savannah, GA 31406
912 920-1656

*Piggly Wiggly #107
202 Harry Raysor Drive
St. Matthews, SC 29135
803 874-1212

*Piggly Wiggly #108
Dorchester - Trolley Roads
Summerville, SC 29483
803 873-1173

*Piggly Wiggly #109
Brandywine - Highway 52
Goose Creek, SC 29445
803 572-1422

*Piggly Wiggly #110
1305 West Main Street
Chesterfield, SC 29709
803 623-6590

Piggly Wiggly #112
Main Street - Railroad Av.
Lamar, SC 29069
803 326-7117

**Greenbax Enterprises,
  Inc.**
4567 Piggly Wiggly Drive
Charleston, SC 29405
803 554-9880

**Greenbax
  Gift Center #04**
655 St. Andrews Road
Columbia, SC 29210
803 772-6258

**Greenbax
  Gift Center #05**
426 Coleman Boulevard
Mt. Pleasant, SC 29464
803 884-0200

**Greenbax
  Gift Center #06**
1610 Sam Rittenberg Blvd.
Charleston, SC 29407
803 766-6422

**Greenbax
  Gift Center #07**
1612-B Fourth Avenue
Conway, SC 29526
803 248-9324

**Greenbax
  Gift Center #08**
Florence Mall
Florence, SC 29501
803 662-1383

**Orvin's Appliance
  Center #9**
Main Street
Moncks Corner, SC 29461
803 761-8268

**Greenbax
  Gift Center #10**
49 W. Montgomery
  Crossroads
Savannah, GA 31406
912 925-6719

**Greenbax
  Gift Center #12**
1021 Broad Street
Sumter, SC 29150
803 775-5156

**Greenbax
  Gift Center #15**
2050 Columbia Road
Orangeburg, SC 29115
803 536-0221

* Company owned stores

~ 24 hour stores

INDEX

ORDER FORM

By Special Request

Piggly Wiggly Carolina Company, Inc.
Post Office Box 118047
Charleston, SC 29423

Please send me ___ copy(ies) of **By Special Request** at: $15.95 each _____
Postage & Handling   3.00 each _____
S.C. Residents add sales tax   .96 each _____
TOTAL _____

Name _____

Address _____

City _____ State _____ Zip _____

All proceeds will benefit charitable causes elected by Piggly Wiggly employees.

Piggly Wiggly Carolina Company, Inc.
Post Office Box 118047
Charleston, SC 29423

Please send me ___ copy(ies) of **By Special Request** at: $15.95 each _____
Postage & Handling   3.00 each _____
S.C. Residents add sales tax   .96 each _____
TOTAL _____

Name _____

Address _____

City _____ State _____ Zip _____

All proceeds will benefit charitable causes elected by Piggly Wiggly employees.

Piggly Wiggly Carolina Company, Inc.
Post Office Box 118047
Charleston, SC 29423

Please send me ___ copy(ies) of **By Special Request** at: $15.95 each _____
Postage & Handling   3.00 each _____
S.C. Residents add sales tax   .96 each _____
TOTAL _____

Name _____

Address _____

City _____ State _____ Zip _____

All proceeds will benefit charitable causes elected by Piggly Wiggly employees.